LEGION

SON OF X

PRODIGAL

PRODIGAL

writer **SI SPURRIER**
pencilers **TAN ENG HUAT** (#1-3) & **JORGE MOLINA** (#4-6)
inkers **CRAIG YEUNG** (#1-3 & #5), **JORGE MOLINA** (#4), **NORMAN LEE** (#5-6) & **WALDEN WONG** (#5-6)
colorists **JOSÉ VILLARRUBIA** (#1-3) & **RACHELLE ROSENBERG** (#4-6)
letterer **VC'S CORY PETIT**
cover artist **MIKE DEL MUNDO**
assistant editor **JENNIFER M. SMITH**
editor **DANIEL KETCHUM**
x-men group editor **NICK LOWE**

Collection Editor: Mark D. Beazley • Assistant Editor: Caitlin O'Connell • Assistant Managing Editor: Kateri Woody
Senior Editor, Special Projects: Jennifer Grünwald • VP Production & Special Projects: Jeff Youngquist
SVP Print, Sales & Marketing: David Gabriel • Book Design: Jeff Powell & Cory Levine

Editor in Chief: C.B. Cebulski • Chief Creative Officer: Joe Quesada
President: Dan Buckley • Executive Producer: Alan Fine

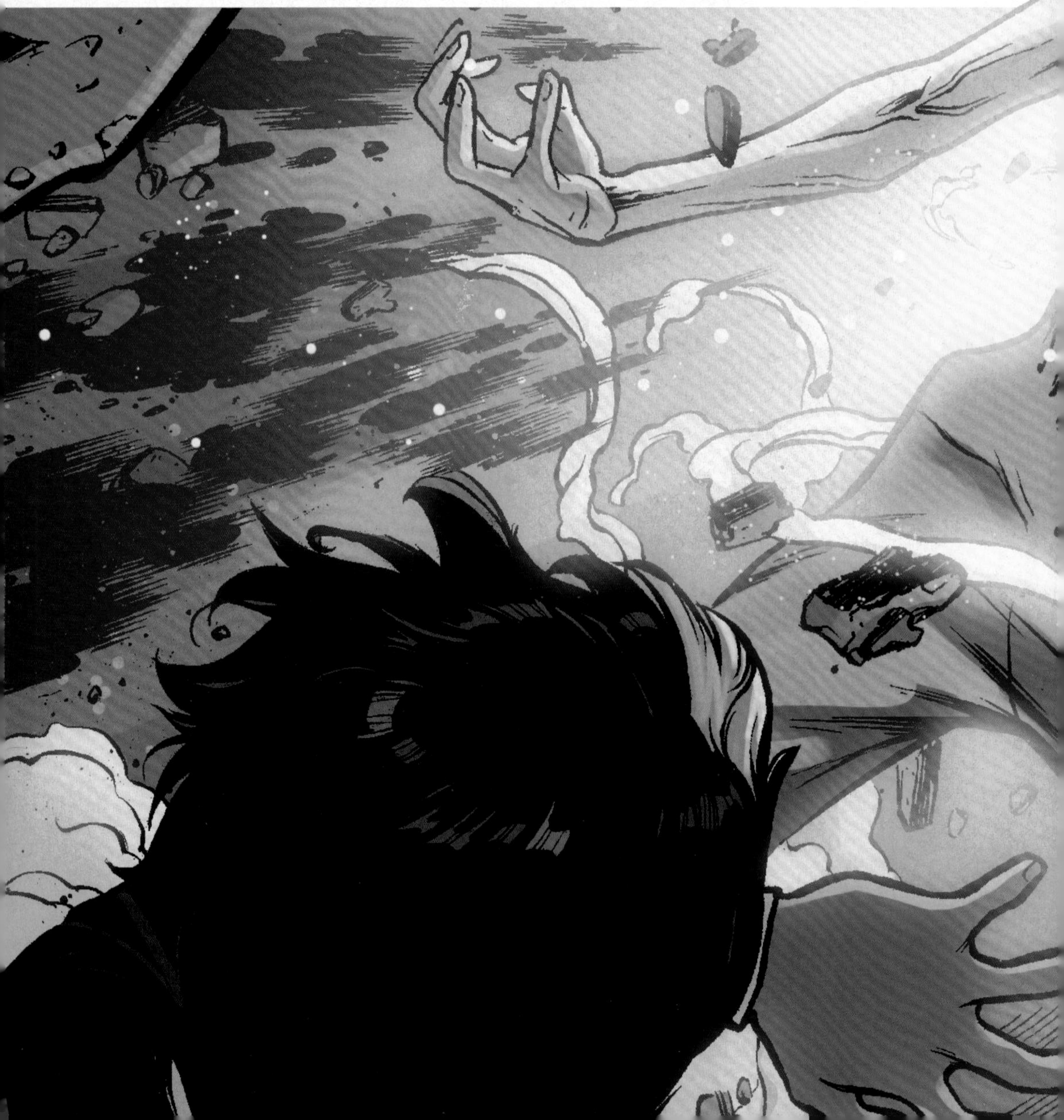

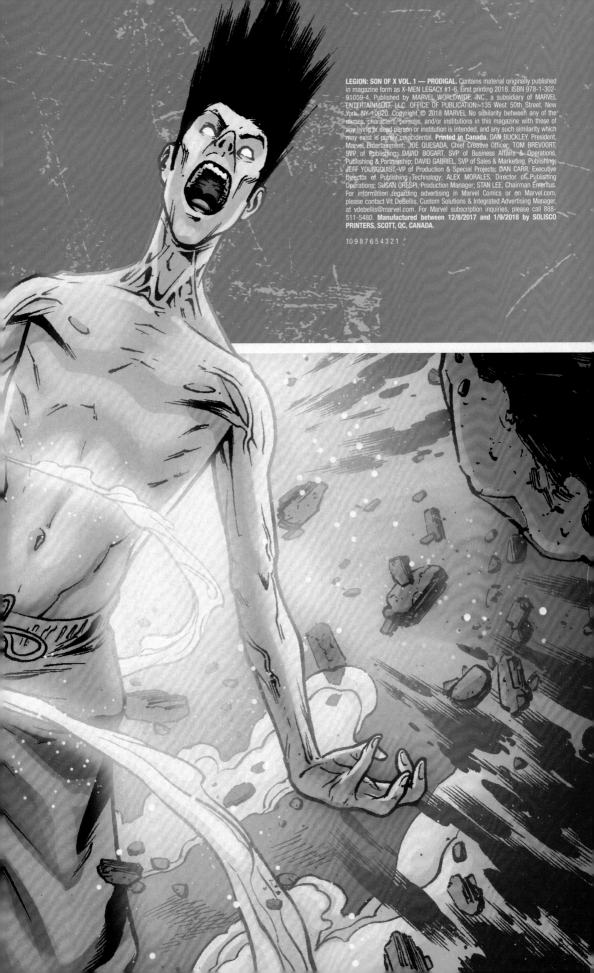

LEGION: SON OF X VOL. 1 — PRODIGAL. Contains material originally published in magazine form as X-MEN LEGACY #1-6. First printing 2018. ISBN 978-1-302-91059-4. Published by MARVEL WORLDWIDE, INC., a subsidiary of MARVEL ENTERTAINMENT, LLC. OFFICE OF PUBLICATION: 135 West 50th Street, New York, NY 10020. Copyright © 2018 MARVEL No similarity between any of the names, characters, persons, and/or institutions in this magazine with those of any living or dead person or institution is intended, and any such similarity which may exist is purely coincidental. **Printed in Canada.** DAN BUCKLEY, President, Marvel Entertainment; JOE QUESADA, Chief Creative Officer; TOM BREVOORT, SVP of Publishing; DAVID BOGART, SVP of Business Affairs & Operations, Publishing & Partnership; DAVID GABRIEL, SVP of Sales & Marketing, Publishing; JEFF YOUNGQUIST, VP of Production & Special Projects; DAN CARR, Executive Director of Publishing Technology; ALEX MORALES, Director of Publishing Operations; SUSAN CRESPI, Production Manager; STAN LEE, Chairman Emeritus. For information regarding advertising in Marvel Comics or on Marvel.com, please contact Vit DeBellis, Custom Solutions & Integrated Advertising Manager, at vdebellis@marvel.com. For Marvel subscription inquiries, please call 888-511-5480. **Manufactured between 12/8/2017 and 1/9/2018 by SOLISCO PRINTERS, SCOTT, QC, CANADA.**

10 9 8 7 6 5 4 3 2 1

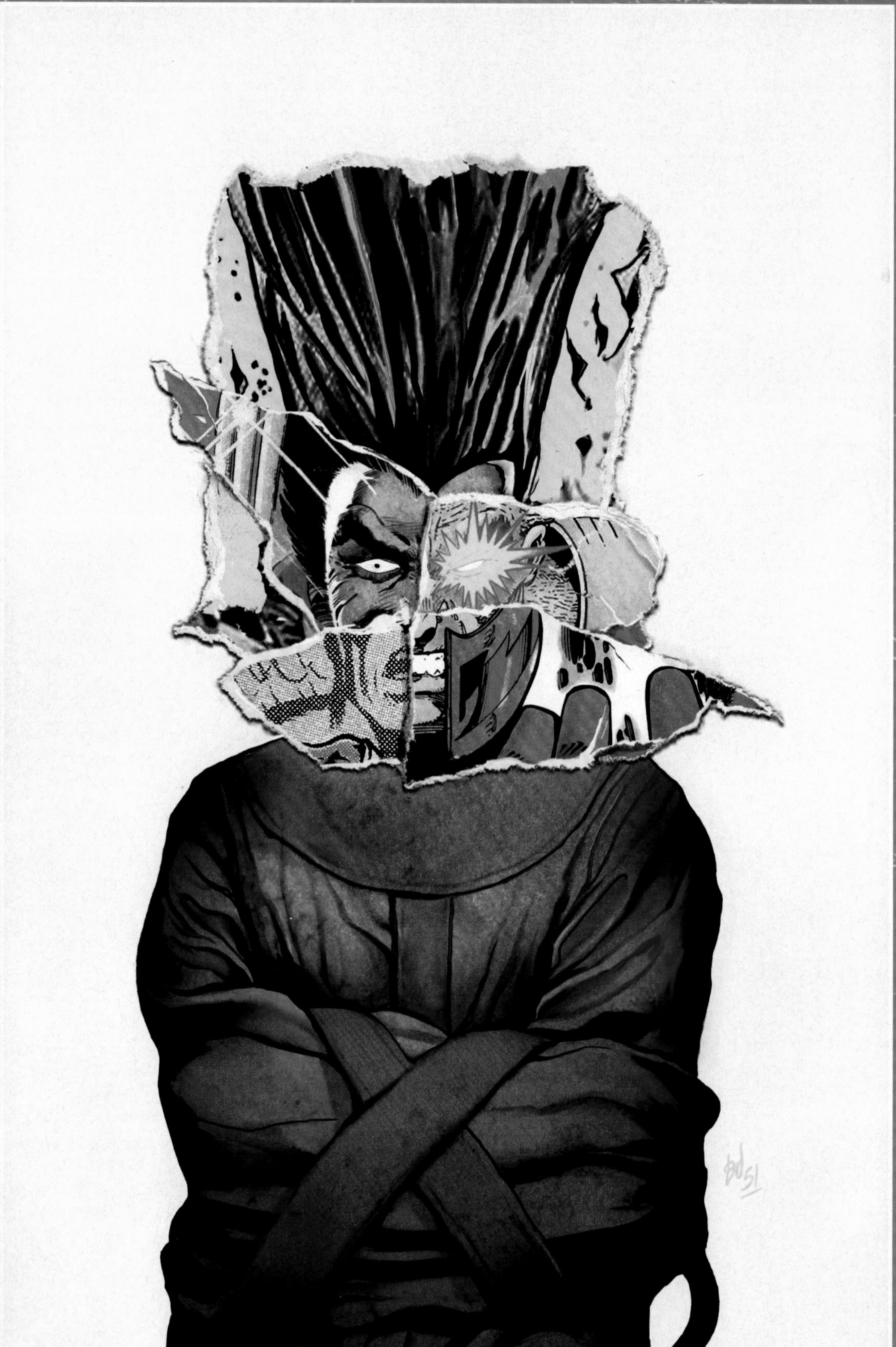

ONE

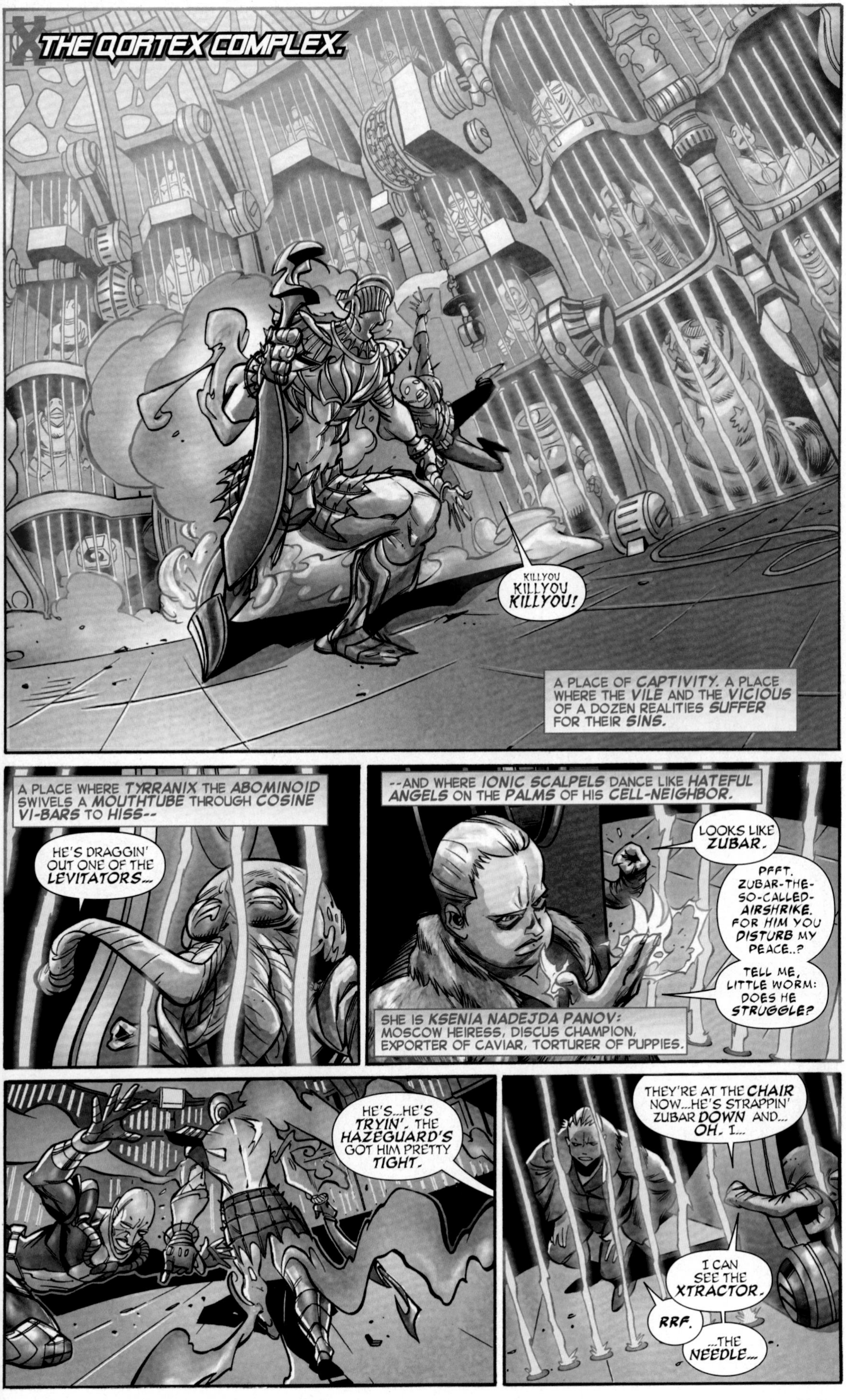
THE QORTEX COMPLEX.
KILLYOU KILLYOU KILLYOU!
A PLACE OF CAPTIVITY. A PLACE WHERE THE VILE AND THE VICIOUS OF A DOZEN REALITIES SUFFER FOR THEIR SINS.
A PLACE WHERE TYRRANIX THE ABOMINOID SWIVELS A MOUTHTUBE THROUGH COSINE VI-BARS TO HISS--
HE'S DRAGGIN' OUT ONE OF THE LEVITATORS...
--AND WHERE IONIC SCALPELS DANCE LIKE HATEFUL ANGELS ON THE PALMS OF HIS CELL-NEIGHBOR.
LOOKS LIKE ZUBAR.
PFFT. ZUBAR-THE-SO-CALLED-AIRSHRIKE. FOR HIM YOU DISTURB MY PEACE..?
TELL ME, LITTLE WORM: DOES HE STRUGGLE?
SHE IS KSENIA NADEJDA PANOV: MOSCOW HEIRESS, DISCUS CHAMPION, EXPORTER OF CAVIAR, TORTURER OF PUPPIES.
HE'S...HE'S TRYIN'. THE HAZEGUARD'S GOT HIM PRETTY TIGHT.
THEY'RE AT THE CHAIR NOW...HE'S STRAPPIN' ZUBAR DOWN AND... OH. I...
I CAN SEE THE XTRACTOR.
RRF.
...THE NEEDLE...

THE XTRACTOR.

AAAAAAAAAA

THE TRUTH IS, *NONE* OF THEM KNOWS *WHAT IT IS.* WHY IT *DRAGS* THEM OUT DAY AFTER DAY; WHAT *SICKLY ESSENCE* IT *DRAINS.*

THEY CAN'T EVEN REMEMBER *HOW* THEY CAME TO *BE* HERE, NOR GUESS WHEN--*IF EVER*-- THEY'LL SEE *RELEASE.*

THEY...THEY SAY IT *SUCKS* OUT THE *BADNESS.* LIKE--PURE *EVIL.*

MAYBE. THERE IS PLENTY TO BE *FOUND* IN THIS PLACE. THOUGH PRECIOUS LITTLE ATTENTION TO *DETAIL.*

LOOK, WORM. LOOK *CLOSE.*

"YOU SEE HOW THE *XTRACTOR* IS *FRAIL,* DA? BENEATH THE ARMOR.

"HOW HE RELIES ON THE *HAZEGUARD* TO SUBDUE US?

"ONLY WHEN THE PRISONERS ARE *EMPTIED*-- EXHAUSTED--DOES HE DARE *HANDLE* THEM *HIMSELF.*

"THAT, MY NOISY LITTLE WORM... *THAT* IS THE *WEAK MOMENT*...

...*THAT* IS THE MOMENT I *AWAIT.*

YOU WILL *NOT DISTURB* ME AGAIN.

MWWAAAAAA!

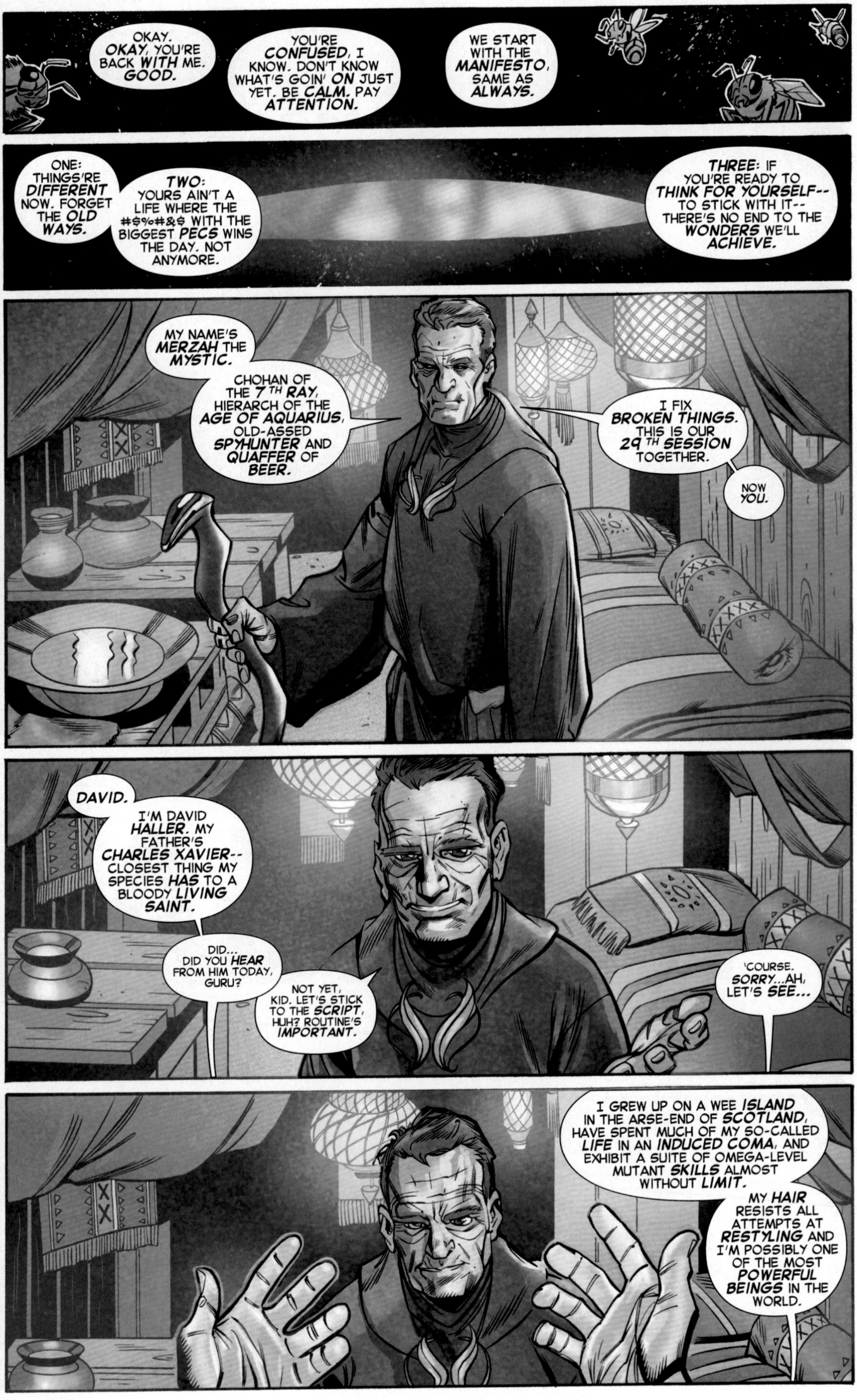
OKAY. OKAY, YOU'RE BACK WITH ME. GOOD.
YOU'RE CONFUSED, I KNOW. DON'T KNOW WHAT'S GOIN' ON JUST YET. BE CALM. PAY ATTENTION.
WE START WITH THE MANIFESTO, SAME AS ALWAYS.
ONE: THINGS'RE DIFFERENT NOW. FORGET THE OLD WAYS.
TWO: YOURS AIN'T A LIFE WHERE THE #$%#&$ WITH THE BIGGEST PECS WINS THE DAY. NOT ANYMORE.
THREE: IF YOU'RE READY TO THINK FOR YOURSELF-- TO STICK WITH IT-- THERE'S NO END TO THE WONDERS WE'LL ACHIEVE.
MY NAME'S MERZAH THE MYSTIC.
CHOHAN OF THE 7TH RAY, HIERARCH OF THE AGE OF AQUARIUS, OLD-ASSED SPYHUNTER AND QUAFFER OF BEER.
I FIX BROKEN THINGS. THIS IS OUR 29TH SESSION TOGETHER.
NOW YOU.
DAVID.
I'M DAVID HALLER. MY FATHER'S CHARLES XAVIER-- CLOSEST THING MY SPECIES HAS TO A BLOODY LIVING SAINT.
DID... DID YOU HEAR FROM HIM TODAY, GURU?
NOT YET, KID. LET'S STICK TO THE SCRIPT, HUH? ROUTINE'S IMPORTANT.
'COURSE. SORRY...AH, LET'S SEE...
I GREW UP ON A WEE ISLAND IN THE ARSE-END OF SCOTLAND, HAVE SPENT MUCH OF MY SO-CALLED LIFE IN AN INDUCED COMA, AND EXHIBIT A SUITE OF OMEGA-LEVEL MUTANT SKILLS ALMOST WITHOUT LIMIT.
MY HAIR RESISTS ALL ATTEMPTS AT RESTYLING AND I'M POSSIBLY ONE OF THE MOST POWERFUL BEINGS IN THE WORLD.

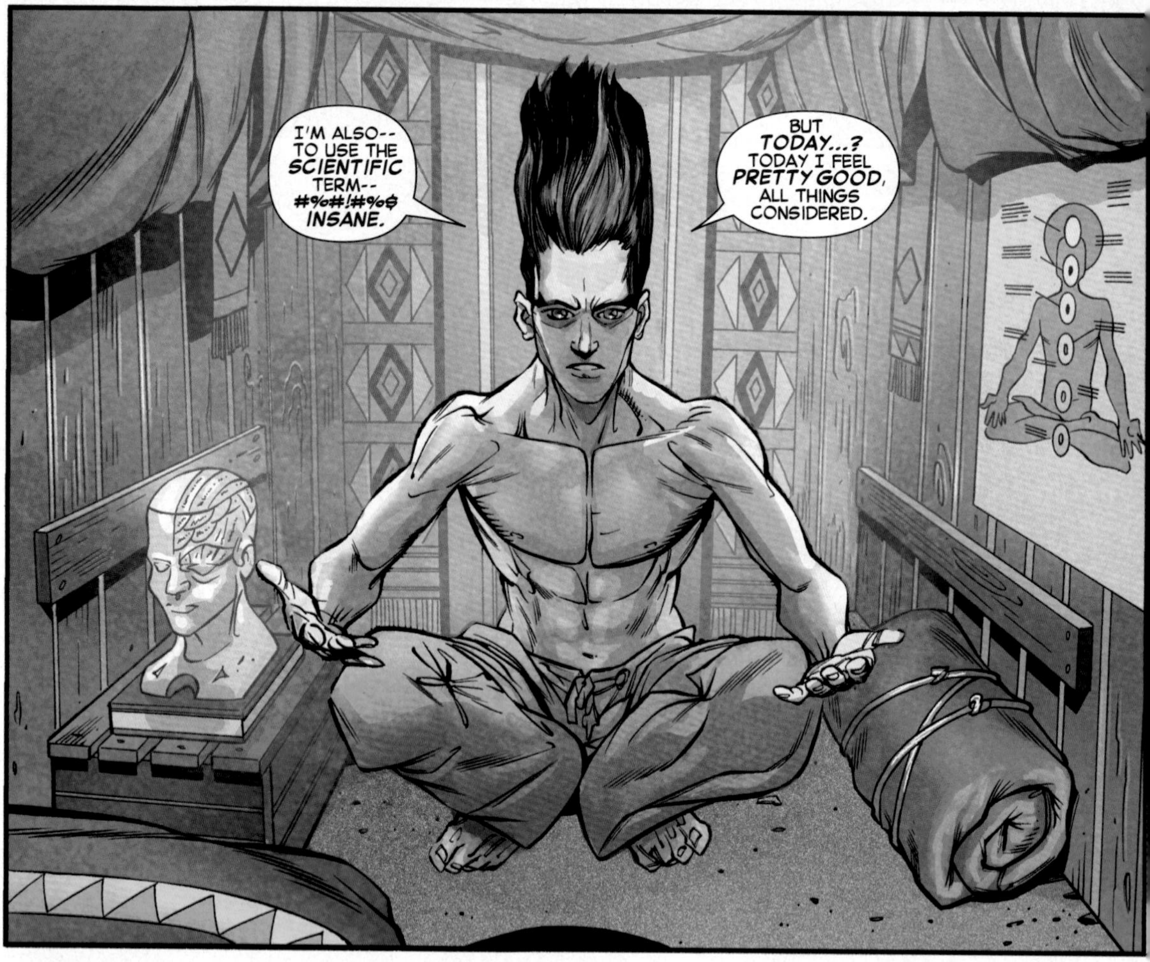
I'M ALSO-- TO USE THE SCIENTIFIC TERM-- #%#!#%$ INSANE.
BUT TODAY...? TODAY I FEEL PRETTY GOOD, ALL THINGS CONSIDERED.

PRODIGAL

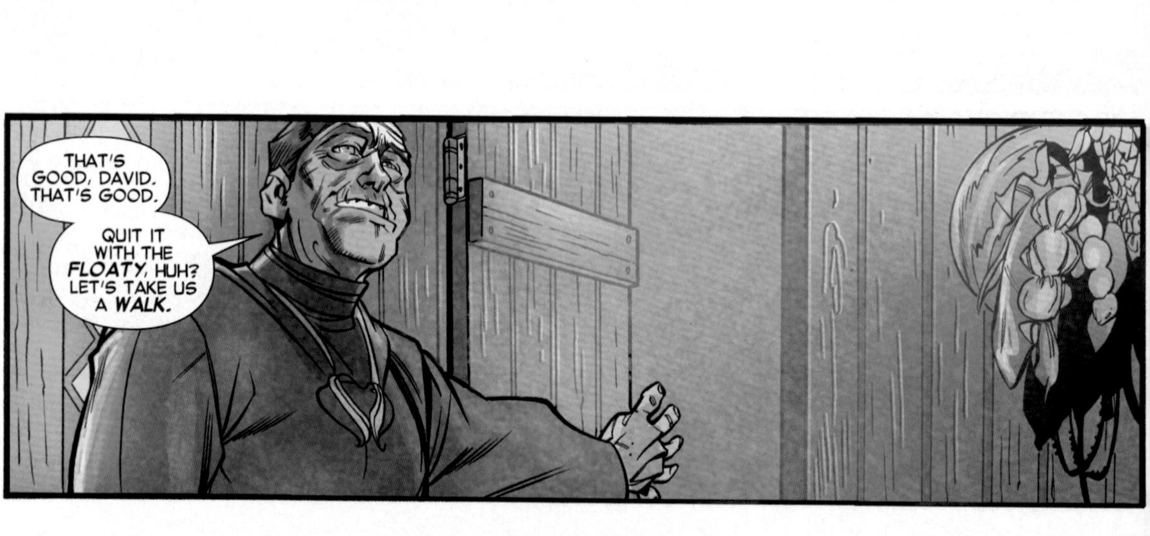
THAT'S GOOD, DAVID. THAT'S GOOD.
QUIT IT WITH THE FLOATY, HUH? LET'S TAKE US A WALK.

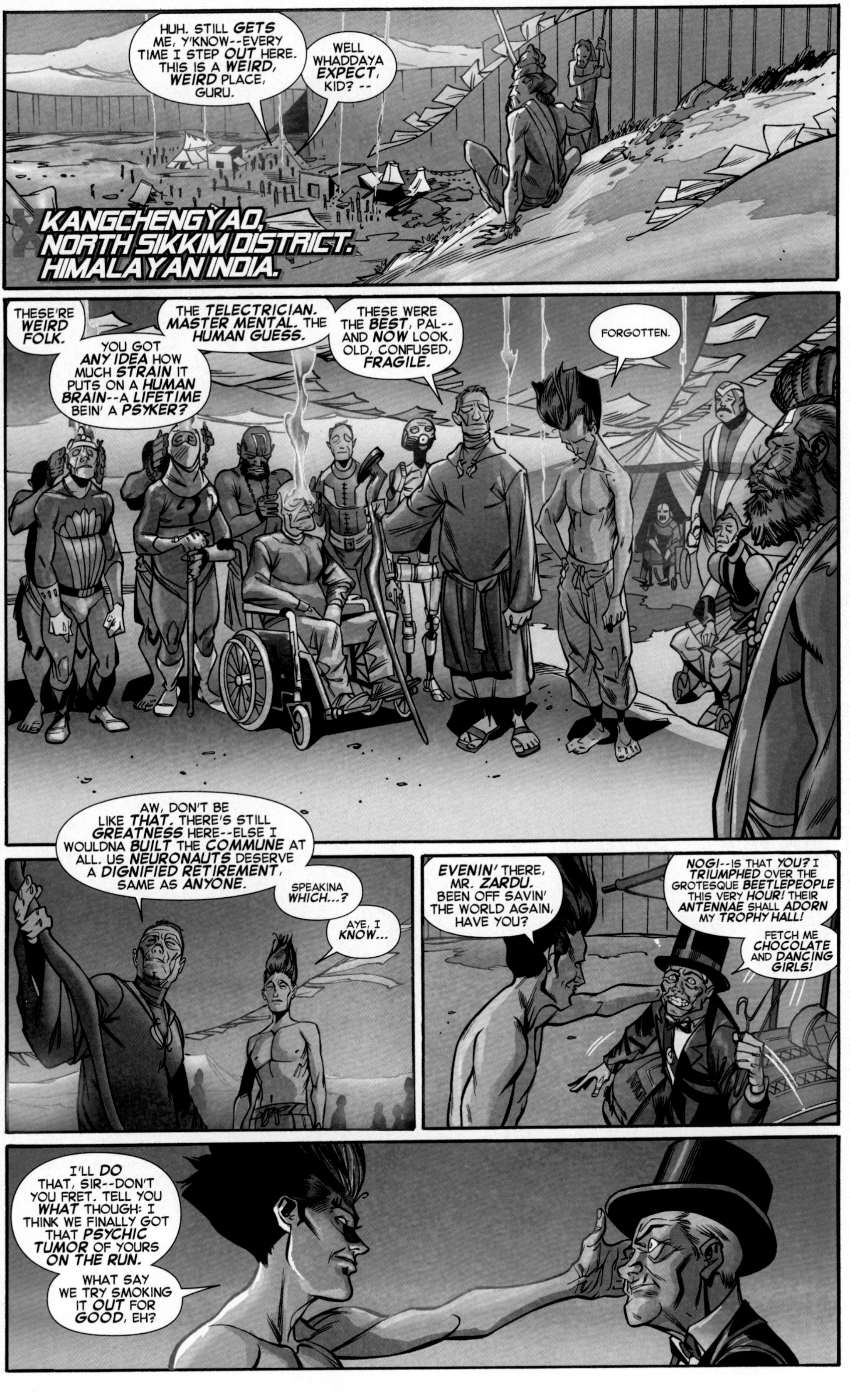
HUH. STILL GETS ME, Y'KNOW--EVERY TIME I STEP OUT HERE. THIS IS A WEIRD, WEIRD PLACE, GURU.
WELL WHADDAYA EXPECT, KID? --
KANGCHENGYAO, NORTH SIKKIM DISTRICT. HIMALAYAN INDIA.
THESE'RE WEIRD FOLK.
YOU GOT ANY IDEA HOW MUCH STRAIN IT PUTS ON A HUMAN BRAIN--A LIFETIME BEIN' A PSYKER?
THE TELECTRICIAN. MASTER MENTAL. THE HUMAN GUESS.
THESE WERE THE BEST, PAL--AND NOW LOOK. OLD, CONFUSED, FRAGILE.
FORGOTTEN.
AW, DON'T BE LIKE THAT. THERE'S STILL GREATNESS HERE--ELSE I WOULDNA BUILT THE COMMUNE AT ALL. US NEURONAUTS DESERVE A DIGNIFIED RETIREMENT, SAME AS ANYONE.
SPEAKINA WHICH...?
AYE, I KNOW...
EVENIN' THERE, MR. ZARDU. BEEN OFF SAVIN' THE WORLD AGAIN, HAVE YOU?
NOGI--IS THAT YOU? I TRIUMPHED OVER THE GROTESQUE BEETLEPEOPLE THIS VERY HOUR! THEIR ANTENNAE SHALL ADORN MY TROPHY HALL!
FETCH ME CHOCOLATE AND DANCING GIRLS!
I'LL DO THAT, SIR--DON'T YOU FRET. TELL YOU WHAT THOUGH: I THINK WE FINALLY GOT THAT PSYCHIC TUMOR OF YOURS ON THE RUN.
WHAT SAY WE TRY SMOKING IT OUT FOR GOOD, EH?

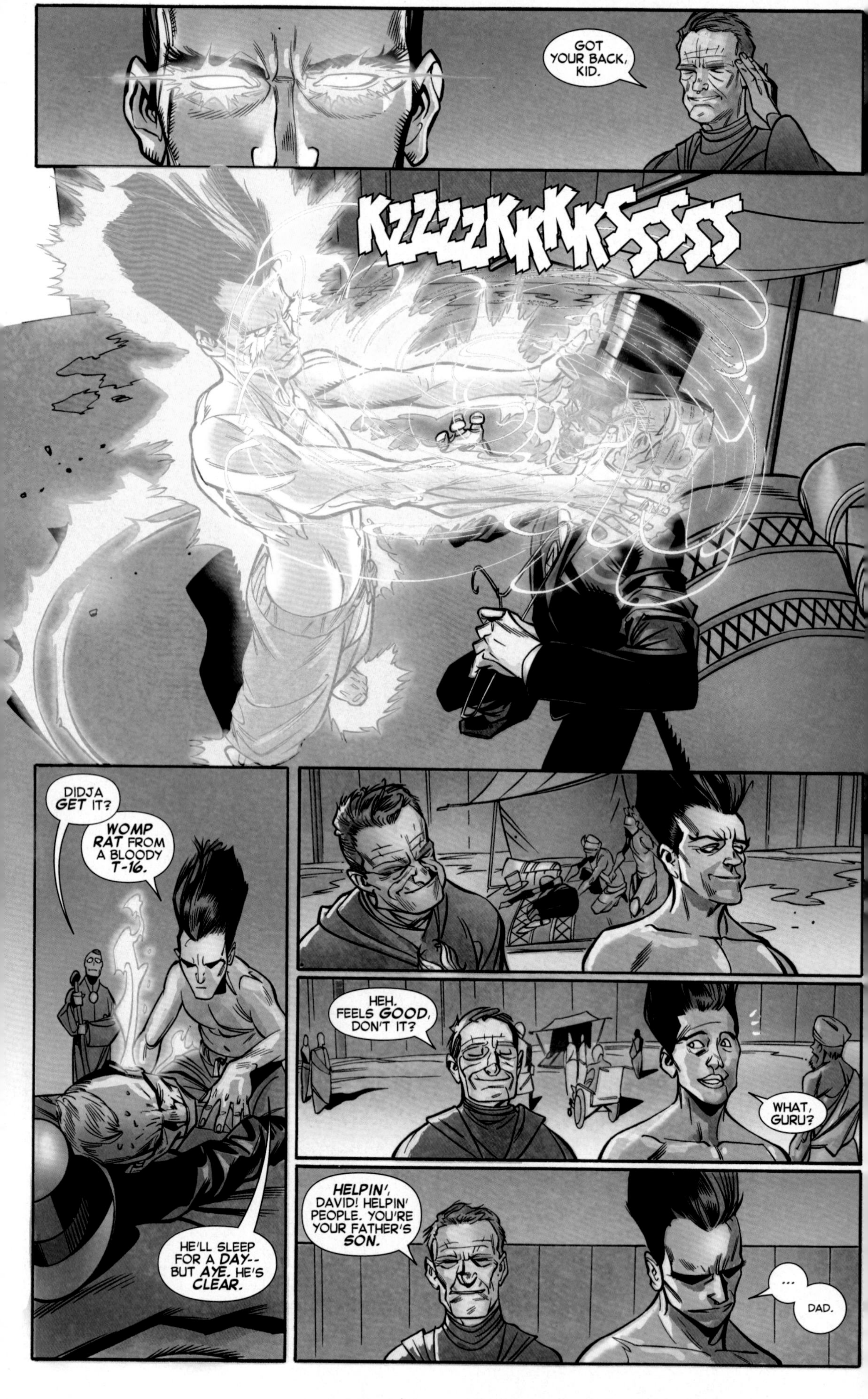
GOT YOUR BACK, KID.
KZZZZKKKKSSSSS
DIDJA GET IT?
WOMP RAT FROM A BLOODY T-16.
HE'LL SLEEP FOR A DAY-- BUT AYE. HE'S CLEAR.
HEH. FEELS GOOD, DON'T IT?
WHAT, GURU?
HELPIN', DAVID! HELPIN' PEOPLE. YOU'RE YOUR FATHER'S SON.
...
DAD.

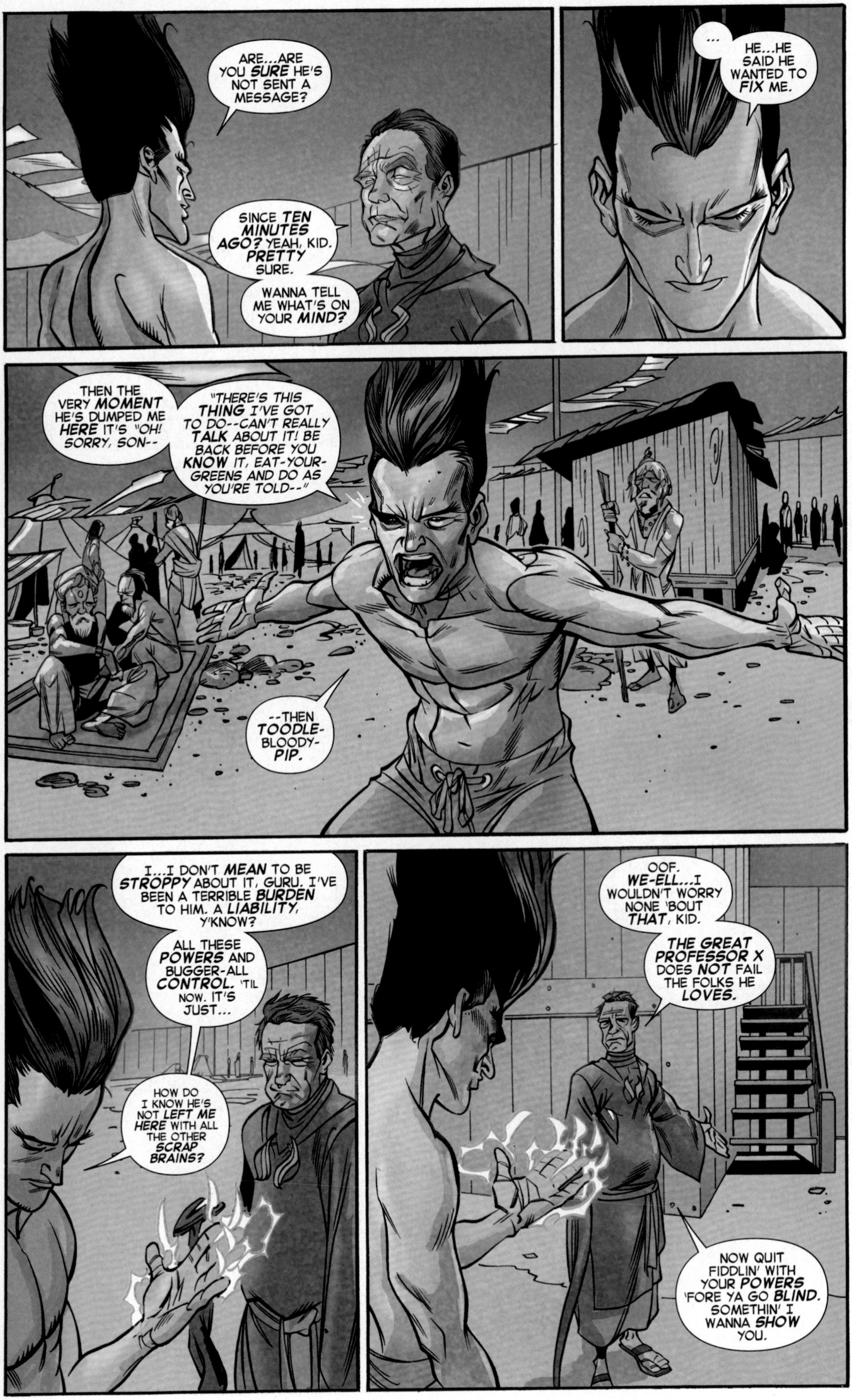

ARE...ARE YOU SURE HE'S NOT SENT A MESSAGE?
SINCE TEN MINUTES AGO? YEAH, KID. PRETTY SURE.
WANNA TELL ME WHAT'S ON YOUR MIND?
...
HE...HE SAID HE WANTED TO FIX ME.
THEN THE VERY MOMENT HE'S DUMPED ME HERE IT'S "OH! SORRY, SON--
"THERE'S THIS THING I'VE GOT TO DO--CAN'T REALLY TALK ABOUT IT! BE BACK BEFORE YOU KNOW IT, EAT-YOUR-GREENS AND DO AS YOU'RE TOLD--"
--THEN TOODLE-BLOODY-PIP.
I...I DON'T MEAN TO BE STROPPY ABOUT IT, GURU. I'VE BEEN A TERRIBLE BURDEN TO HIM. A LIABILITY, Y'KNOW?
ALL THESE POWERS AND BUGGER-ALL CONTROL. 'TIL NOW. IT'S JUST...
HOW DO I KNOW HE'S NOT LEFT ME HERE WITH ALL THE OTHER SCRAP BRAINS?
OOF. WE-ELL...I WOULDN'T WORRY NONE 'BOUT THAT, KID.
THE GREAT PROFESSOR X DOES NOT FAIL THE FOLKS HE LOVES.
NOW QUIT FIDDLIN' WITH YOUR POWERS 'FORE YA GO BLIND. SOMETHIN' I WANNA SHOW YOU.

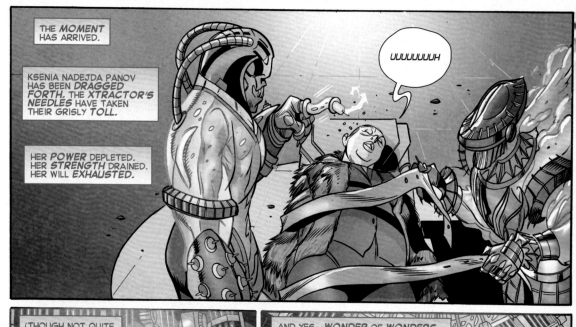

THE *MOMENT* HAS ARRIVED.

KSENIA NADEJDA PANOV HAS BEEN *DRAGGED FORTH.* THE *XTRACTOR'S NEEDLES* HAVE TAKEN THEIR GRISLY *TOLL.*

HER *POWER* DEPLETED. HER *STRENGTH* DRAINED. HER WILL *EXHAUSTED.*

UUUUUUUH

(THOUGH NOT QUITE AS EXHAUSTED AS SHE PRETENDS.)

I'VE GOT IT FROM HERE. *CHEERS.*

AND YES--*WONDER* OF *WONDERS*-- AS THE GREAT *XTRACTOR* RETURNS HER TO *HELL* SHE FEELS IT *PAUSE...*

...SENSES ITS *GRIP SLACKEN,* AS IF DISTRACTED BY A *THOUGHT.*

...AND HEARS ITS VOICE--*THICK* WITH *BITTERNESS*--WHISPER:

"THE GREAT *PROFESSOR X* DOES NOT FAIL THE FOLKS HE *LOVES.*"

HH.

MY *ARSE.*

THWUK

HA!

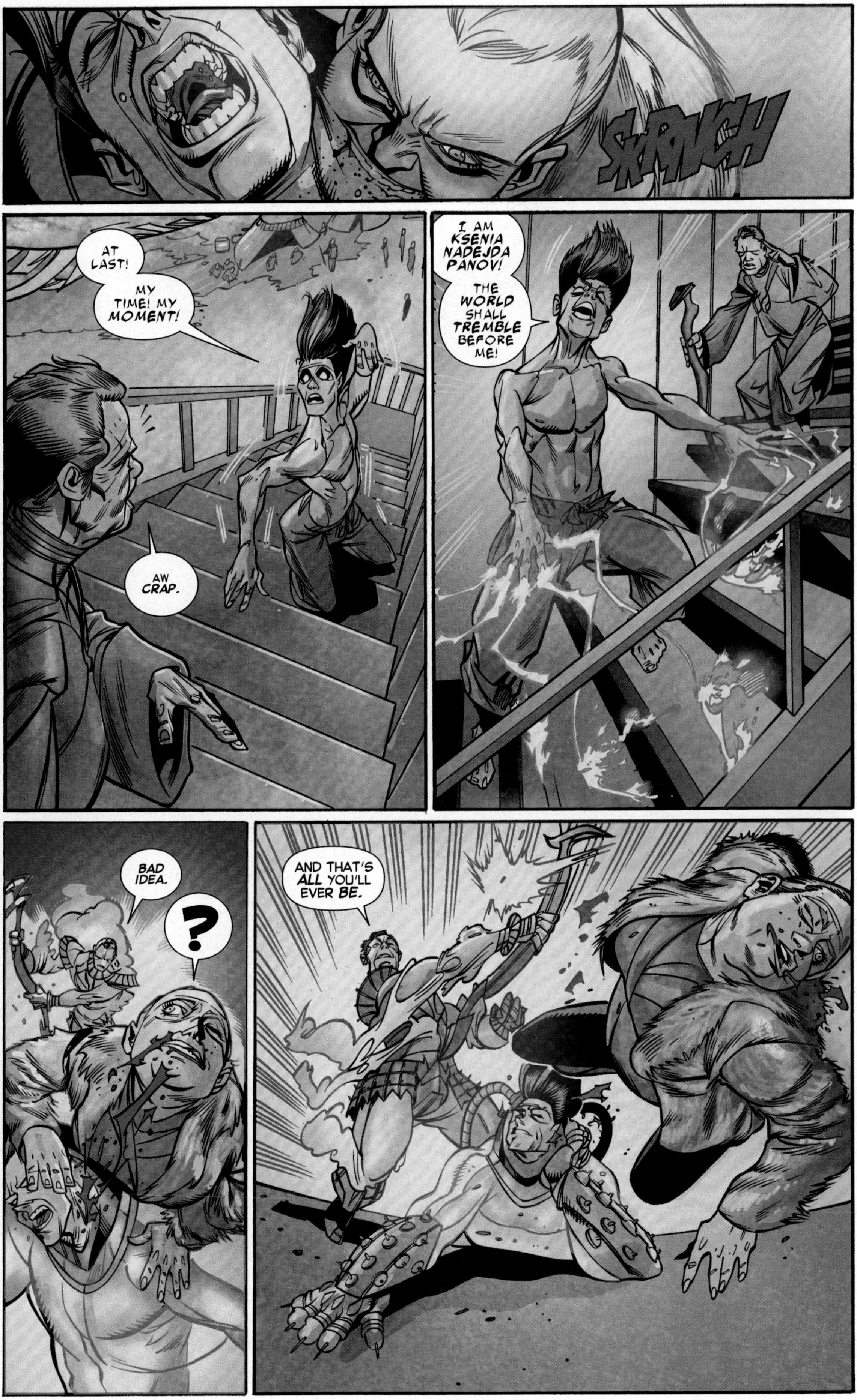
SKRUNCH
AT LAST!
MY TIME! MY MOMENT!
AW CRAP.
I AM KSENIA NADEJDA PANOV!
THE WORLD SHALL TREMBLE BEFORE ME!
BAD IDEA.
?
AND THAT'S ALL YOU'LL EVER BE.

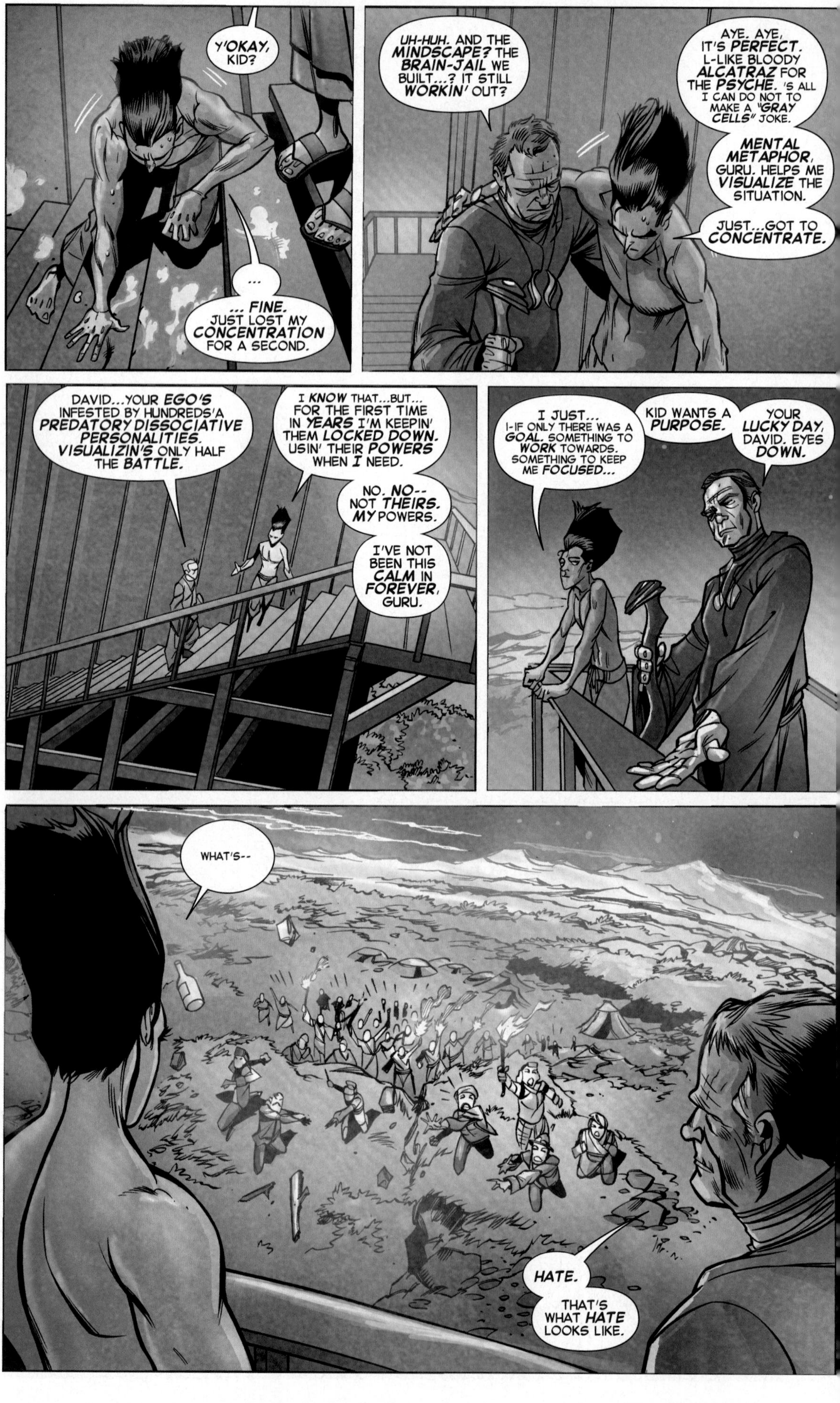
Y'OKAY, KID?
...
... FINE. JUST LOST MY CONCENTRATION FOR A SECOND.
UH-HUH. AND THE MINDSCAPE? THE BRAIN-JAIL WE BUILT...? IT STILL WORKIN' OUT?
AYE. AYE, IT'S PERFECT. L-LIKE BLOODY ALCATRAZ FOR THE PSYCHE. 'S ALL I CAN DO NOT TO MAKE A "GRAY CELLS" JOKE.
MENTAL METAPHOR, GURU. HELPS ME VISUALIZE THE SITUATION.
JUST...GOT TO CONCENTRATE.
DAVID...YOUR EGO'S INFESTED BY HUNDREDS'A PREDATORY DISSOCIATIVE PERSONALITIES. VISUALIZIN'S ONLY HALF THE BATTLE.
I KNOW THAT...BUT... FOR THE FIRST TIME IN YEARS I'M KEEPIN' THEM LOCKED DOWN. USIN' THEIR POWERS WHEN I NEED.
NO. NO-- NOT THEIRS. MY POWERS.
I'VE NOT BEEN THIS CALM IN FOREVER, GURU.
I JUST... I-IF ONLY THERE WAS A GOAL. SOMETHING TO WORK TOWARDS. SOMETHING TO KEEP ME FOCUSED...
KID WANTS A PURPOSE.
YOUR LUCKY DAY, DAVID. EYES DOWN.
WHAT'S--
HATE.
THAT'S WHAT HATE LOOKS LIKE.

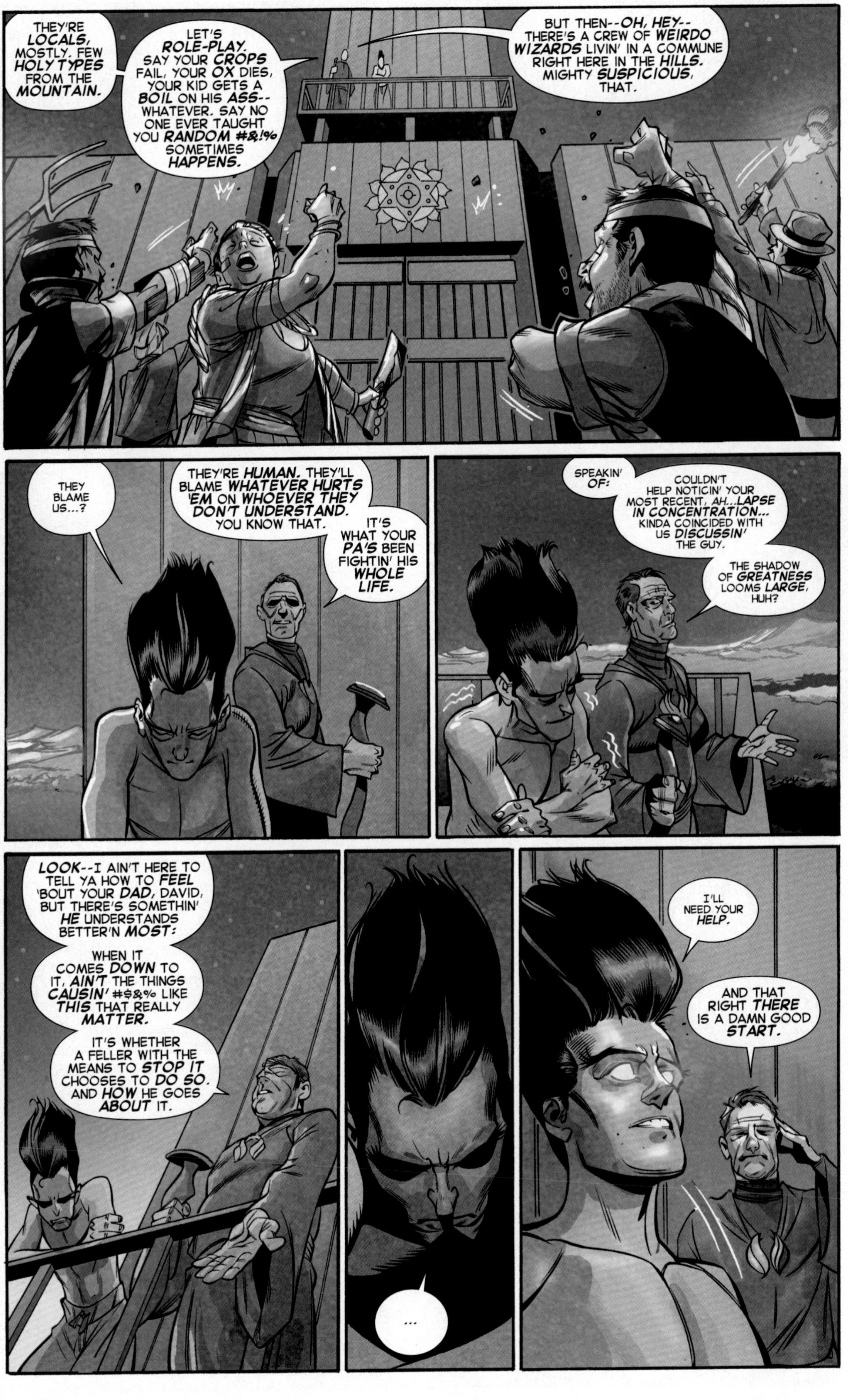
THEY'RE LOCALS, MOSTLY. FEW HOLY TYPES FROM THE MOUNTAIN.
LET'S ROLE-PLAY. SAY YOUR CROPS FAIL, YOUR OX DIES, YOUR KID GETS A BOIL ON HIS ASS-- WHATEVER. SAY NO ONE EVER TAUGHT YOU RANDOM #&!% SOMETIMES HAPPENS.
BUT THEN--OH, HEY-- THERE'S A CREW OF WEIRDO WIZARDS LIVIN' IN A COMMUNE RIGHT HERE IN THE HILLS. MIGHTY SUSPICIOUS, THAT.
THEY BLAME US...?
THEY'RE HUMAN. THEY'LL BLAME WHATEVER HURTS 'EM ON WHOEVER THEY DON'T UNDERSTAND. YOU KNOW THAT.
IT'S WHAT YOUR PA'S BEEN FIGHTIN' HIS WHOLE LIFE.
SPEAKIN' OF:
COULDN'T HELP NOTICIN' YOUR MOST RECENT, AH...LAPSE IN CONCENTRATION... KINDA COINCIDED WITH US DISCUSSIN' THE GUY.
THE SHADOW OF GREATNESS LOOMS LARGE, HUH?
LOOK--I AIN'T HERE TO TELL YA HOW TO FEEL 'BOUT YOUR DAD, DAVID, BUT THERE'S SOMETHIN' HE UNDERSTANDS BETTER'N MOST:
WHEN IT COMES DOWN TO IT, AIN'T THE THINGS CAUSIN' #$&% LIKE THIS THAT REALLY MATTER.
IT'S WHETHER A FELLER WITH THE MEANS TO STOP IT CHOOSES TO DO SO. AND HOW HE GOES ABOUT IT.
...
I'LL NEED YOUR HELP.
AND THAT RIGHT THERE IS A DAMN GOOD START.

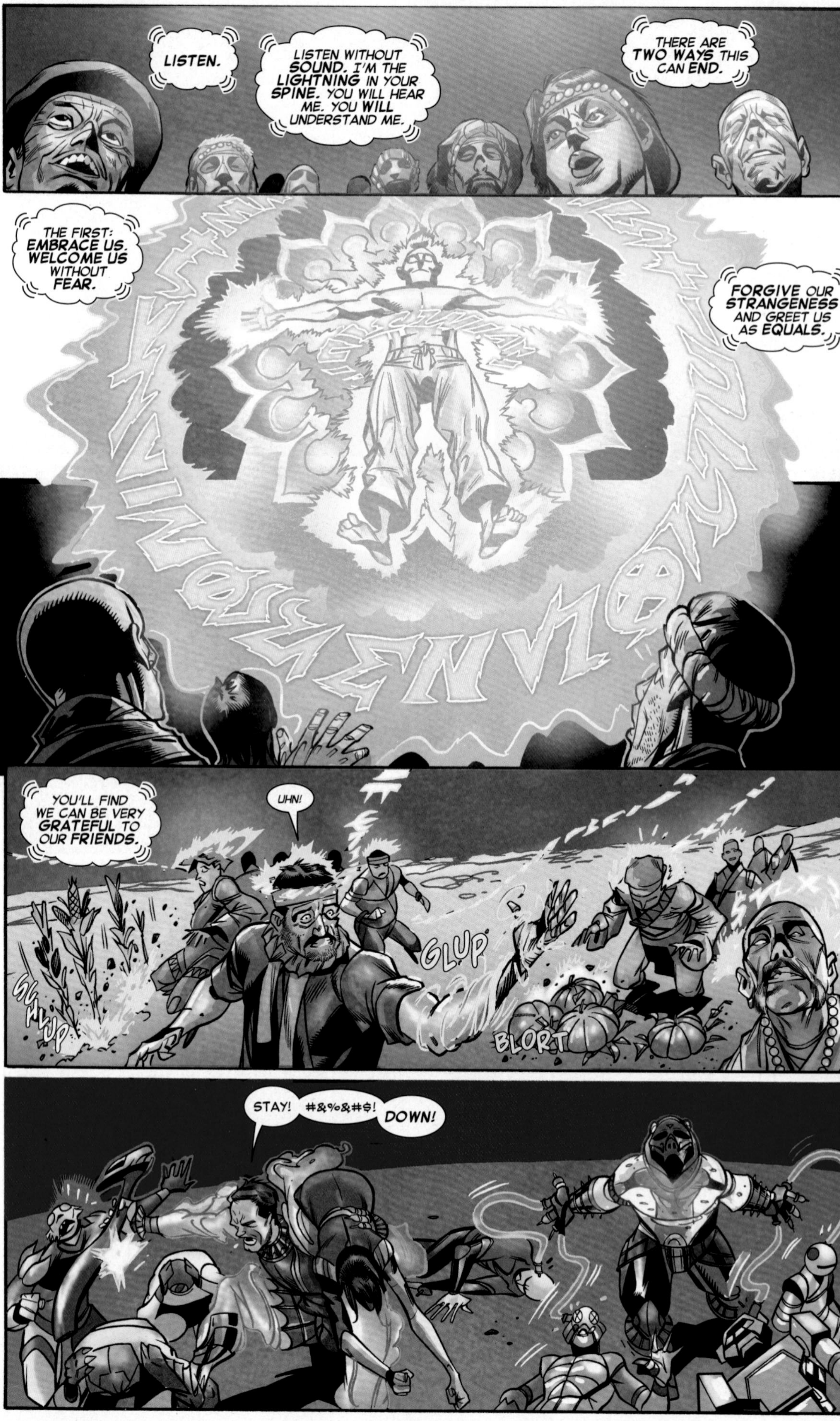
LISTEN.
LISTEN WITHOUT SOUND. I'M THE LIGHTNING IN YOUR SPINE. YOU WILL HEAR ME. YOU WILL UNDERSTAND ME.
THERE ARE TWO WAYS THIS CAN END.
THE FIRST: EMBRACE US. WELCOME US WITHOUT FEAR.
FORGIVE OUR STRANGENESS AND GREET US AS EQUALS.
YOU'LL FIND WE CAN BE VERY GRATEFUL TO OUR FRIENDS.
UHN!
GLUP
SCHLUP
BLORT
STAY!
#&%&#$!
DOWN!

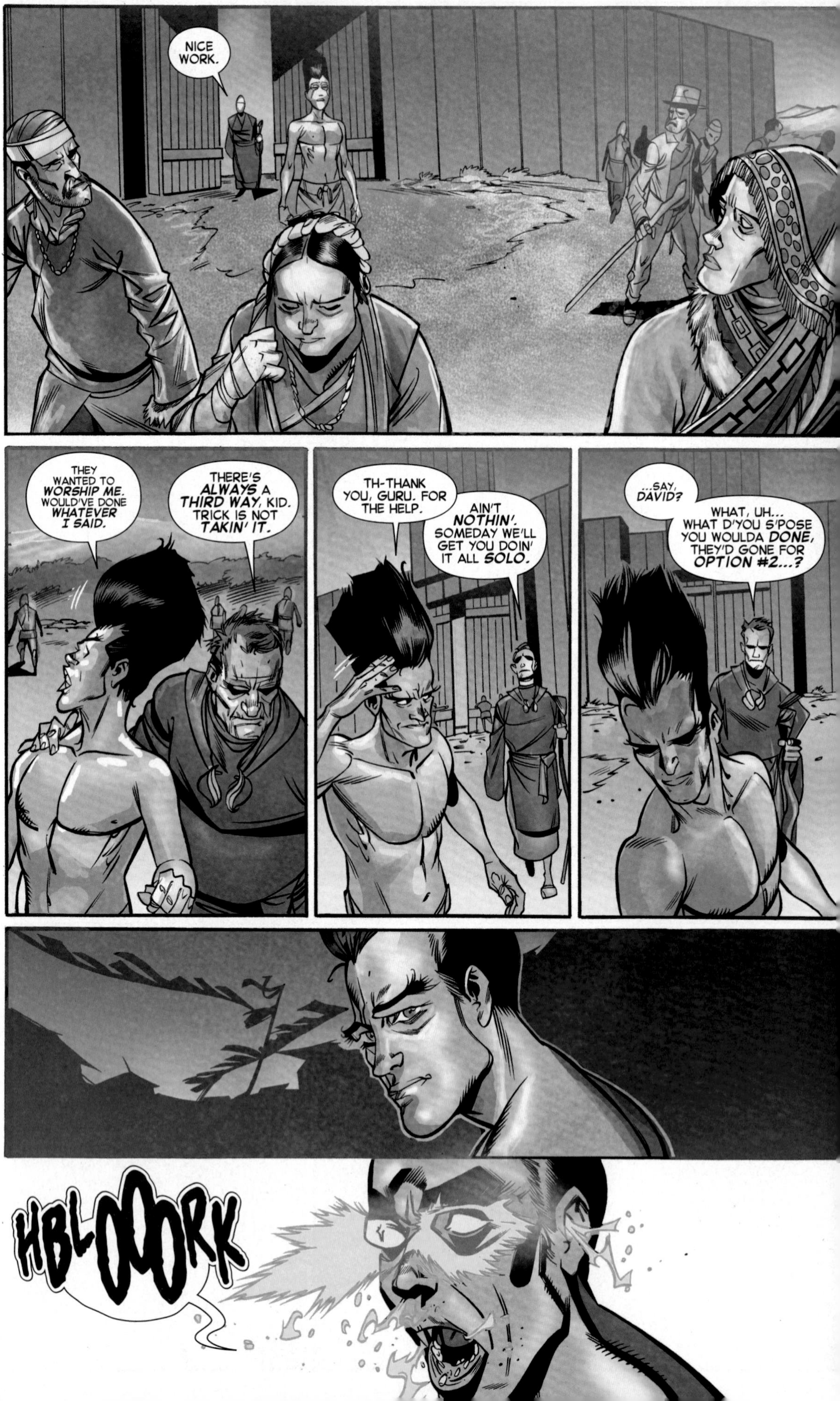
NICE WORK.
THEY WANTED TO WORSHIP ME. WOULD'VE DONE WHATEVER I SAID.
THERE'S ALWAYS A THIRD WAY, KID. TRICK IS NOT TAKIN' IT.
TH-THANK YOU, GURU. FOR THE HELP.
AIN'T NOTHIN'. SOMEDAY WE'LL GET YOU DOIN' IT ALL SOLO.
...SAY, DAVID?
WHAT, UH... WHAT D'YOU S'POSE YOU WOULDA DONE, THEY'D GONE FOR OPTION #2...?
HBLOOORK

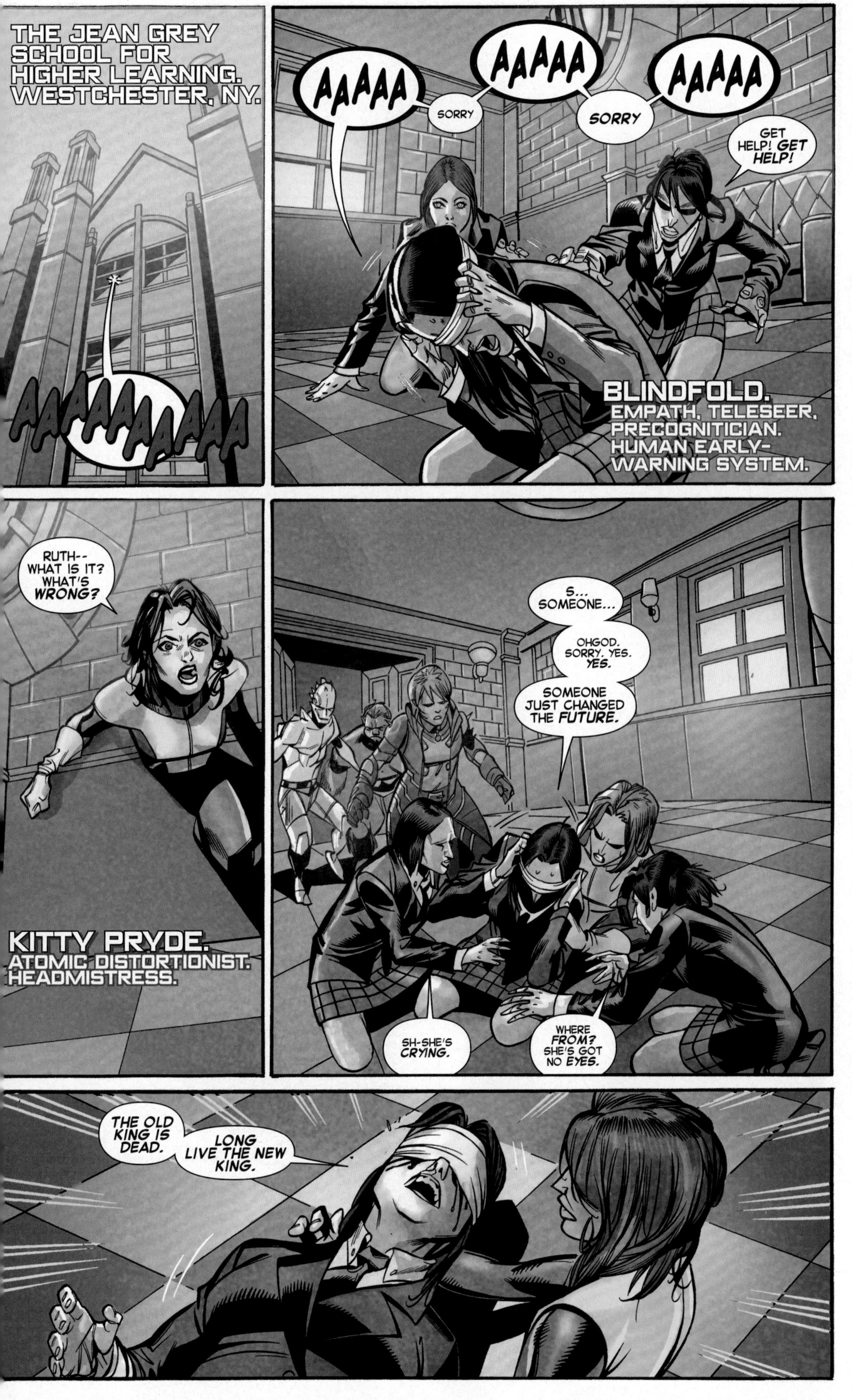
THE JEAN GREY SCHOOL FOR HIGHER LEARNING. WESTCHESTER, NY.
AAAAAAAAAA
AAAAA
SORRY
AAAAA
SORRY
AAAAA
GET HELP! GET HELP!
BLINDFOLD.
EMPATH, TELESEER, PRECOGNITICIAN. HUMAN EARLY-WARNING SYSTEM.
RUTH-- WHAT IS IT? WHAT'S WRONG?
KITTY PRYDE.
ATOMIC DISTORTIONIST. HEADMISTRESS.
S... SOMEONE...
OHGOD. SORRY. YES. YES.
SOMEONE JUST CHANGED THE FUTURE.
SH-SHE'S CRYING.
WHERE FROM? SHE'S GOT NO EYES.
THE OLD KING IS DEAD.
LONG LIVE THE NEW KING.

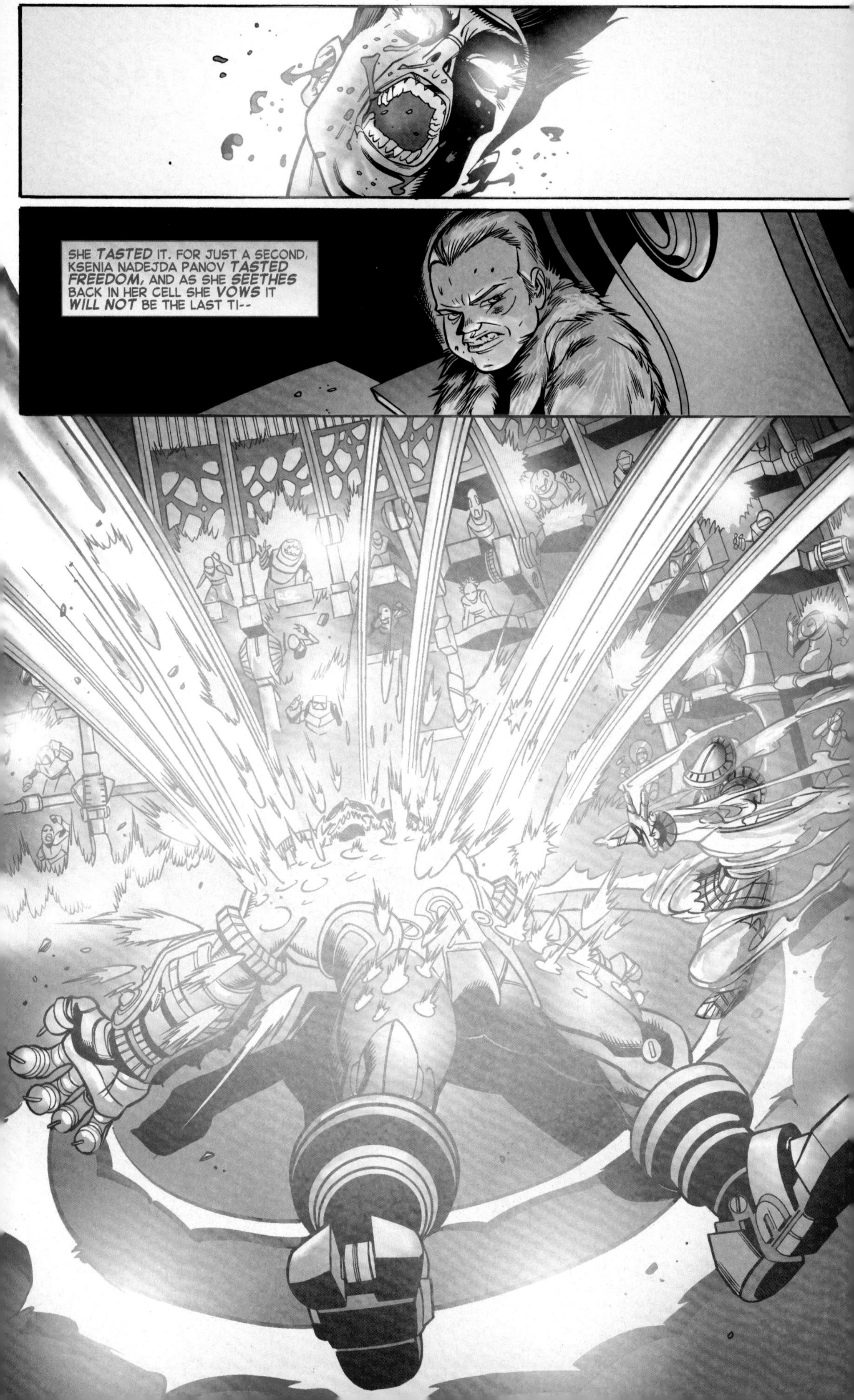
SHE TASTED IT. FOR JUST A SECOND, KSENIA NADEJDA PANOV TASTED FREEDOM, AND AS SHE SEETHES BACK IN HER CELL SHE VOWS IT WILL NOT BE THE LAST TI--

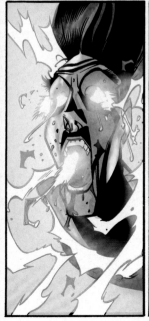

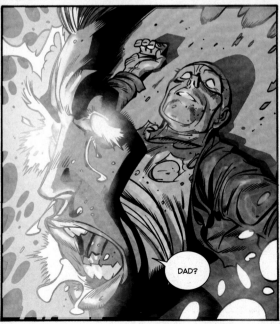

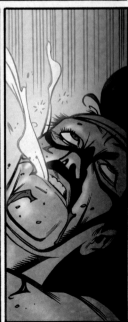

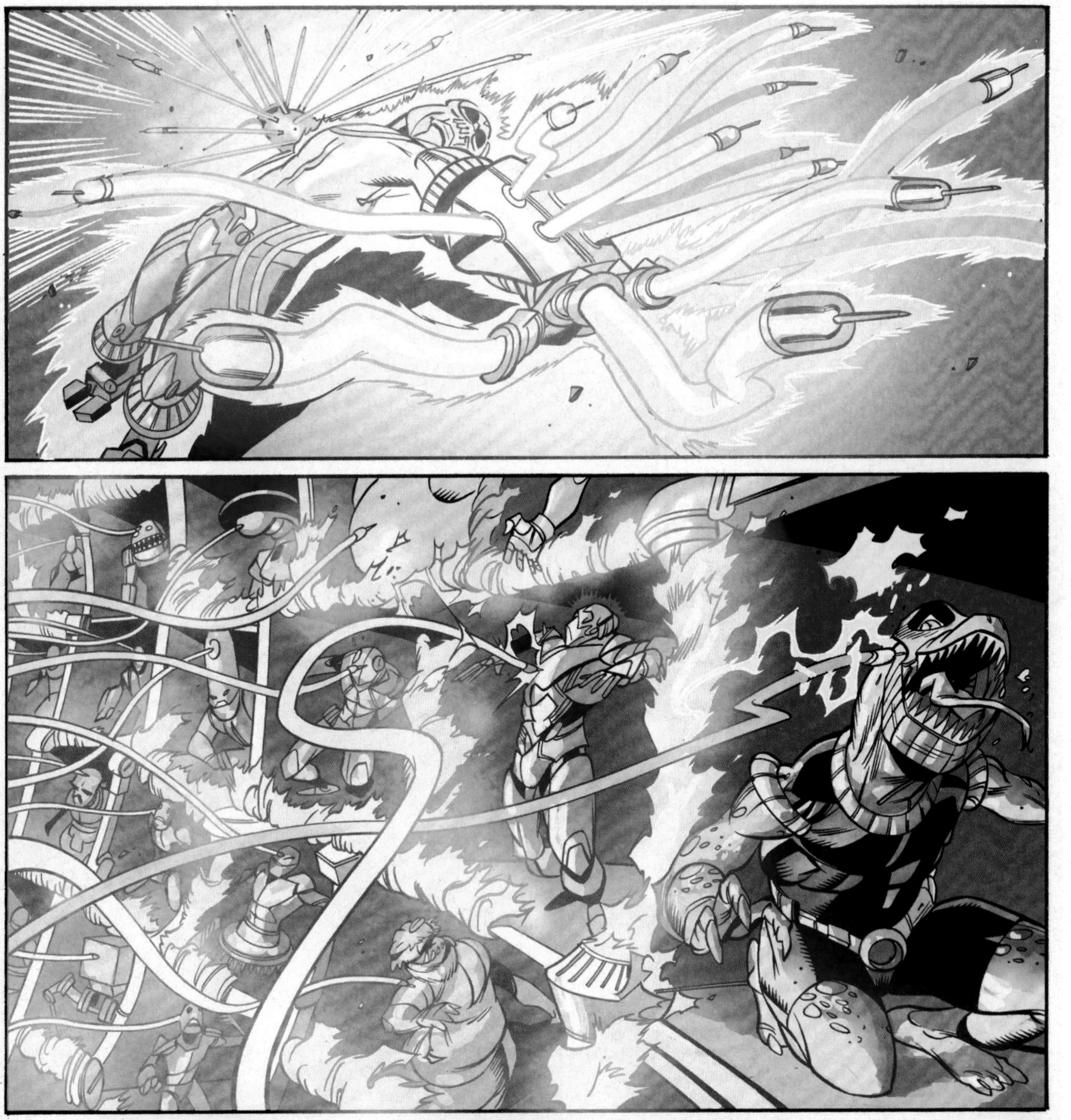
DAD?

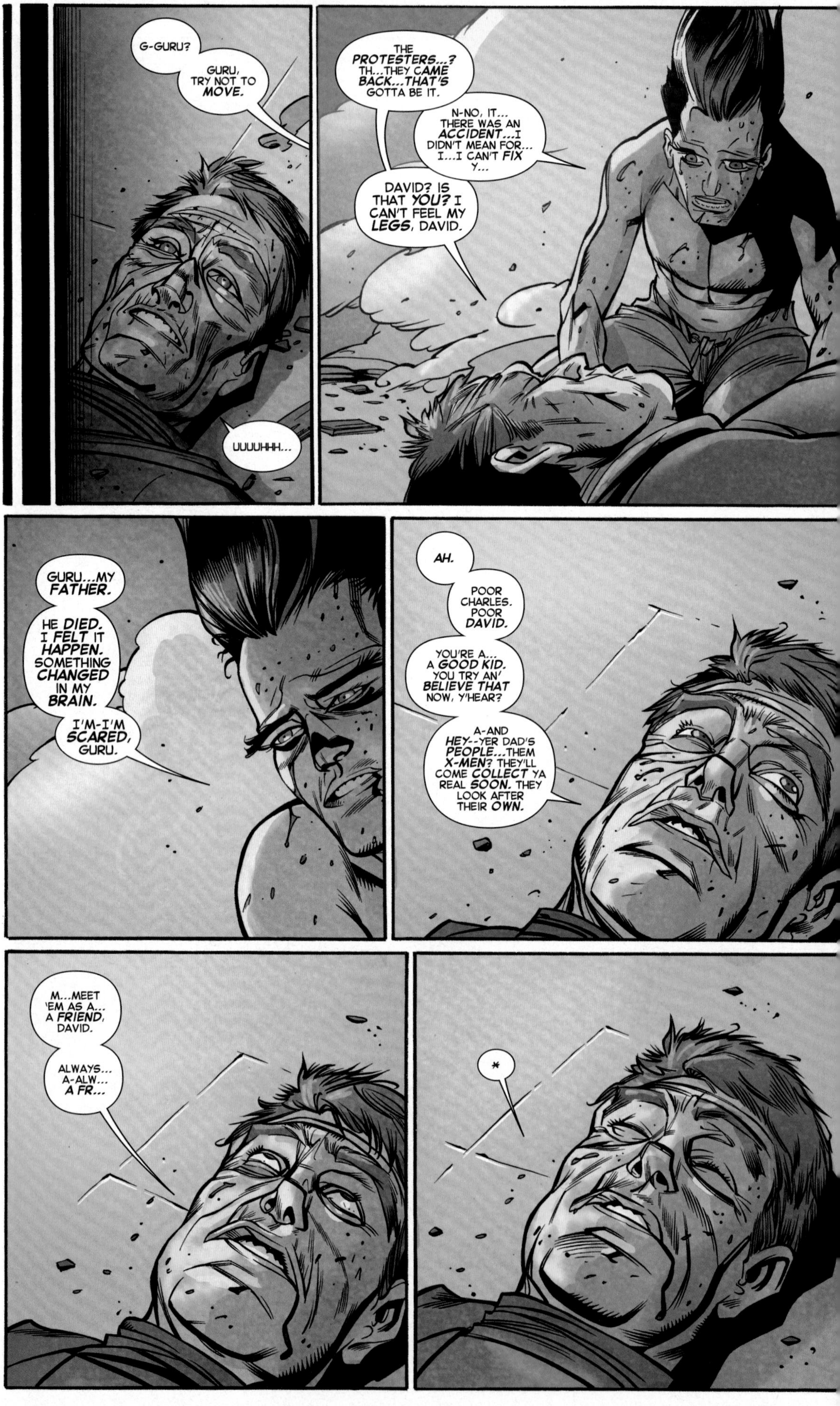
G-GURU?
GURU, TRY NOT TO MOVE.
UUUUHHH...
THE PROTESTERS...? TH...THEY CAME BACK...THAT'S GOTTA BE IT.
N-NO, IT... THERE WAS AN ACCIDENT...I DIDN'T MEAN FOR... I...I CAN'T FIX Y...
DAVID? IS THAT YOU? I CAN'T FEEL MY LEGS, DAVID.
GURU...MY FATHER.
HE DIED. I FELT IT HAPPEN. SOMETHING CHANGED IN MY BRAIN.
I'M-I'M SCARED, GURU.
AH.
POOR CHARLES. POOR DAVID.
YOU'RE A... A GOOD KID. YOU TRY AN' BELIEVE THAT NOW, Y'HEAR?
A-AND HEY--YER DAD'S PEOPLE...THEM X-MEN? THEY'LL COME COLLECT YA REAL SOON. THEY LOOK AFTER THEIR OWN.
M...MEET 'EM AS A... A FRIEND, DAVID.
ALWAYS... A-ALW... A FR...
*

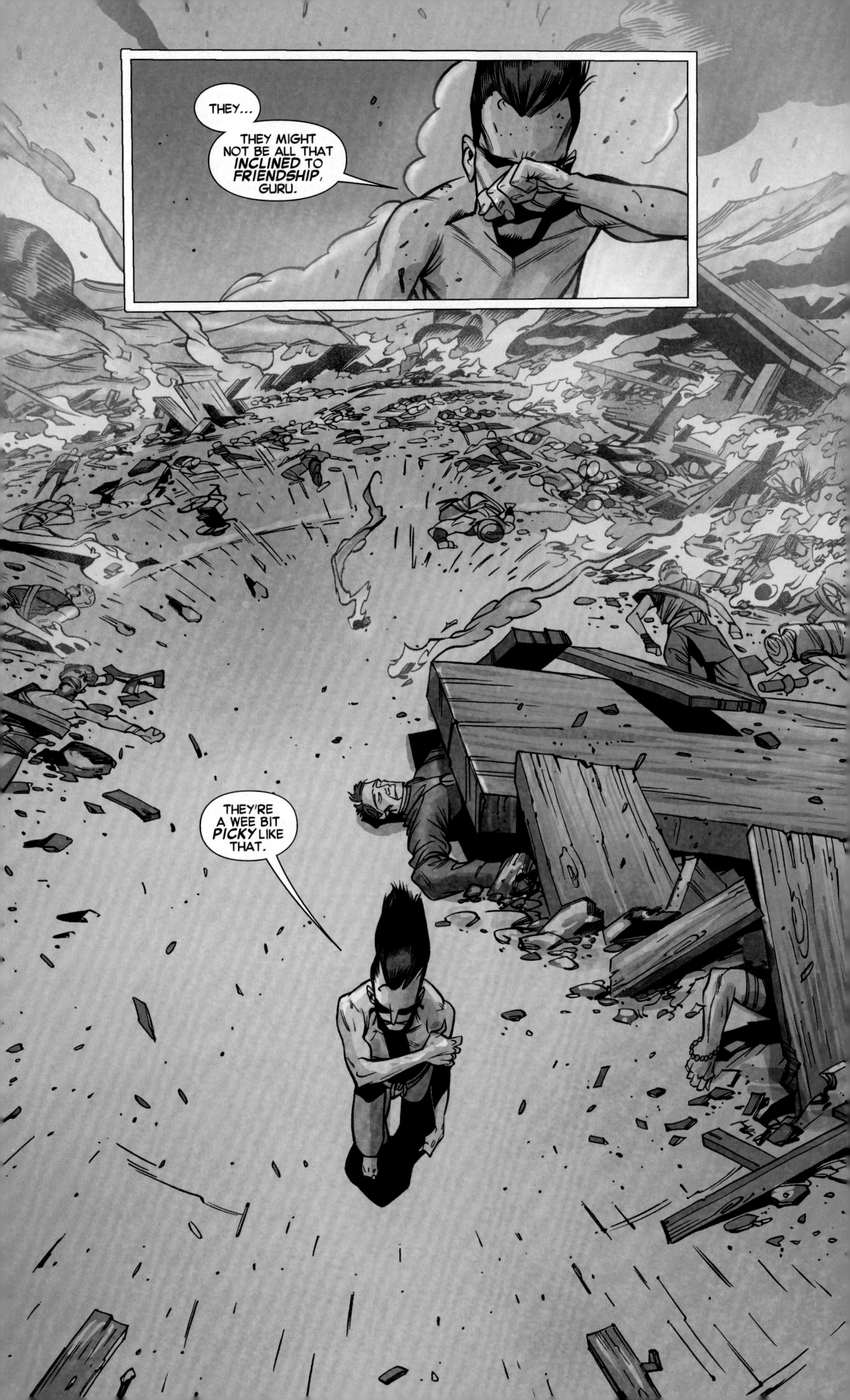
THEY...
THEY MIGHT NOT BE ALL THAT INCLINED TO FRIENDSHIP, GURU.
THEY'RE A WEE BIT PICKY LIKE THAT.

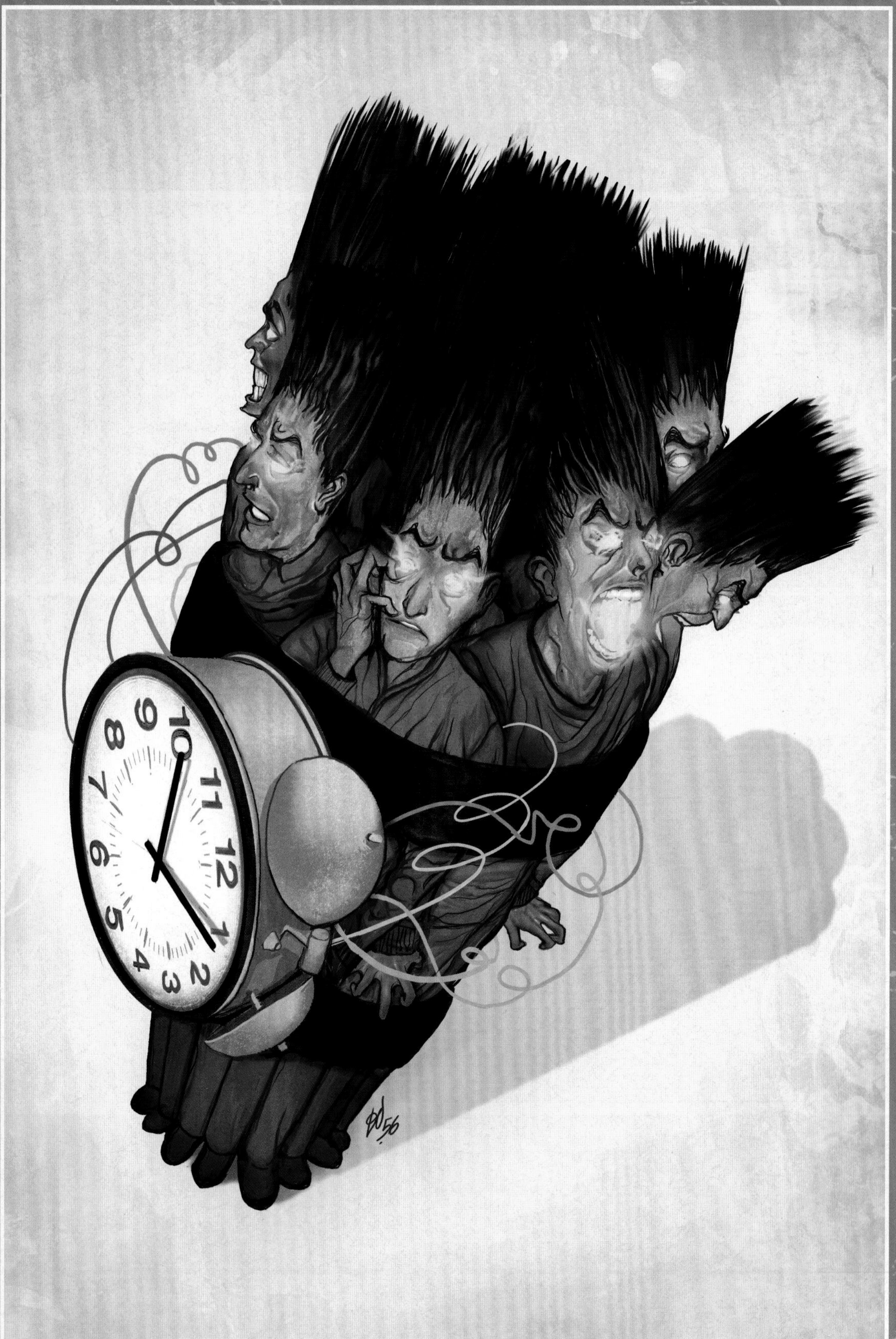

TWO

HERE'S A *THING:*

WHEN YOUR *DAD'S* THE PLANET'S FOREMOST *PSYCHIC MINDBOTHERER,* YOU GET A WEE BIT BLOODY *USED* TO THINGS BEIN' *WEIRD.* FOR INSTANCE:

THERE'S A *PLACE* MY MOST *SECRET THOUGHTS'RE* BROADCAST LIKE A BALLGAME ANNOUNCEMENT.

THERE'S A *CONCEPTUAL REALM* INSIDE MY *BROKEN BRAIN,* WITH EVERY APPEARANCE OF A *CRAPPY B-MOVIE SCI-FI PRISON.*

WEIRD, NO? I *WARNED* YOU.

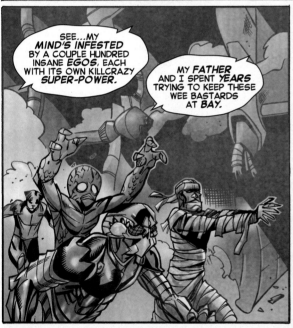

SEE...MY *MIND'S* INFESTED BY A COUPLE HUNDRED INSANE *EGOS,* EACH WITH ITS OWN KILLCRAZY *SUPER-POWER.*

MY *FATHER* AND I SPENT *YEARS* TRYING TO KEEP THESE WEE BASTARDS AT *BAY.*

YEARS OF... OF *TOO MANY ACCIDENTS.* TOO MUCH *TRAGEDY.* YEARS WHICH I *THOUGHT* FINALLY *PAID OFF* WHEN THIS *PLACE* WAS *CONCEIVED.*

A *JAIL'S* AS GOOD A WAY AS *ANY* TO *CONTROL* THE *UNRULY.*

MY *NAME'S DAVID HALLER.* OUT IN THE *REAL WORLD* PEOPLE IN DAFT COSTUMES CALL ME *LEGION.* I WISH THEY BLOODY *WOULDN'T.*

MY *FATHER'S DEAD.* HE'S *DEAD,* AND I'M NOT ENTIRELY READY TO *THINK* ABOUT THAT, EXCEPT THAT THE *SHOCKWAVE* OF IT APPEARS TO'VE *BUGGERED* EVERYTHING *UP.*

SO... THIS WHOLE *"PRISON-FOR-A-BRAIN"* IDEA?

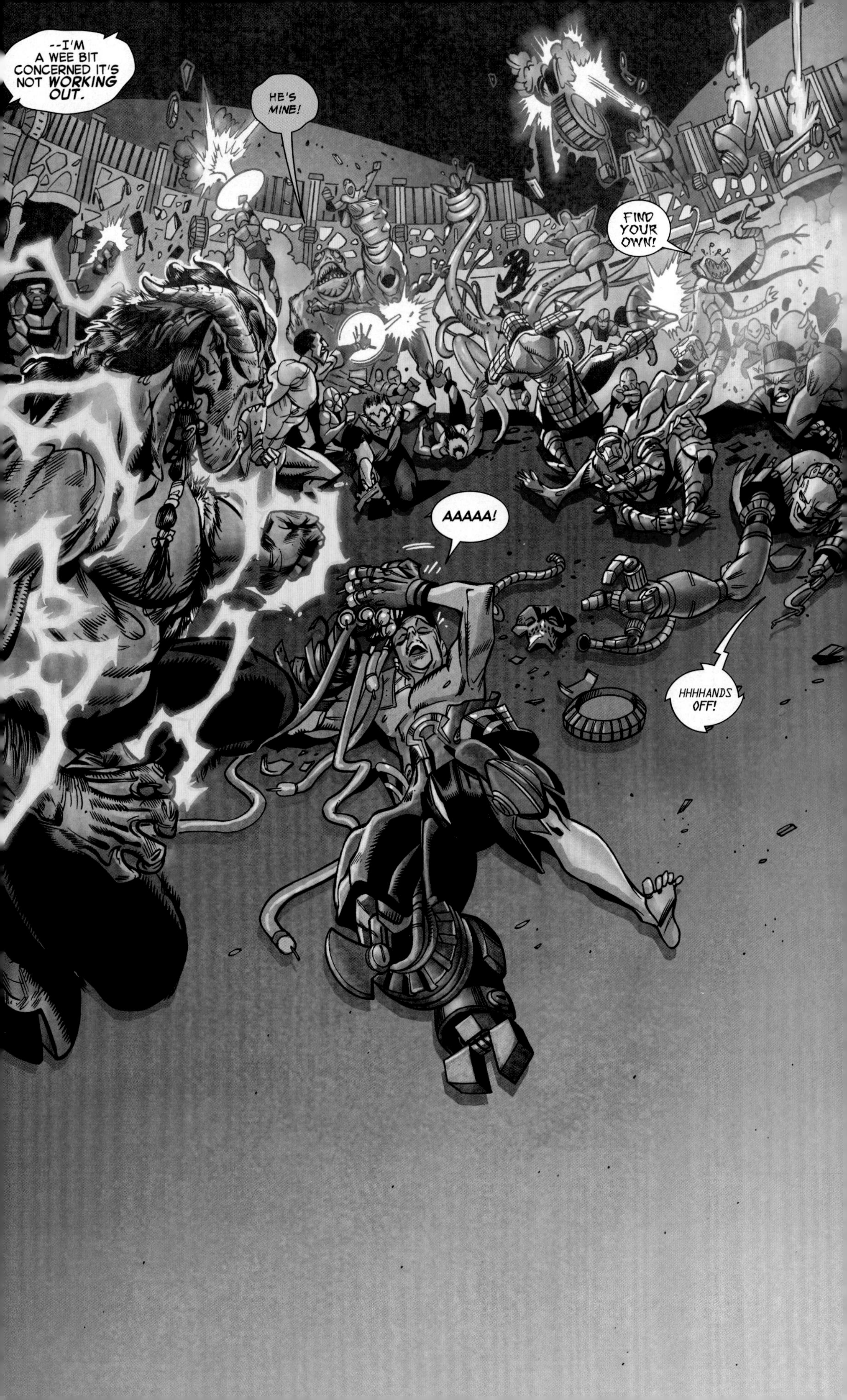
--I'M A WEE BIT CONCERNED IT'S NOT WORKING OUT.
HE'S MINE!
FIND YOUR OWN!
AAAAA!
HHHHANDS OFF!

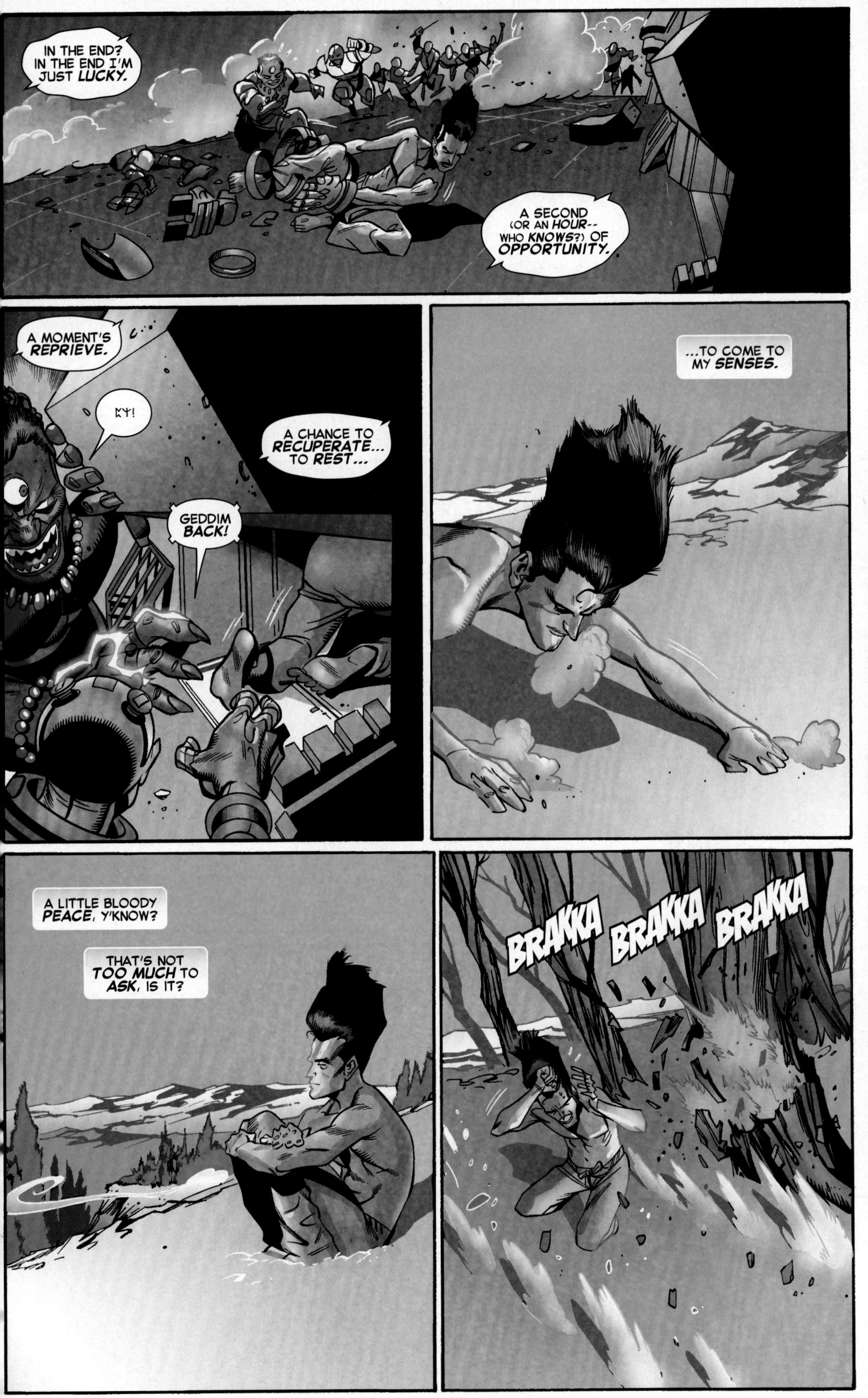
IN THE END? IN THE END I'M JUST LUCKY.
A SECOND (OR AN HOUR-- WHO KNOWS?) OF OPPORTUNITY.
A MOMENT'S REPRIEVE.
A CHANCE TO RECUPERATE... TO REST...
GEDDIM BACK!
...TO COME TO MY SENSES.
A LITTLE BLOODY PEACE, Y'KNOW?
THAT'S NOT TOO MUCH TO ASK, IS IT?
BRAKKA BRAKKA BRAKKA

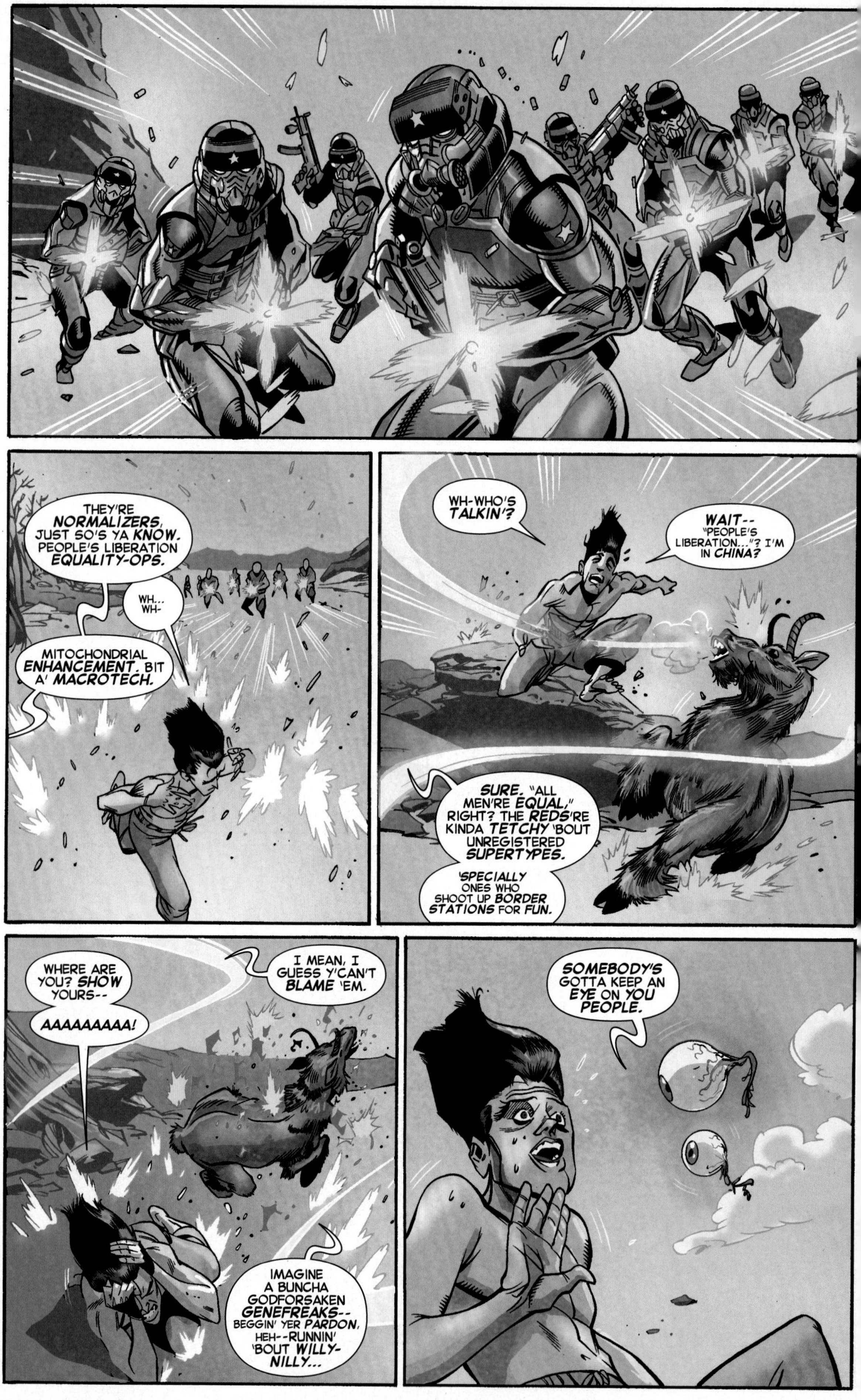
THEY'RE NORMALIZERS, JUST SO'S YA KNOW. PEOPLE'S LIBERATION EQUALITY-OPS.
WH... WH-
MITOCHONDRIAL ENHANCEMENT. BIT A' MACROTECH.
WH-WHO'S TALKIN'?
WAIT-- "PEOPLE'S LIBERATION..."? I'M IN CHINA?
SURE. "ALL MEN'RE EQUAL," RIGHT? THE REDS'RE KINDA TETCHY 'BOUT UNREGISTERED SUPERTYPES.
'SPECIALLY ONES WHO SHOOT UP BORDER STATIONS FOR FUN.
WHERE ARE YOU? SHOW YOURS--
AAAAAAAAA!
I MEAN, I GUESS Y'CAN'T BLAME 'EM.
IMAGINE A BUNCHA GODFORSAKEN GENEFREAKS-- BEGGIN' YER PARDON, HEH--RUNNIN' 'BOUT WILLY-NILLY...
SOMEBODY'S GOTTA KEEP AN EYE ON YOU PEOPLE.

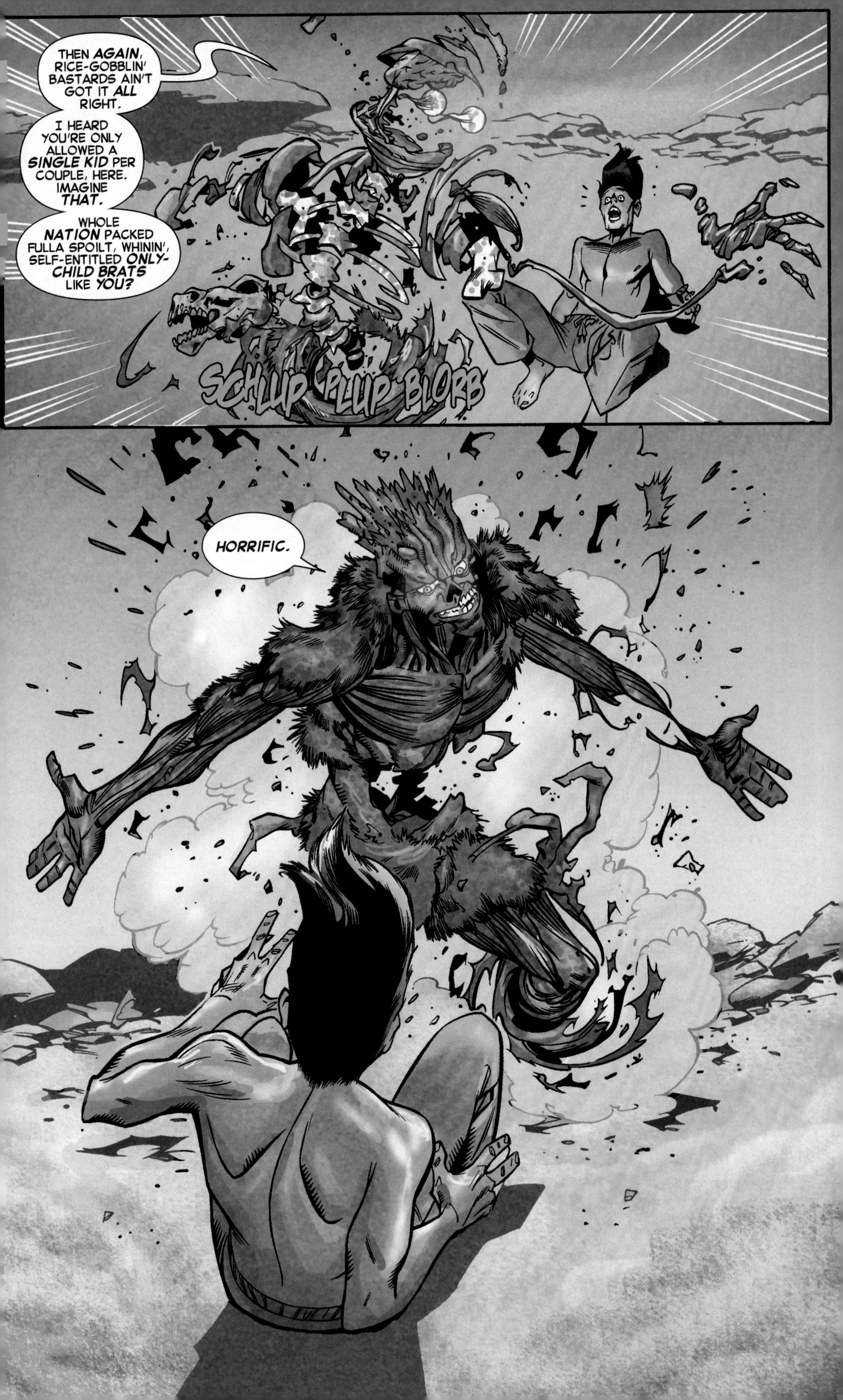
THEN AGAIN, RICE-GOBBLIN' BASTARDS AIN'T GOT IT ALL RIGHT.
I HEARD YOU'RE ONLY ALLOWED A SINGLE KID PER COUPLE, HERE. IMAGINE THAT.
WHOLE NATION PACKED FULLA SPOILT, WHININ', SELF-ENTITLED ONLY-CHILD BRATS LIKE YOU?
SCHLUP PLUP BLORB
HORRIFIC.

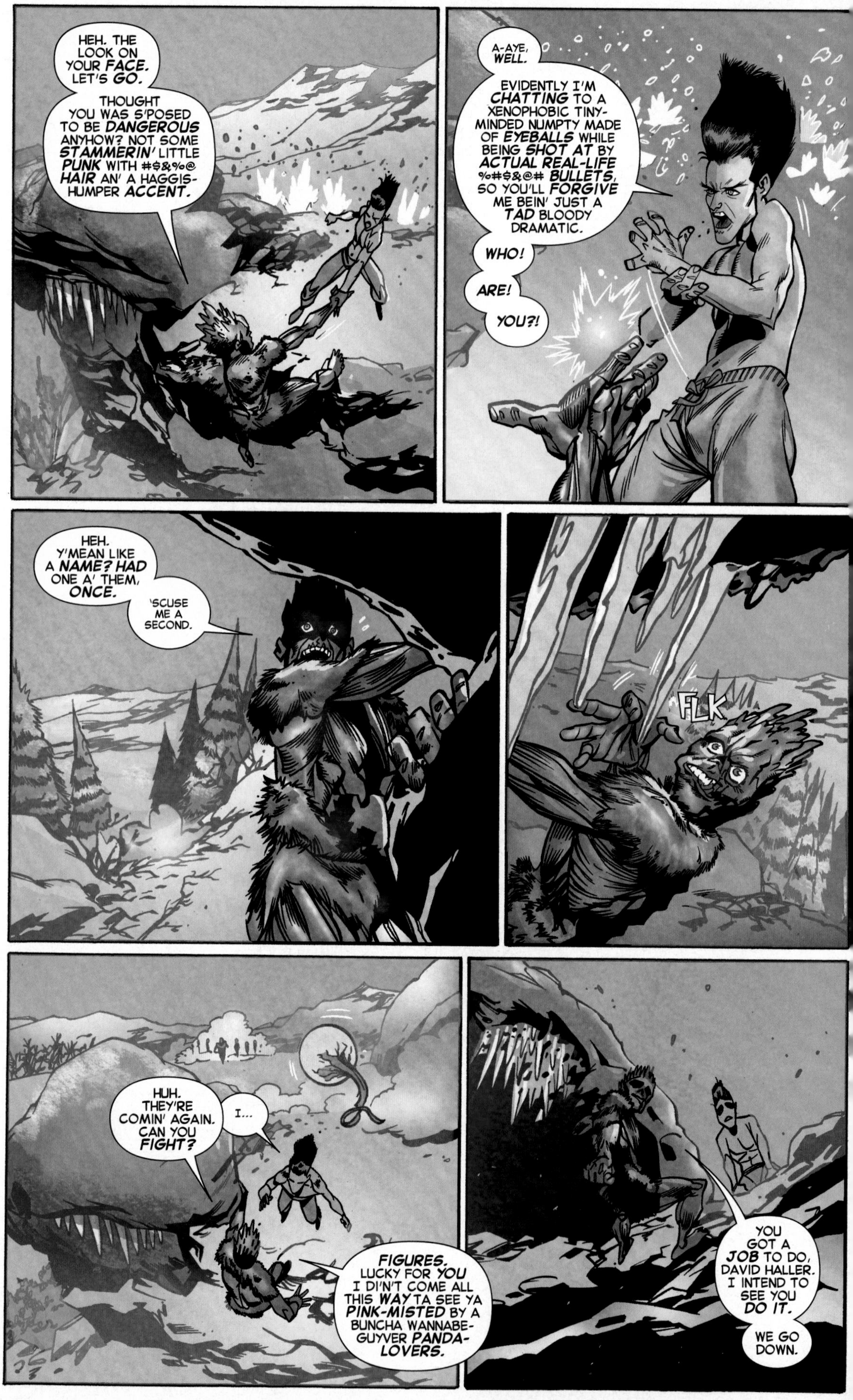
HEH. THE LOOK ON YOUR FACE. LET'S GO.
THOUGHT YOU WAS S'POSED TO BE DANGEROUS ANYHOW? NOT SOME STAMMERIN' LITTLE PUNK WITH #$&%@ HAIR AN' A HAGGIS-HUMPER ACCENT.
A-AYE, WELL.
EVIDENTLY I'M CHATTING TO A XENOPHOBIC TINY-MINDED NUMPTY MADE OF EYEBALLS WHILE BEING SHOT AT BY ACTUAL REAL-LIFE %#$&@# BULLETS, SO YOU'LL FORGIVE ME BEIN' JUST A TAD BLOODY DRAMATIC.
WHO!
ARE!
YOU?!
HEH. Y'MEAN LIKE A NAME? HAD ONE A' THEM, ONCE.
'SCUSE ME A SECOND.
FLK
HUH. THEY'RE COMIN' AGAIN. CAN YOU FIGHT?
I...
FIGURES. LUCKY FOR YOU I DI'N'T COME ALL THIS WAY TA SEE YA PINK-MISTED BY A BUNCHA WANNABE-GUYVER PANDA-LOVERS.
YOU GOT A JOB TO DO, DAVID HALLER. I INTEND TO SEE YOU DO IT.
WE GO DOWN.

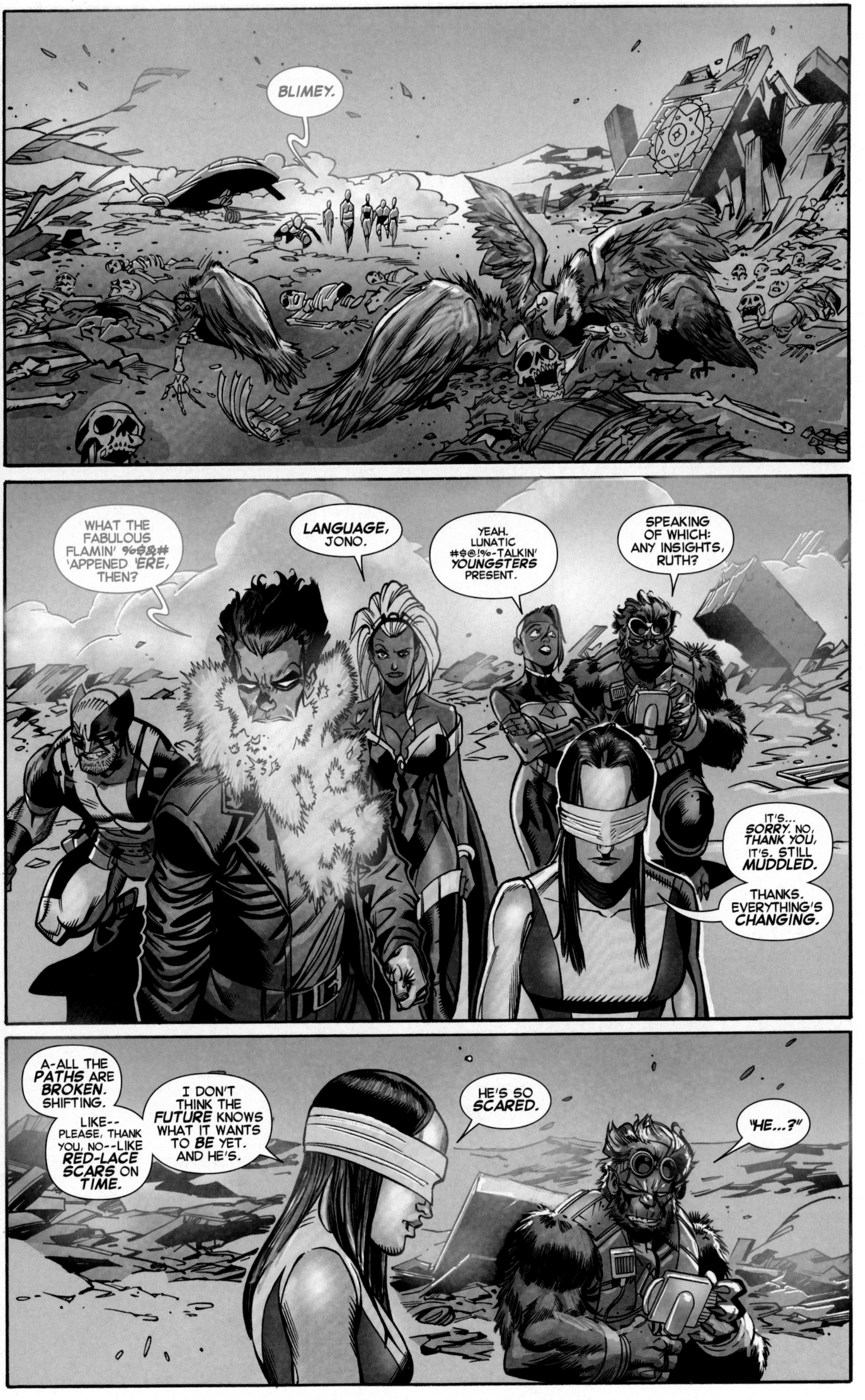
BLIMEY.
WHAT THE FABULOUS FLAMIN' %$&# 'APPENED 'ERE, THEN?
LANGUAGE, JONO.
YEAH. LUNATIC #$@!%-TALKIN' YOUNGSTERS PRESENT.
SPEAKING OF WHICH: ANY INSIGHTS, RUTH?
IT'S... SORRY. NO, THANK YOU, IT'S. STILL MUDDLED.
THANKS. EVERYTHING'S CHANGING.
A-ALL THE PATHS ARE BROKEN. SHIFTING.
LIKE-- PLEASE, THANK YOU, NO--LIKE RED-LACE SCARS ON TIME.
I DON'T THINK THE FUTURE KNOWS WHAT IT WANTS TO BE YET. AND HE'S.
HE'S SO SCARED.
"HE...?"

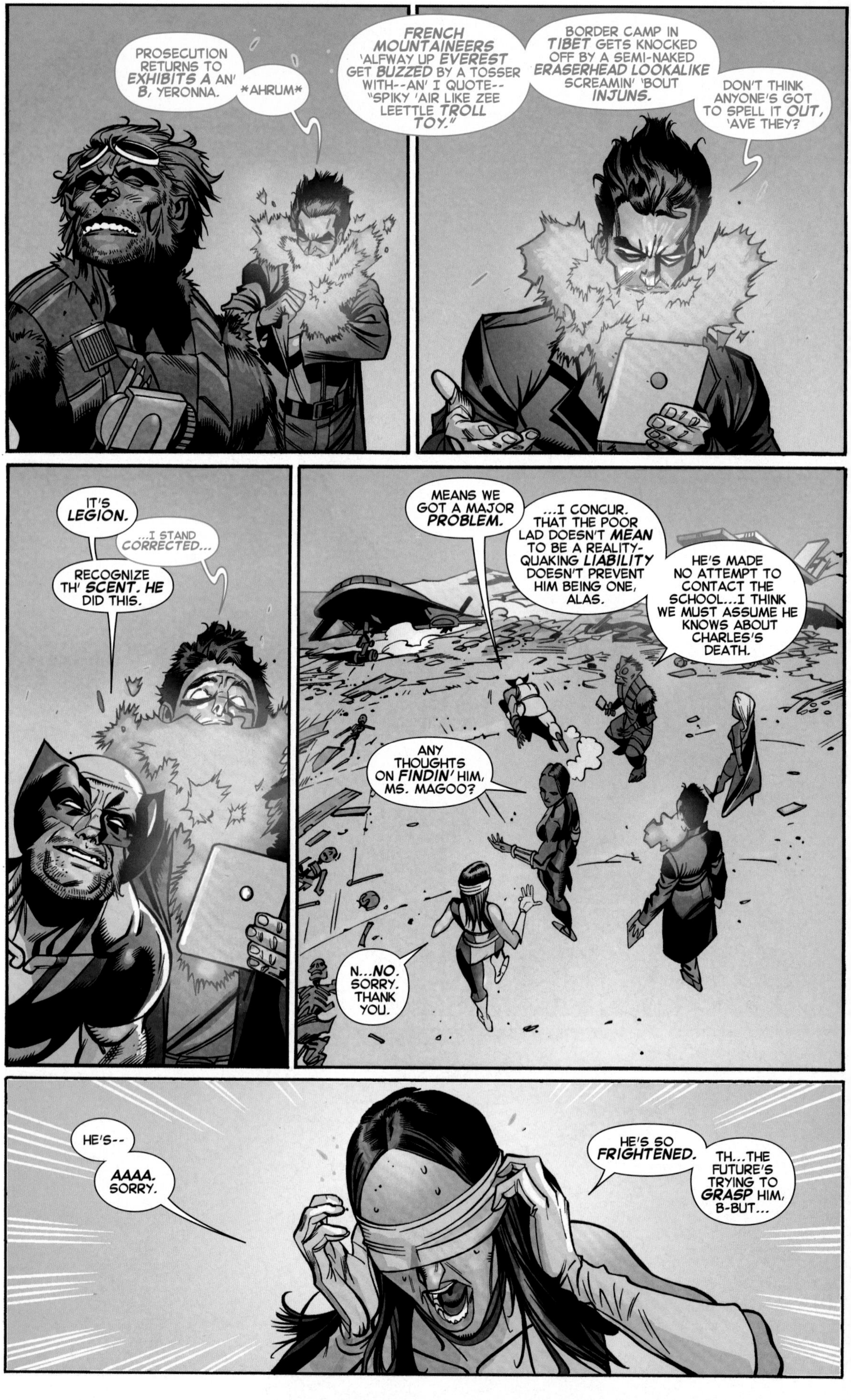
PROSECUTION RETURNS TO EXHIBITS A AN' B, YERONNA.
AHRUM
FRENCH MOUNTAINEERS 'ALFWAY UP EVEREST GET BUZZED BY A TOSSER WITH--AN' I QUOTE-- "SPIKY 'AIR LIKE ZEE LEETTLE TROLL TOY."
BORDER CAMP IN TIBET GETS KNOCKED OFF BY A SEMI-NAKED ERASERHEAD LOOKALIKE SCREAMIN' 'BOUT INJUNS.
DON'T THINK ANYONE'S GOT TO SPELL IT OUT, 'AVE THEY?
IT'S LEGION.
RECOGNIZE TH' SCENT. HE DID THIS.
...I STAND CORRECTED...
MEANS WE GOT A MAJOR PROBLEM.
...I CONCUR. THAT THE POOR LAD DOESN'T MEAN TO BE A REALITY-QUAKING LIABILITY DOESN'T PREVENT HIM BEING ONE, ALAS.
HE'S MADE NO ATTEMPT TO CONTACT THE SCHOOL...I THINK WE MUST ASSUME HE KNOWS ABOUT CHARLES'S DEATH.
ANY THOUGHTS ON FINDIN' HIM, MS. MAGOO?
N...NO. SORRY. THANK YOU.
HE'S--
AAAA. SORRY.
HE'S SO FRIGHTENED.
TH...THE FUTURE'S TRYING TO GRASP HIM, B-BUT...

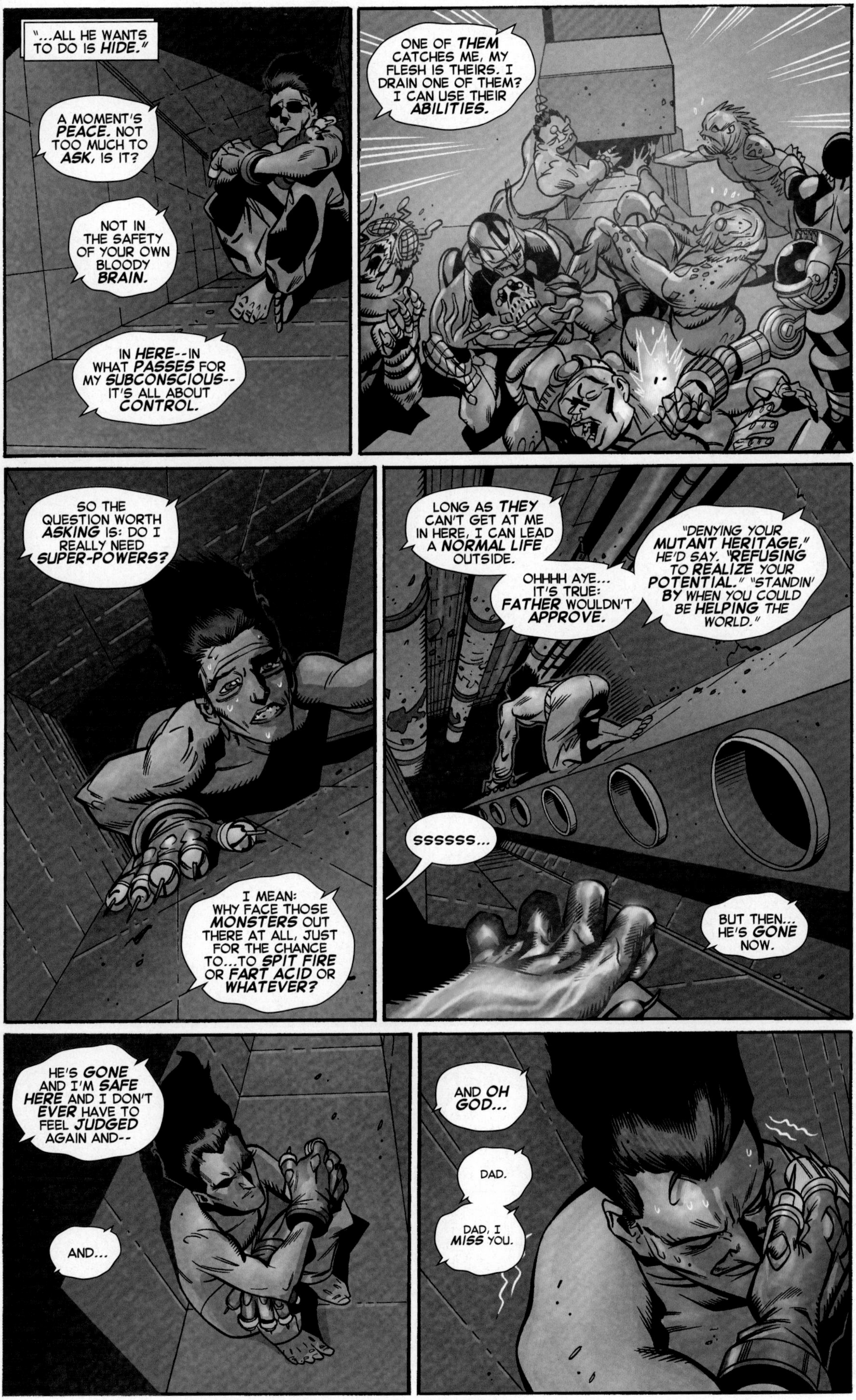
"...ALL HE WANTS TO DO IS HIDE."
A MOMENT'S PEACE. NOT TOO MUCH TO ASK, IS IT?
NOT IN THE SAFETY OF YOUR OWN BLOODY BRAIN.
IN HERE--IN WHAT PASSES FOR MY SUBCONSCIOUS--IT'S ALL ABOUT CONTROL.
ONE OF THEM CATCHES ME, MY FLESH IS THEIRS. I DRAIN ONE OF THEM? I CAN USE THEIR ABILITIES.
SO THE QUESTION WORTH ASKING IS: DO I REALLY NEED SUPER-POWERS?
I MEAN: WHY FACE THOSE MONSTERS OUT THERE AT ALL, JUST FOR THE CHANCE TO...TO SPIT FIRE OR FART ACID OR WHATEVER?
LONG AS THEY CAN'T GET AT ME IN HERE, I CAN LEAD A NORMAL LIFE OUTSIDE.
OHHHH AYE... IT'S TRUE: FATHER WOULDN'T APPROVE.
"DENYING YOUR MUTANT HERITAGE," HE'D SAY. "REFUSING TO REALIZE YOUR POTENTIAL." "STANDIN' BY WHEN YOU COULD BE HELPING THE WORLD."
SSSSSS...
BUT THEN... HE'S GONE NOW.
HE'S GONE AND I'M SAFE HERE AND I DON'T EVER HAVE TO FEEL JUDGED AGAIN AND--
AND...
AND OH GOD...
DAD.
DAD, I MISS YOU.

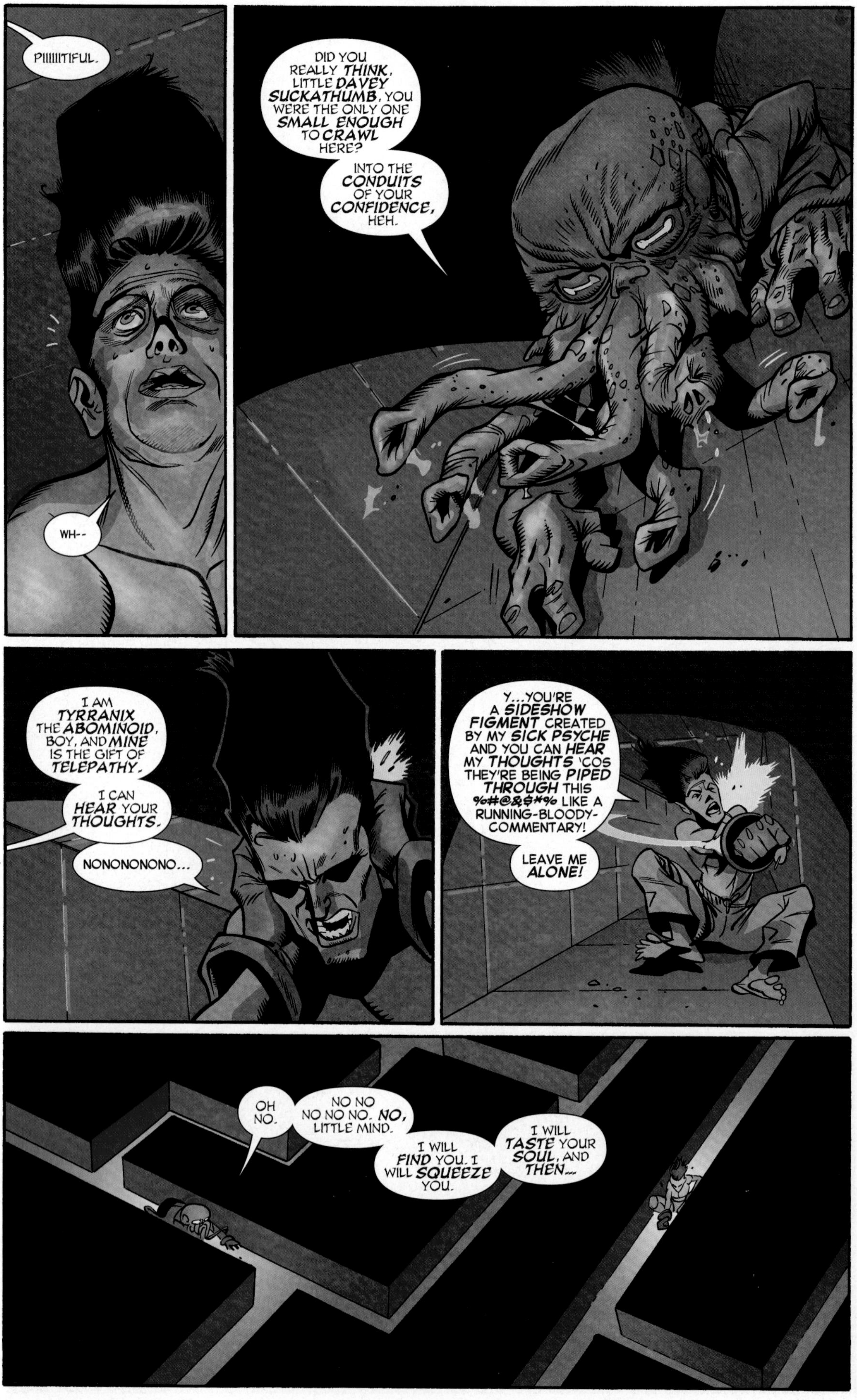
PIIIIITIFUL.
WH--
DID YOU REALLY THINK, LITTLE DAVEY SUCKATHUMB, YOU WERE THE ONLY ONE SMALL ENOUGH TO CRAWL HERE?
INTO THE CONDUITS OF YOUR CONFIDENCE, HEH.
I AM TYRRANIX THE ABOMINOID, BOY, AND MINE IS THE GIFT OF TELEPATHY.
I CAN HEAR YOUR THOUGHTS.
NONONONONO...
Y...YOU'RE A SIDESHOW FIGMENT CREATED BY MY SICK PSYCHE AND YOU CAN HEAR MY THOUGHTS 'COS THEY'RE BEING PIPED THROUGH THIS %#@&$*% LIKE A RUNNING-BLOODY-COMMENTARY!
LEAVE ME ALONE!
OH NO.
NO NO NO NO NO. NO, LITTLE MIND.
I WILL FIND YOU. I WILL SQUEEZE YOU.
I WILL TASTE YOUR SOUL, AND THEN...

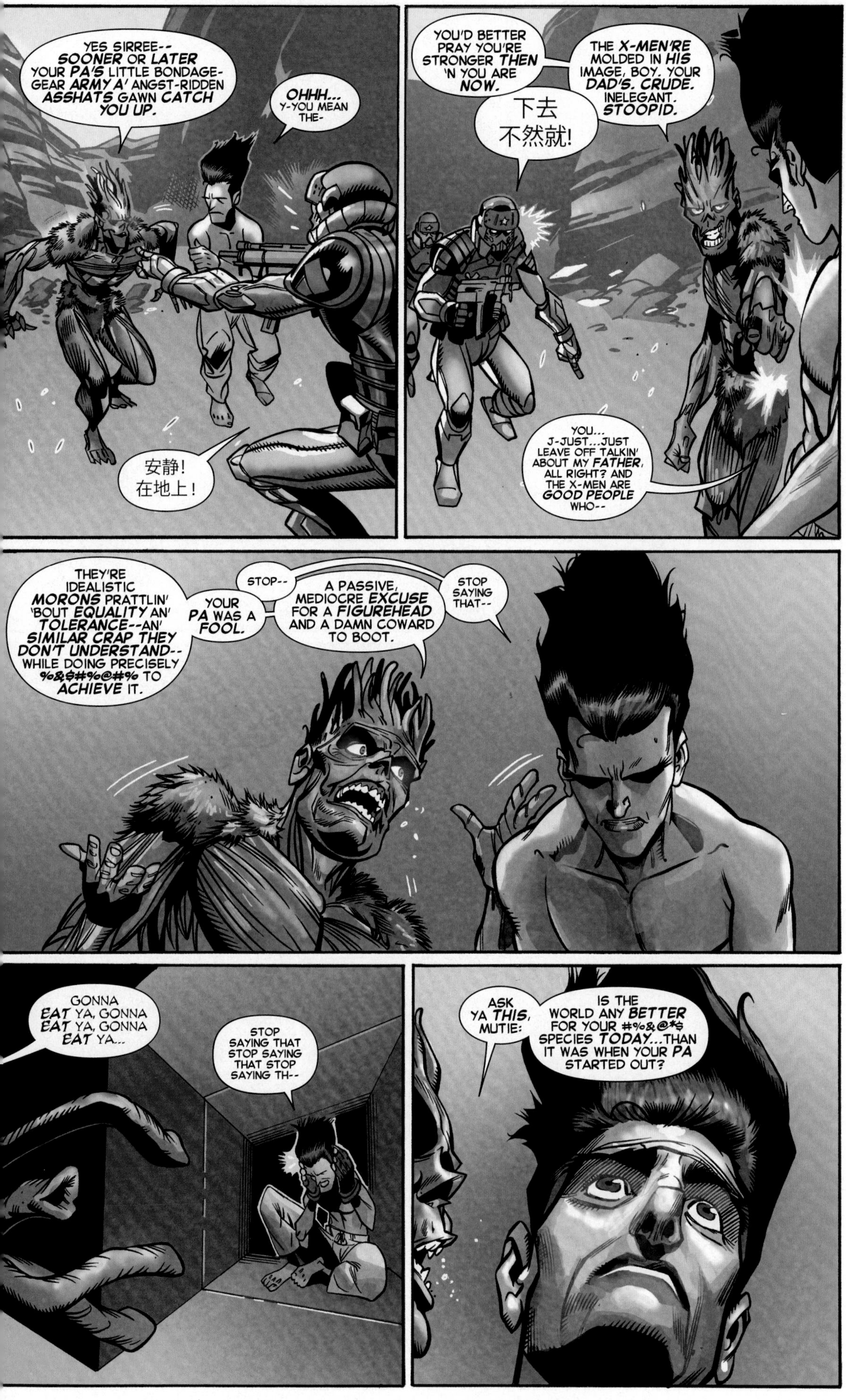
YES SIRREE-- SOONER OR LATER YOUR PA'S LITTLE BONDAGE-GEAR ARMY A' ANGST-RIDDEN ASSHATS GAWN CATCH YOU UP.
OHHH... Y-YOU MEAN THE-
安静! 在地上!
YOU'D BETTER PRAY YOU'RE STRONGER THEN 'N YOU ARE NOW.
THE X-MEN'RE MOLDED IN HIS IMAGE, BOY. YOUR DAD'S. CRUDE. INELEGANT. STOOPID.
下去 不然就!
YOU... J-JUST...JUST LEAVE OFF TALKIN' ABOUT MY FATHER, ALL RIGHT? AND THE X-MEN ARE GOOD PEOPLE WHO--
THEY'RE IDEALISTIC MORONS PRATTLIN' 'BOUT EQUALITY AN' TOLERANCE--AN' SIMILAR CRAP THEY DON'T UNDERSTAND-- WHILE DOING PRECISELY %&$#%@#% TO ACHIEVE IT.
YOUR PA WAS A FOOL.
STOP--
A PASSIVE, MEDIOCRE EXCUSE FOR A FIGUREHEAD AND A DAMN COWARD TO BOOT.
STOP SAYING THAT--
GONNA EAT YA, GONNA EAT YA, GONNA EAT YA...
STOP SAYING THAT STOP SAYING THAT STOP SAYING TH--
ASK YA THIS, MUTIE:
IS THE WORLD ANY BETTER FOR YOUR #%&@*$ SPECIES TODAY...THAN IT WAS WHEN YOUR PA STARTED OUT?

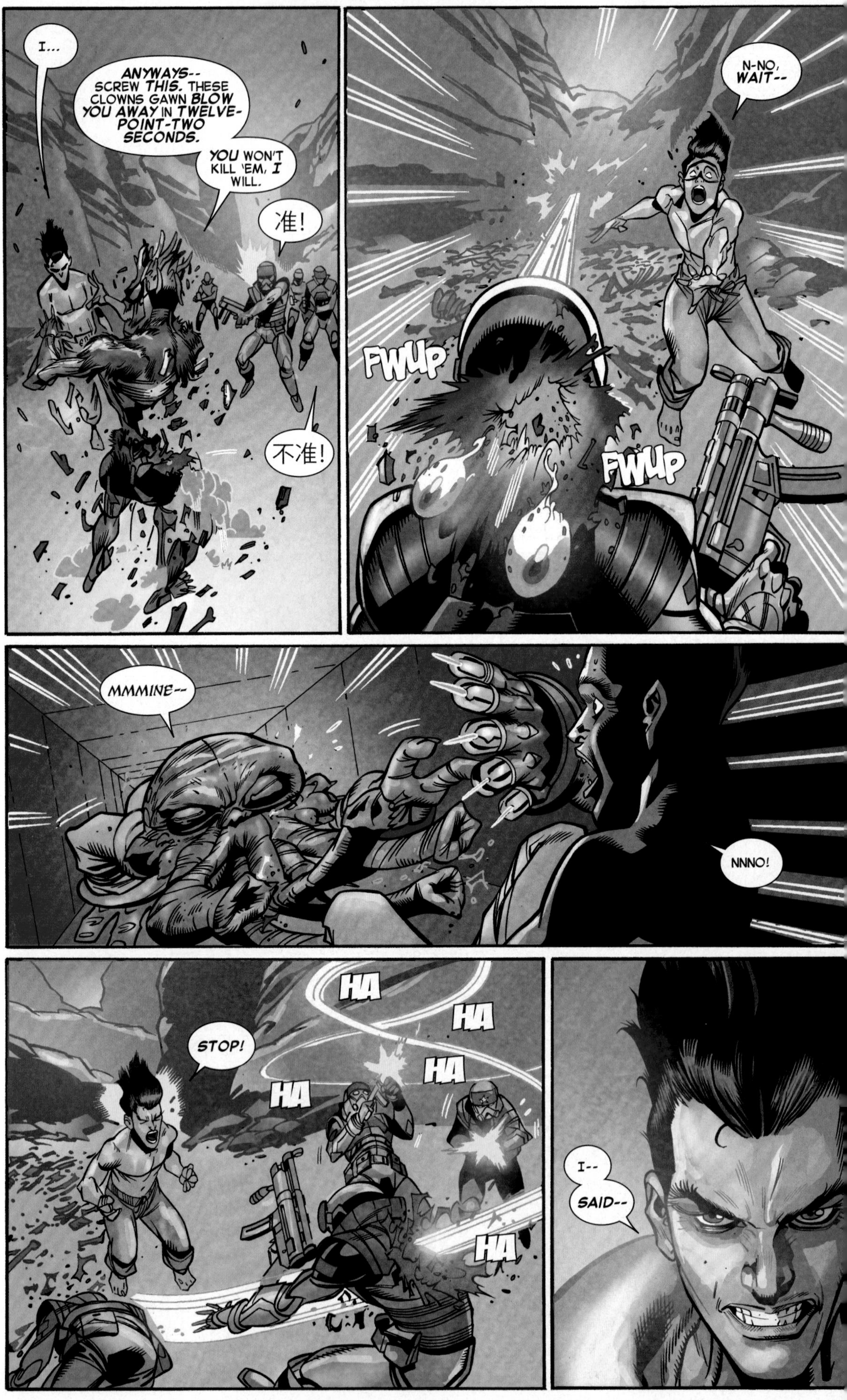

I...
ANYWAYS-- SCREW THIS. THESE CLOWNS GAWN BLOW YOU AWAY IN TWELVE-POINT-TWO SECONDS.
YOU WON'T KILL 'EM, I WILL.
准!
不准!
N-NO, WAIT--
FWUP
FWUP
MMMINE--
NNNO!
STOP!
HA
HA
HA
HA
HA
I--
SAID--

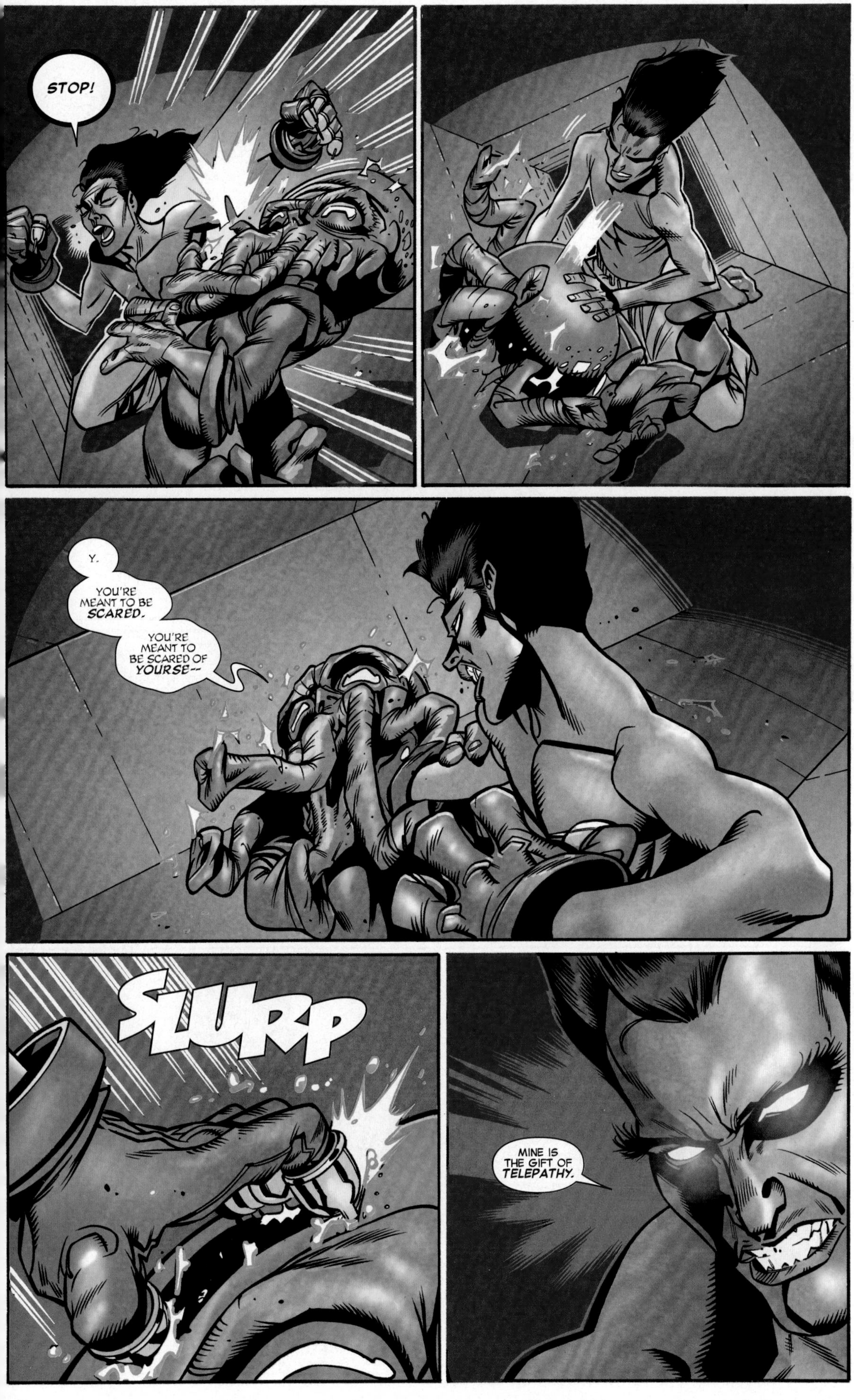
STOP!
Y.
YOU'RE MEANT TO BE SCARED.
YOU'RE MEANT TO BE SCARED OF YOURSE--
SLURP
MINE IS THE GIFT OF TELEPATHY.

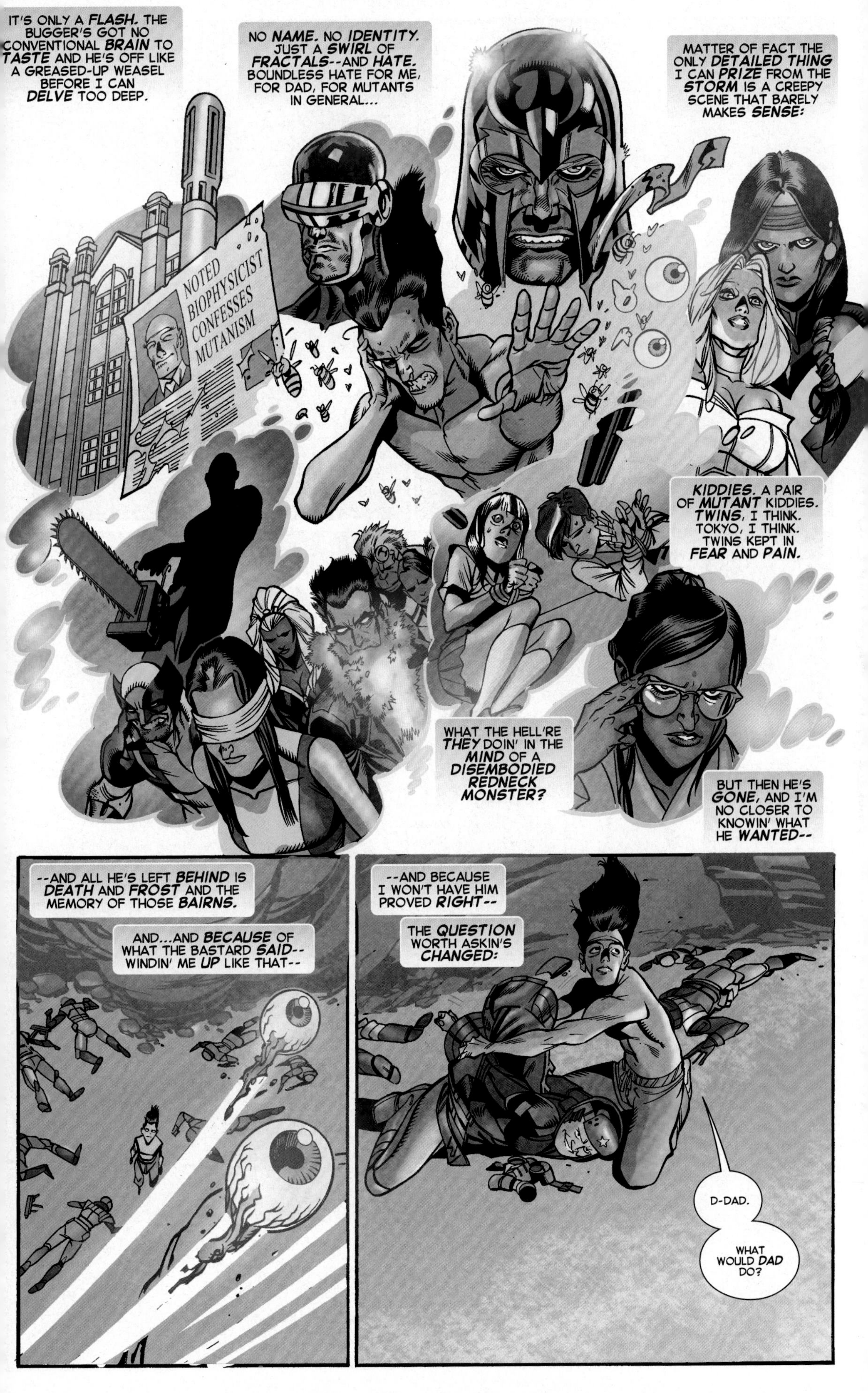
IT'S ONLY A FLASH. THE BUGGER'S GOT NO CONVENTIONAL BRAIN TO TASTE AND HE'S OFF LIKE A GREASED-UP WEASEL BEFORE I CAN DELVE TOO DEEP.
NO NAME. NO IDENTITY. JUST A SWIRL OF FRACTALS--AND HATE. BOUNDLESS HATE FOR ME, FOR DAD, FOR MUTANTS IN GENERAL...
MATTER OF FACT THE ONLY DETAILED THING I CAN PRIZE FROM THE STORM IS A CREEPY SCENE THAT BARELY MAKES SENSE:
NOTED BIOPHYSICIST CONFESSES MUTANISM
KIDDIES. A PAIR OF MUTANT KIDDIES. TWINS, I THINK. TOKYO, I THINK. TWINS KEPT IN FEAR AND PAIN.
WHAT THE HELL'RE THEY DOIN' IN THE MIND OF A DISEMBODIED REDNECK MONSTER?
BUT THEN HE'S GONE, AND I'M NO CLOSER TO KNOWIN' WHAT HE WANTED--
--AND ALL HE'S LEFT BEHIND IS DEATH AND FROST AND THE MEMORY OF THOSE BAIRNS.
AND...AND BECAUSE OF WHAT THE BASTARD SAID--WINDIN' ME UP LIKE THAT--
--AND BECAUSE I WON'T HAVE HIM PROVED RIGHT--
THE QUESTION WORTH ASKIN'S CHANGED:
D-DAD.
WHAT WOULD DAD DO?

AND I THINK WE ALL BLOODY *KNOW* THE *ANSWER* TO THAT.

I WILL *HELP* THOSE CHILDREN.

uuuuu

"TYRRANIX THE *ABOMINOID,*" EH? YOU GOT IT *WRONG,* Y'DAFT WEE *PEST.*

MINE IS THE GIFT OF *TELEPATHY.* *MINE.*

AND FROM *NOW ON* I'LL TAKE IT FROM YOU WHENEVER I BLOODY *WANT.*

WVBBB

HHH.

RIGHT. WELL.

THAT'S *ONE* POWER SORTED.

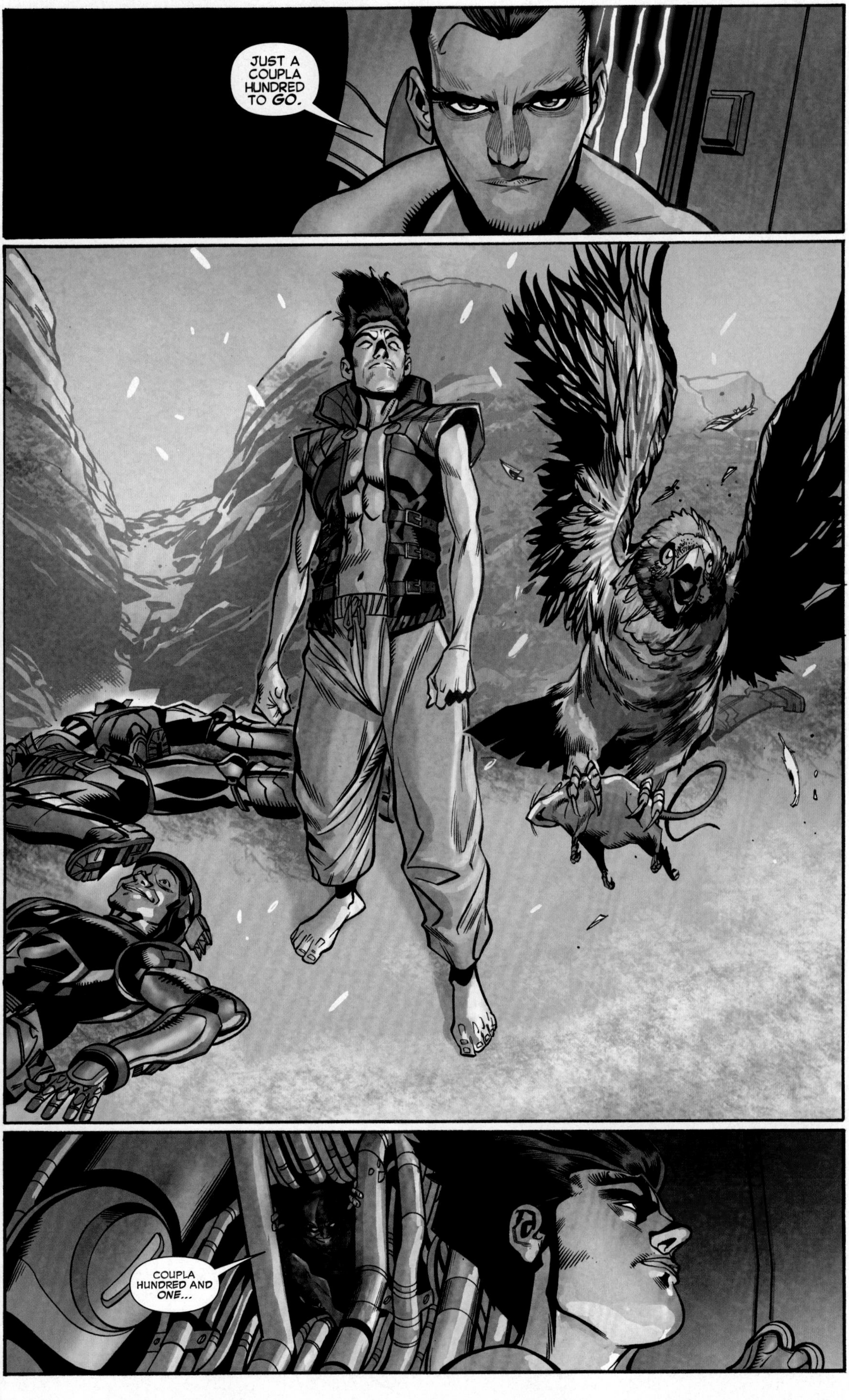
JUST A COUPLA HUNDRED TO GO.
COUPLA HUNDRED AND ONE...

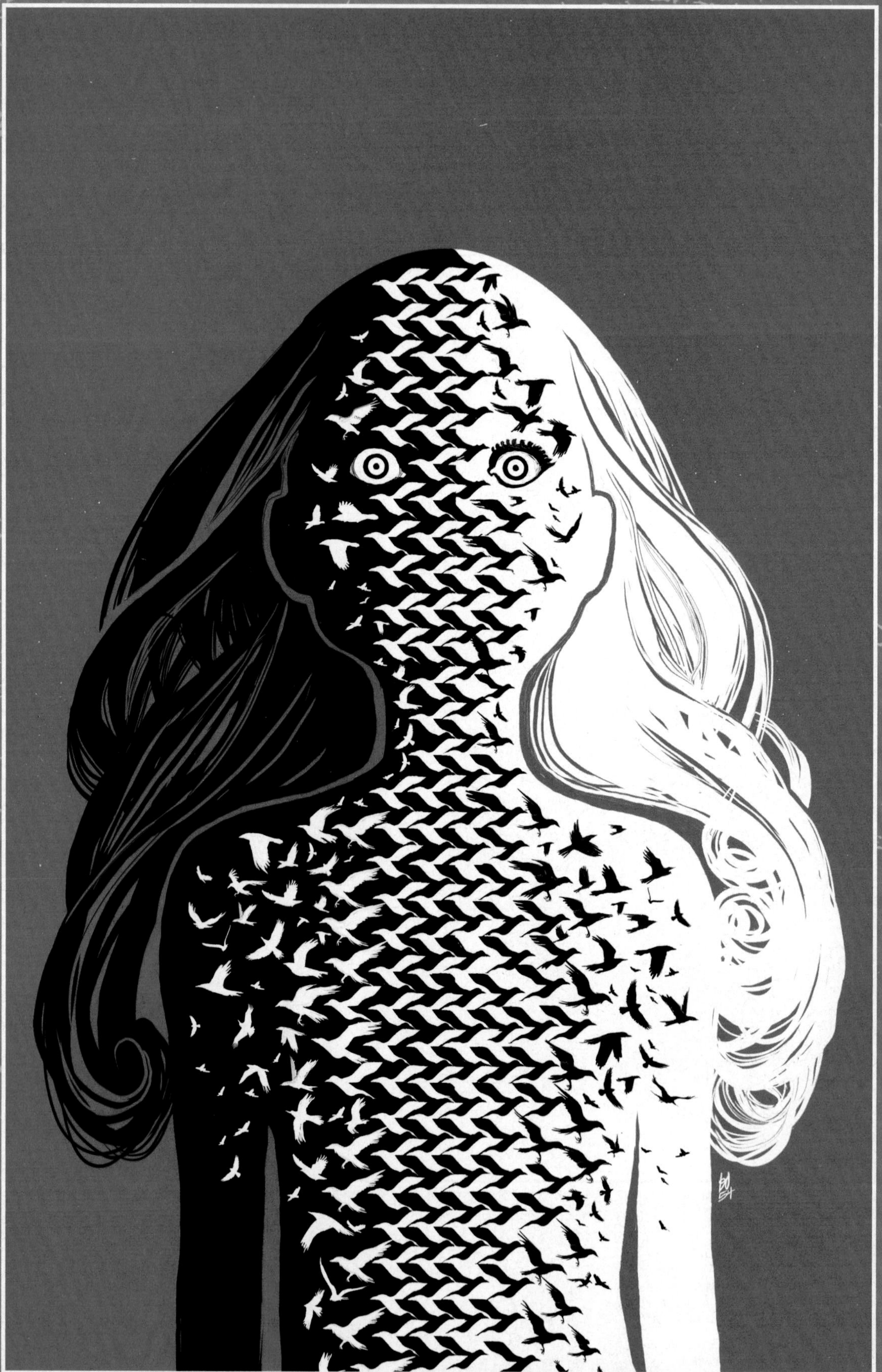

THREE

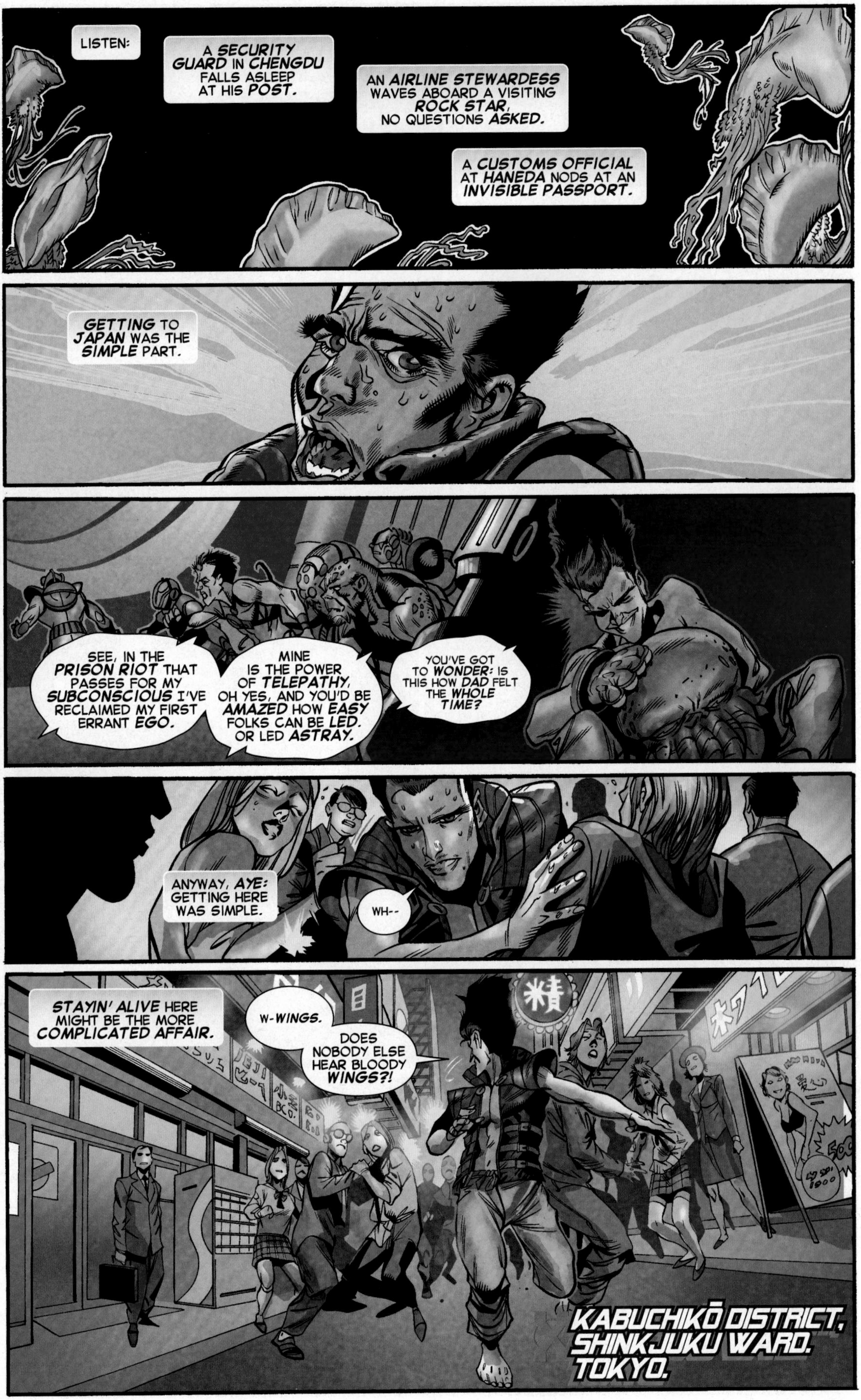
LISTEN:
A SECURITY GUARD IN CHENGDU FALLS ASLEEP AT HIS POST.
AN AIRLINE STEWARDESS WAVES ABOARD A VISITING ROCK STAR, NO QUESTIONS ASKED.
A CUSTOMS OFFICIAL AT HANEDA NODS AT AN INVISIBLE PASSPORT.
GETTING TO JAPAN WAS THE SIMPLE PART.
SEE, IN THE PRISON RIOT THAT PASSES FOR MY SUBCONSCIOUS I'VE RECLAIMED MY FIRST ERRANT EGO.
MINE IS THE POWER OF TELEPATHY, OH YES, AND YOU'D BE AMAZED HOW EASY FOLKS CAN BE LED. OR LED ASTRAY.
YOU'VE GOT TO WONDER: IS THIS HOW DAD FELT THE WHOLE TIME?
ANYWAY, AYE: GETTING HERE WAS SIMPLE.
WH--
STAYIN' ALIVE HERE MIGHT BE THE MORE COMPLICATED AFFAIR.
W-WINGS.
DOES NOBODY ELSE HEAR BLOODY WINGS?!
KABUCHIKŌ DISTRICT, SHINKJUKU WARD. TOKYO.

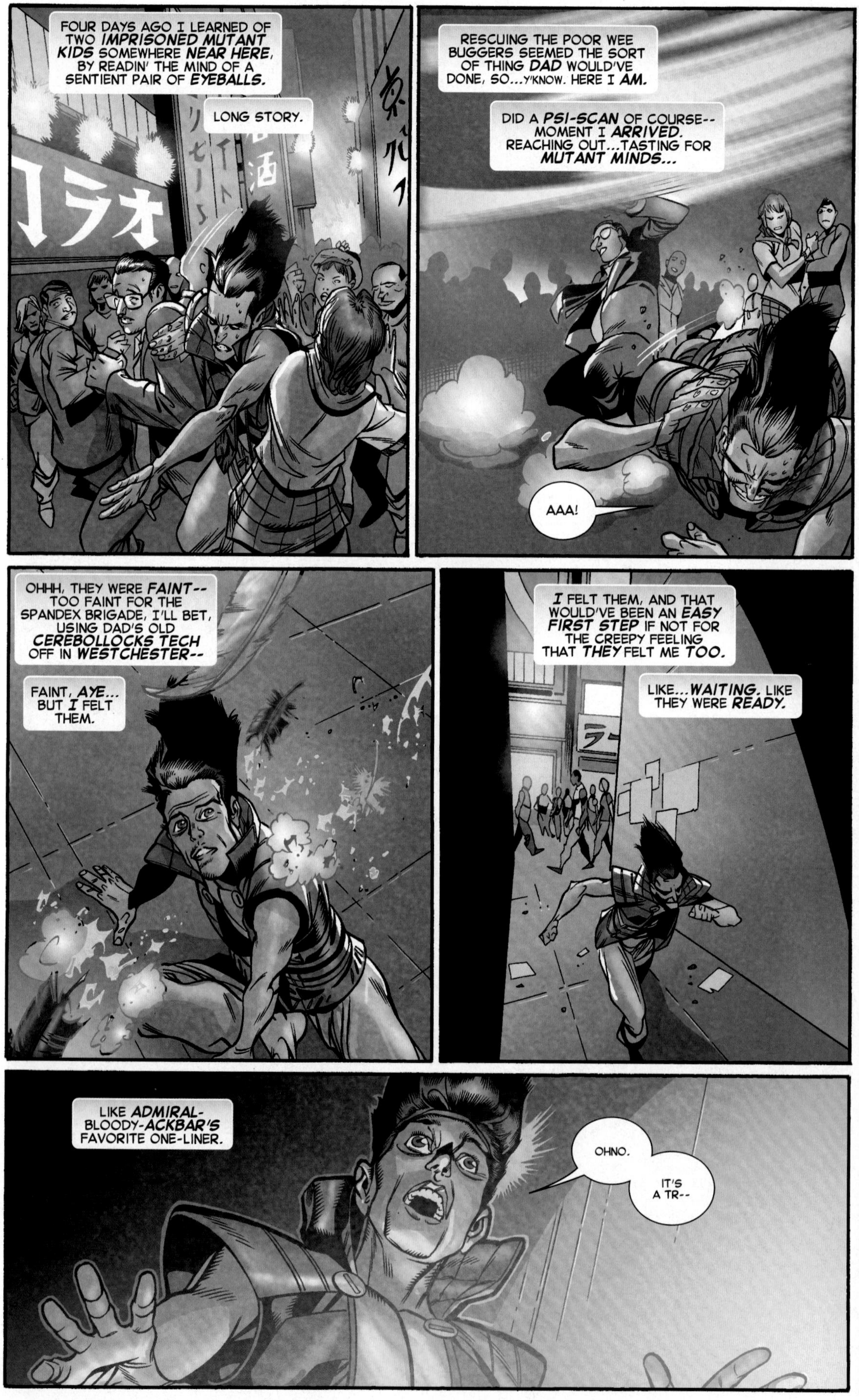
FOUR DAYS AGO I LEARNED OF TWO IMPRISONED MUTANT KIDS SOMEWHERE NEAR HERE, BY READIN' THE MIND OF A SENTIENT PAIR OF EYEBALLS.
LONG STORY.
RESCUING THE POOR WEE BUGGERS SEEMED THE SORT OF THING DAD WOULD'VE DONE, SO...Y'KNOW. HERE I AM.
DID A PSI-SCAN OF COURSE-- MOMENT I ARRIVED. REACHING OUT...TASTING FOR MUTANT MINDS...
AAA!
OHHH, THEY WERE FAINT-- TOO FAINT FOR THE SPANDEX BRIGADE, I'LL BET, USING DAD'S OLD CEREBOLLOCKS TECH OFF IN WESTCHESTER--
FAINT, AYE... BUT I FELT THEM.
I FELT THEM, AND THAT WOULD'VE BEEN AN EASY FIRST STEP IF NOT FOR THE CREEPY FEELING THAT THEY FELT ME TOO.
LIKE...WAITING. LIKE THEY WERE READY.
LIKE ADMIRAL-BLOODY-ACKBAR'S FAVORITE ONE-LINER.
OHNO.
IT'S A TR--

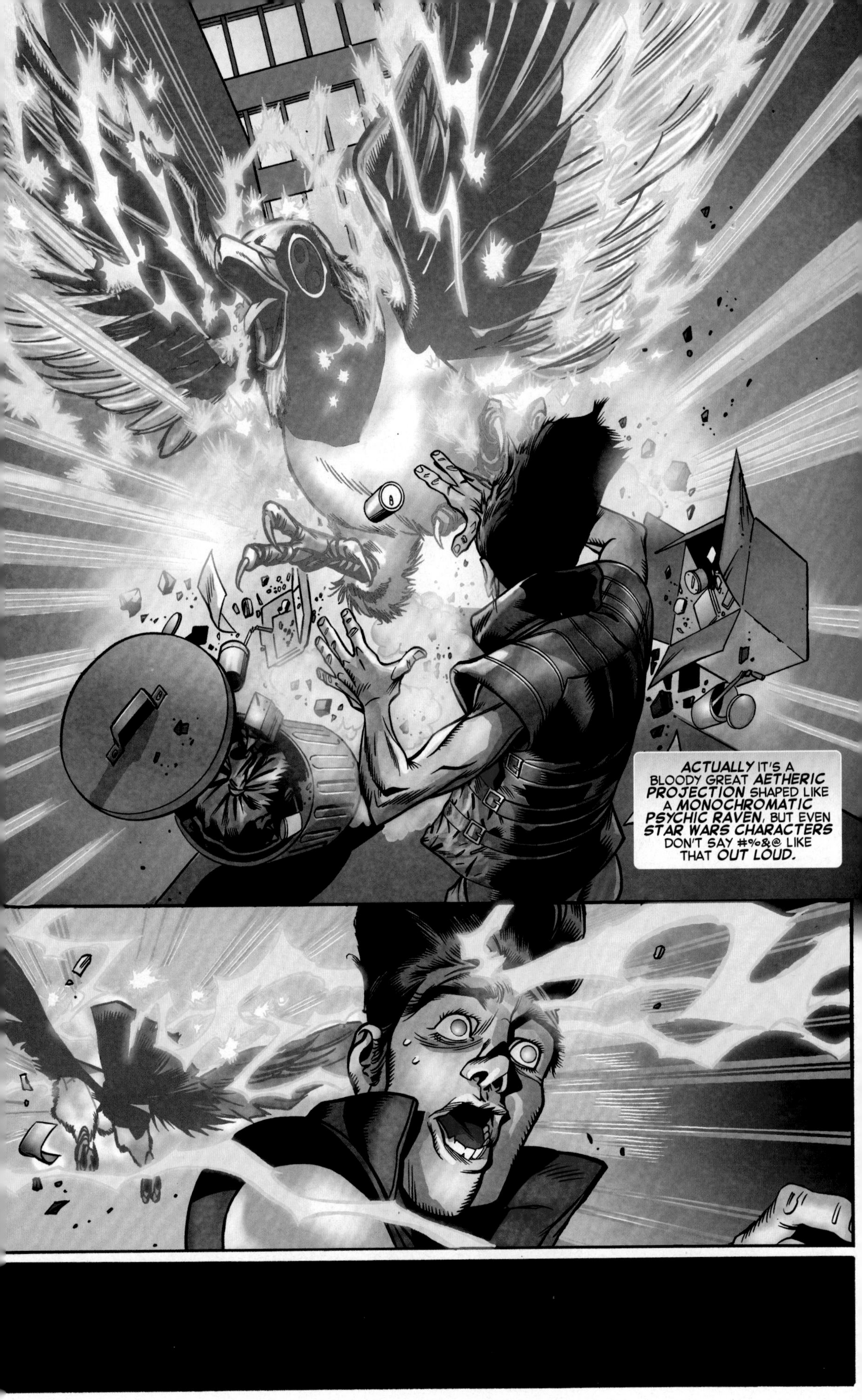
ACTUALLY IT'S A BLOODY GREAT AETHERIC PROJECTION SHAPED LIKE A MONOCHROMATIC PSYCHIC RAVEN, BUT EVEN STAR WARS CHARACTERS DON'T SAY #%&@ LIKE THAT OUT LOUD.

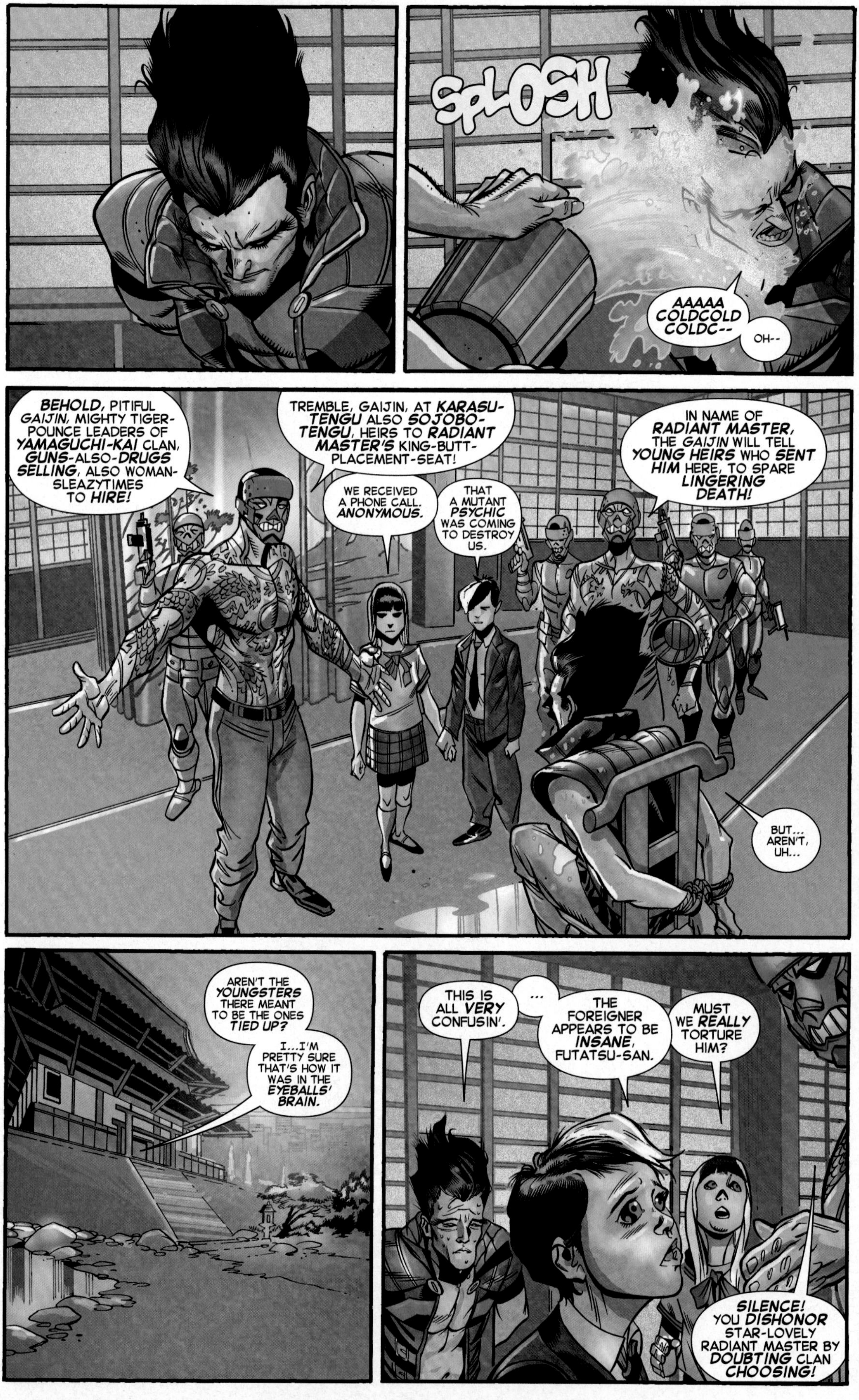
SPLOSH
AAAAA COLDCOLD COLDC--
OH--
BEHOLD, PITIFUL GAIJIN, MIGHTY TIGER-POUNCE LEADERS OF YAMAGUCHI-KAI CLAN, GUNS-ALSO-DRUGS SELLING, ALSO WOMAN-SLEAZYTIMES TO HIRE!
TREMBLE, GAIJIN, AT KARASU-TENGU ALSO SOJOBO-TENGU, HEIRS TO RADIANT MASTER'S KING-BUTT-PLACEMENT-SEAT!
WE RECEIVED A PHONE CALL. ANONYMOUS.
THAT A MUTANT PSYCHIC WAS COMING TO DESTROY US.
IN NAME OF RADIANT MASTER, THE GAIJIN WILL TELL YOUNG HEIRS WHO SENT HIM HERE, TO SPARE LINGERING DEATH!
BUT... AREN'T, UH...
AREN'T THE YOUNGSTERS THERE MEANT TO BE THE ONES TIED UP?
I...I'M PRETTY SURE THAT'S HOW IT WAS IN THE EYEBALLS' BRAIN.
THIS IS ALL VERY CONFUSIN'.
...
THE FOREIGNER APPEARS TO BE INSANE, FUTATSU-SAN.
MUST WE REALLY TORTURE HIM?
SILENCE! YOU DISHONOR STAR-LOVELY RADIANT MASTER BY DOUBTING CLAN CHOOSING!

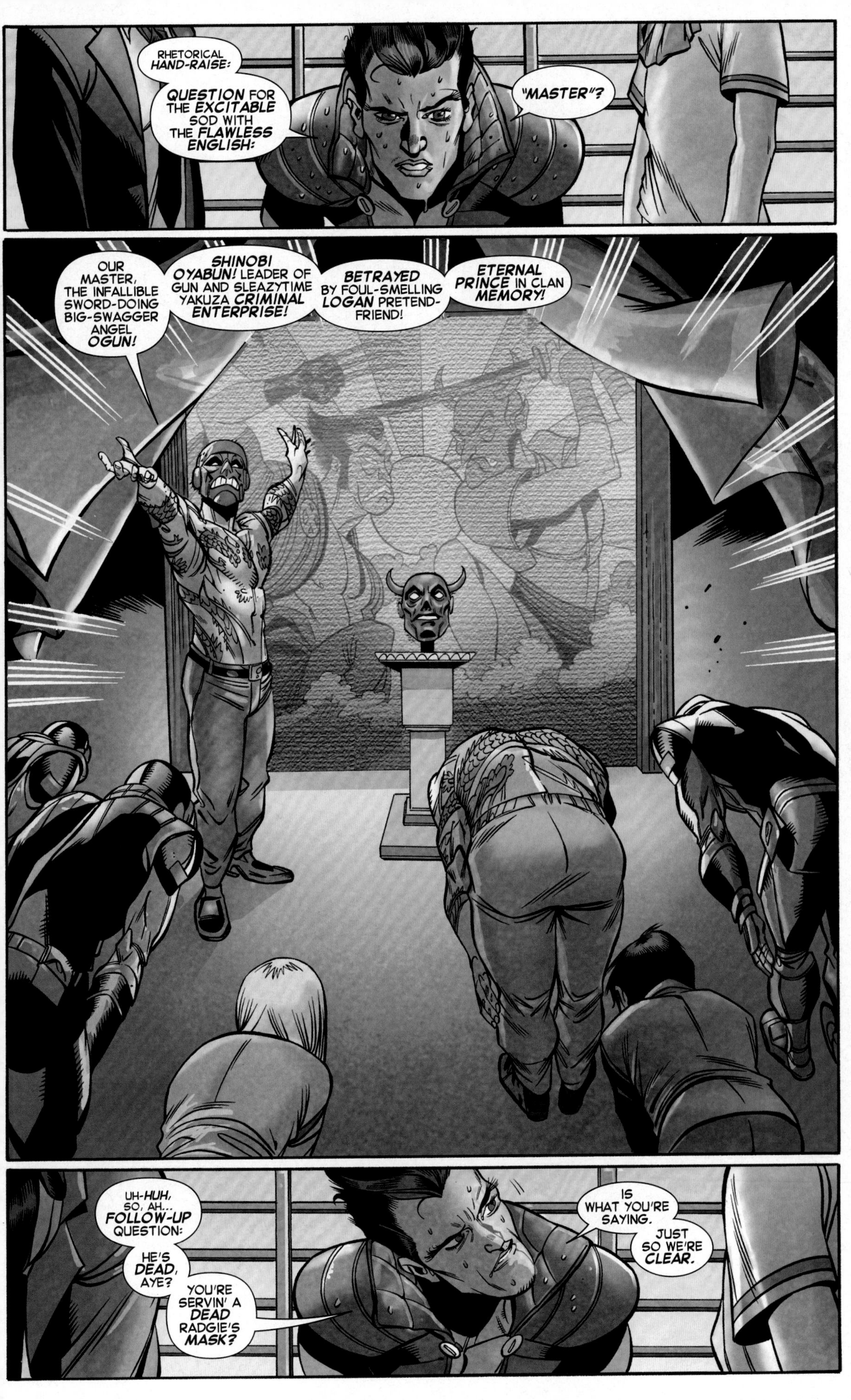
RHETORICAL HAND-RAISE:
QUESTION FOR THE EXCITABLE SOD WITH THE FLAWLESS ENGLISH:
"MASTER"?
OUR MASTER, THE INFALLIBLE SWORD-DOING BIG-SWAGGER ANGEL OGUN!
SHINOBI OYABUN! LEADER OF GUN AND SLEAZYTIME YAKUZA CRIMINAL ENTERPRISE!
BETRAYED BY FOUL-SMELLING LOGAN PRETEND-FRIEND!
ETERNAL PRINCE IN CLAN MEMORY!
UH-HUH, SO, AH... FOLLOW-UP QUESTION:
HE'S DEAD, AYE?
YOU'RE SERVIN' A DEAD RADGIE'S MASK?
IS WHAT YOU'RE SAYING.
JUST SO WE'RE CLEAR.

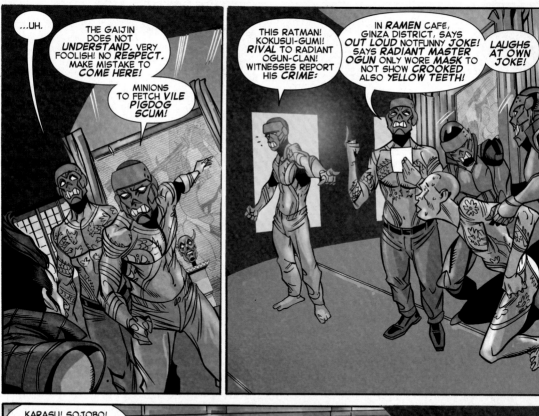

...UH.

THE GAIJIN DOES NOT *UNDERSTAND.* VERY *FOOLISH!* NO *RESPECT.* MAKE MISTAKE TO *COME HERE!*

MINIONS TO FETCH *VILE PIGDOG SCUM!*

THIS *RATMAN! KOKUSUI-GUMI! RIVAL* TO *RADIANT OGUN-CLAN!* WITNESSES REPORT HIS *CRIME:*

IN *RAMEN* CAFE, GINZA DISTRICT, SAYS *OUT LOUD NOTFUNNY JOKE!* SAYS *RADIANT MASTER OGUN* ONLY WORE *MASK* TO NOT SHOW *CROOKED* ALSO *YELLOW TEETH!*

LAUGHS AT OWN JOKE!

KARASU! SOJOBO! PLEASE TO SHOW *NOTNORMAL-HAIR MAN* WHAT IS *FATE* FOR *SLIMEPIG* INSULTING *MEMORY* OF *RADIANT MASTER!*

P-PLEASE, *FUTATSU-SAN...*

WE DO NOT *WANT* TO HURT THIS MA--

IMPUDENTING! THINK OF *OYABUN OGUN!* GREAT LEADER WHO TOOK YOU *IN!* SAVED AS *BABYTWINS* FROM *POVERTY* ALSO *DEATH!* RAISED IN GLORIOUS *YAKUZA-CLAN* LIKE *OWN SON* ALSO *DAUGHTER!*

WHAT *HELL* IS WORSE THAN *NOT-TO-MAKE-HONOR* IN DEBT?

AND *SO.*

SO THE POOR WEE SODS BEND THEIR NECKS, TAKE A LONG *BREATH...*

AND BLOODY *DO IT.*

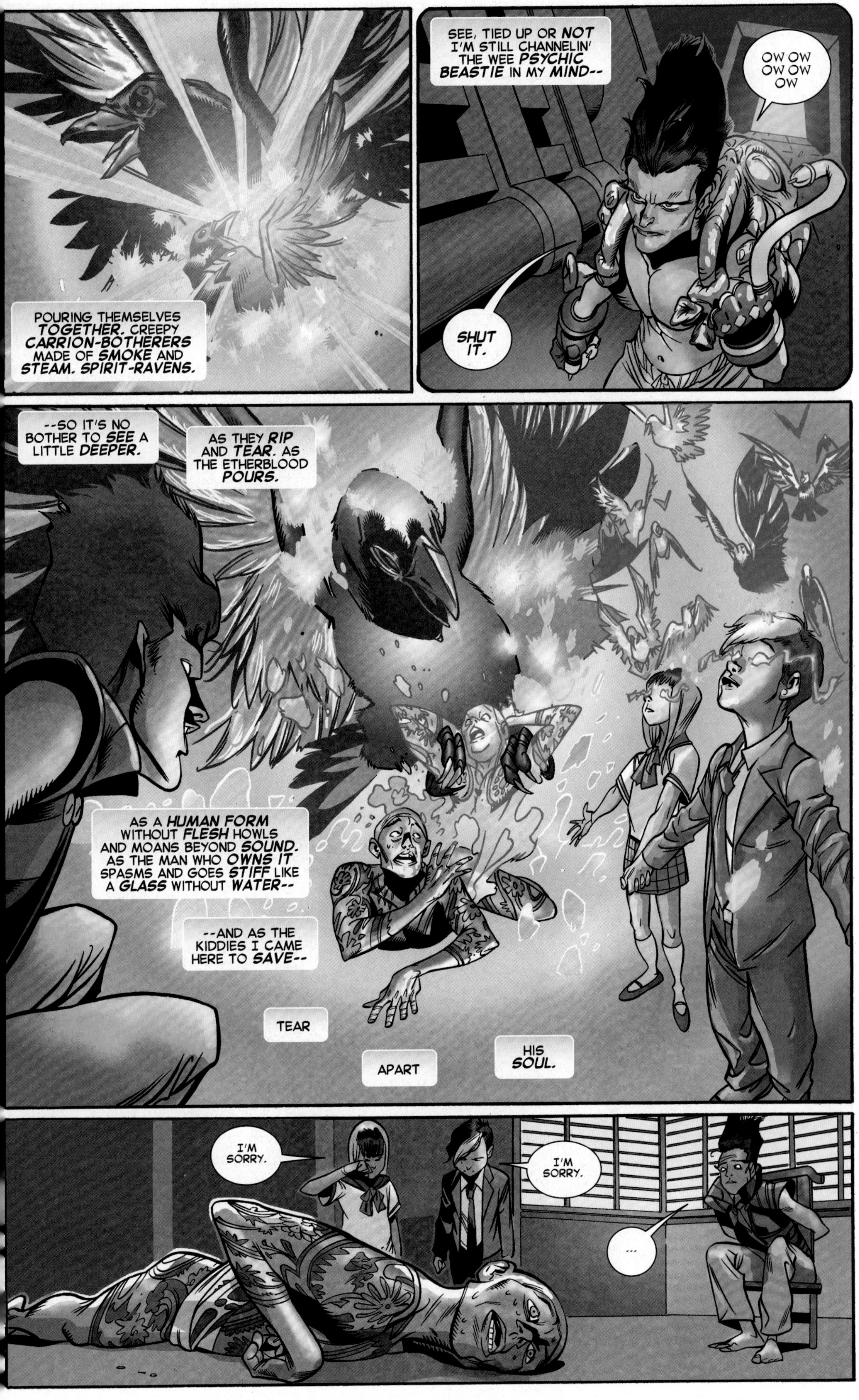
POURING THEMSELVES TOGETHER. CREEPY CARRION-BOTHERERS MADE OF SMOKE AND STEAM. SPIRIT-RAVENS.
SEE, TIED UP OR NOT I'M STILL CHANNELIN' THE WEE PSYCHIC BEASTIE IN MY MIND--
OW OW OW OW OW
SHUT IT.
--SO IT'S NO BOTHER TO SEE A LITTLE DEEPER.
AS THEY RIP AND TEAR. AS THE ETHERBLOOD POURS.
AS A HUMAN FORM WITHOUT FLESH HOWLS AND MOANS BEYOND SOUND. AS THE MAN WHO OWNS IT SPASMS AND GOES STIFF LIKE A GLASS WITHOUT WATER--
--AND AS THE KIDDIES I CAME HERE TO SAVE--
TEAR
APART
HIS SOUL.
I'M SORRY.
I'M SORRY.
...

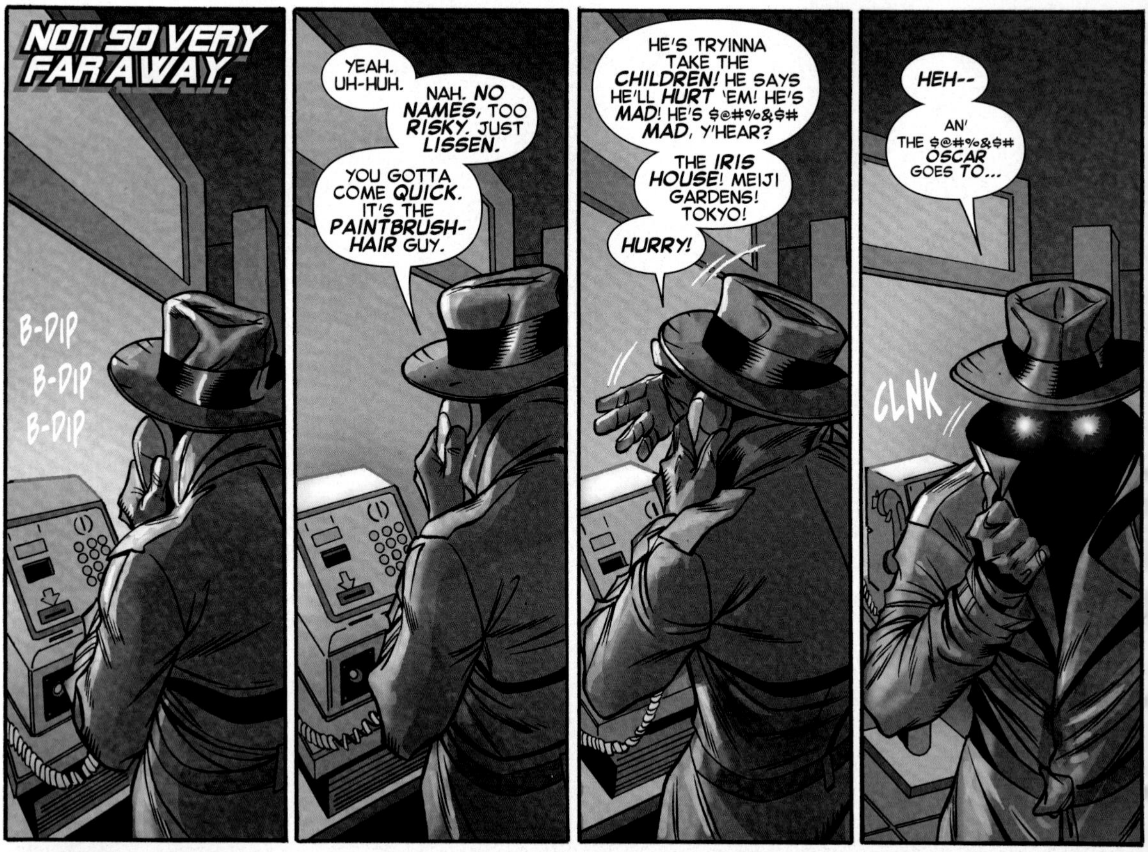
NOT SO VERY FAR AWAY.
B-DIP
B-DIP
B-DIP
YEAH. UH-HUH.
NAH. NO NAMES, TOO RISKY. JUST LISSEN.
YOU GOTTA COME QUICK. IT'S THE PAINTBRUSH-HAIR GUY.
HE'S TRYINNA TAKE THE CHILDREN! HE SAYS HE'LL HURT 'EM! HE'S MAD! HE'S $@#%&$# MAD, Y'HEAR?
THE IRIS HOUSE! MEIJI GARDENS! TOKYO!
HURRY!
HEH--
AN' THE $@#%&$# OSCAR GOES TO...
CLNK

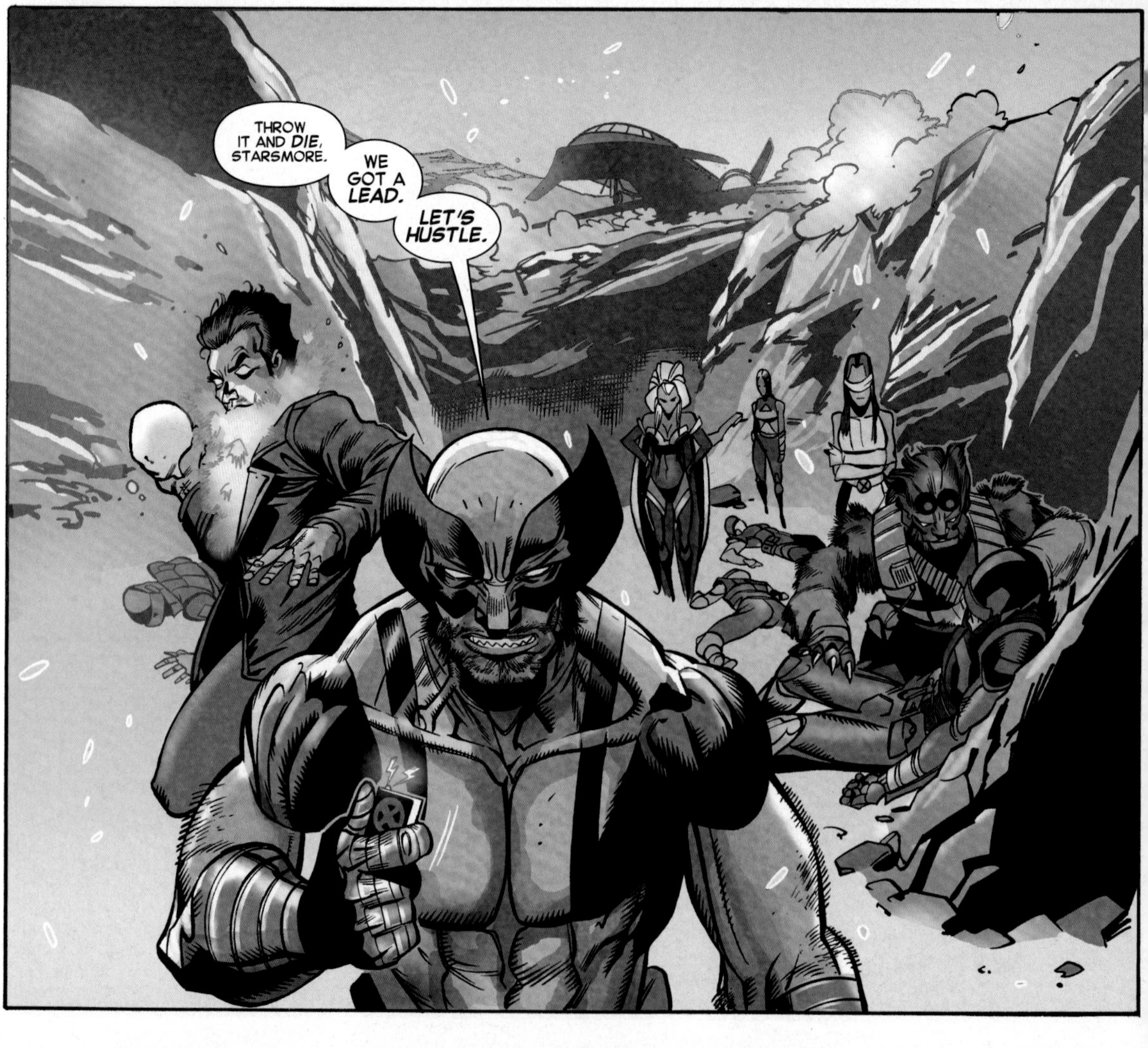
THROW IT AND DIE, STARSMORE.
WE GOT A LEAD.
LET'S HUSTLE.

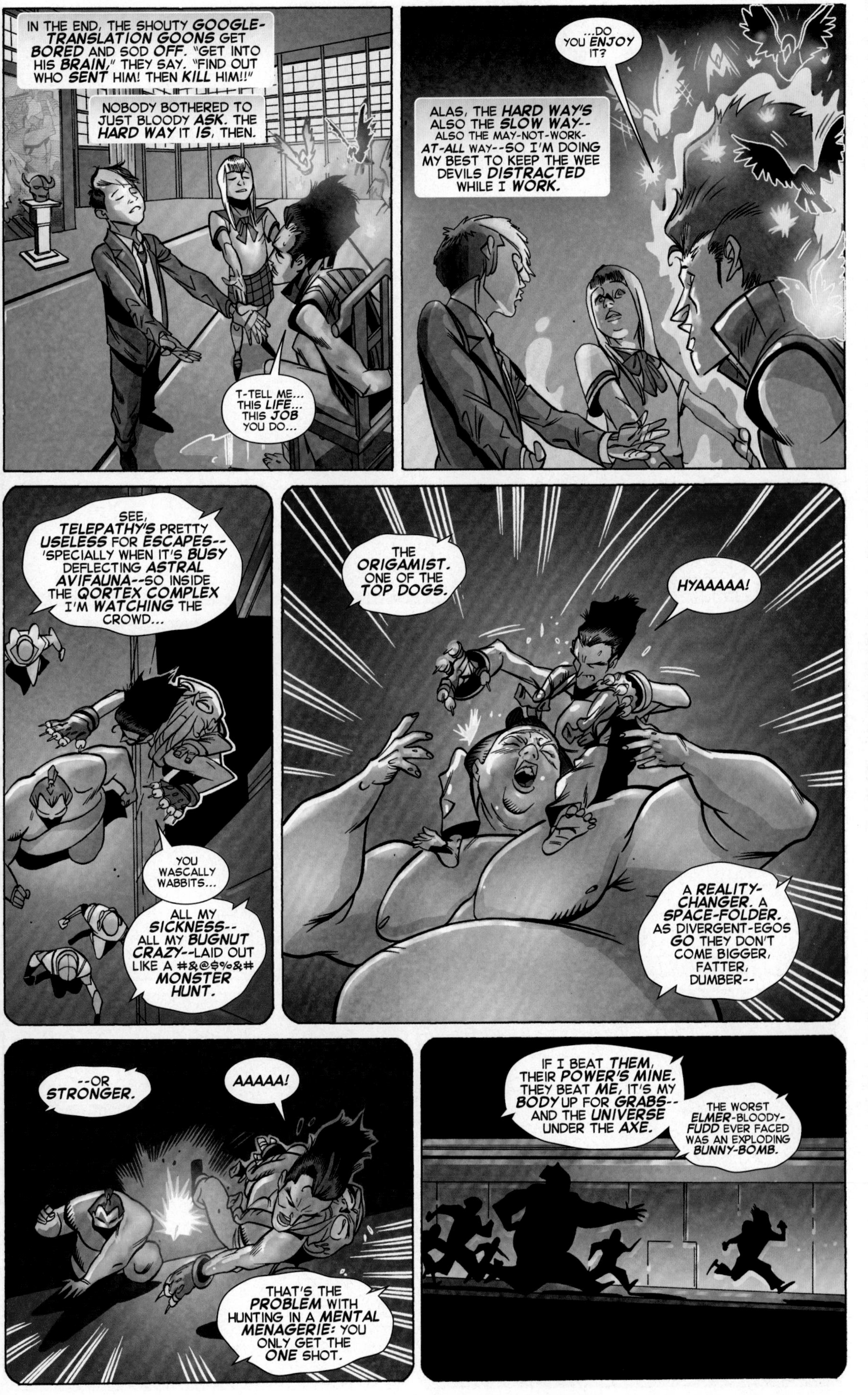
IN THE END, THE SHOUTY GOOGLE-TRANSLATION GOONS GET BORED AND SOD OFF. "GET INTO HIS BRAIN," THEY SAY. "FIND OUT WHO SENT HIM! THEN KILL HIM!!"
NOBODY BOTHERED TO JUST BLOODY ASK. THE HARD WAY IT IS, THEN.
T-TELL ME... THIS LIFE... THIS JOB YOU DO...
...DO YOU ENJOY IT?
ALAS, THE HARD WAY'S ALSO THE SLOW WAY--ALSO THE MAY-NOT-WORK-AT-ALL WAY--SO I'M DOING MY BEST TO KEEP THE WEE DEVILS DISTRACTED WHILE I WORK.
SEE, TELEPATHY'S PRETTY USELESS FOR ESCAPES--'SPECIALLY WHEN IT'S BUSY DEFLECTING ASTRAL AVIFAUNA--SO INSIDE THE QORTEX COMPLEX I'M WATCHING THE CROWD...
YOU WASCALLY WABBITS...
ALL MY SICKNESS--ALL MY BUGNUT CRAZY--LAID OUT LIKE A #&@$%&# MONSTER HUNT.
THE ORIGAMIST. ONE OF THE TOP DOGS.
HYAAAAA!
A REALITY-CHANGER. A SPACE-FOLDER. AS DIVERGENT-EGOS GO THEY DON'T COME BIGGER, FATTER, DUMBER--
--OR STRONGER.
AAAAA!
THAT'S THE PROBLEM WITH HUNTING IN A MENTAL MENAGERIE: YOU ONLY GET THE ONE SHOT.
IF I BEAT THEM, THEIR POWER'S MINE. THEY BEAT ME, IT'S MY BODY UP FOR GRABS--AND THE UNIVERSE UNDER THE AXE.
THE WORST ELMER-BLOODY-FUDD EVER FACED WAS AN EXPLODING BUNNY-BOMB.

DO WE ENJOY IT? OF COURSE NOT.

I-IT'S REVOLTING. IT MAKES US FEEL BAD.

TH... THEN WHY DO IT?

...YOU'RE GAIJIN. IT WOULD MAKE NO SENSE TO YOU.

WE HAVE HEARD ABOUT YOUR WAYS. YOU DO WHAT YOU WISH. YOU HAVE NO RESPECT FOR THOSE THAT CAME BEFORE.

NO OBLIGATION TO HISTORY. NO DEBT TO YOUR FORBEARS.

YOU WOULD NOT UNDERSTAND.

... I MIGHT.

OKAY. SO MAYBE TARGETING THE ORIGAMIST WAS A TAD OVERAMBITIOUS FOR A FIRST ATTEMPT.

CROTCHETY OLD MAX KELVIN'S MORE MY SPEED.

WALA WALAWALA WALAAAAAAA AAAA

OR NOT.

CRAP CRAP CRAP

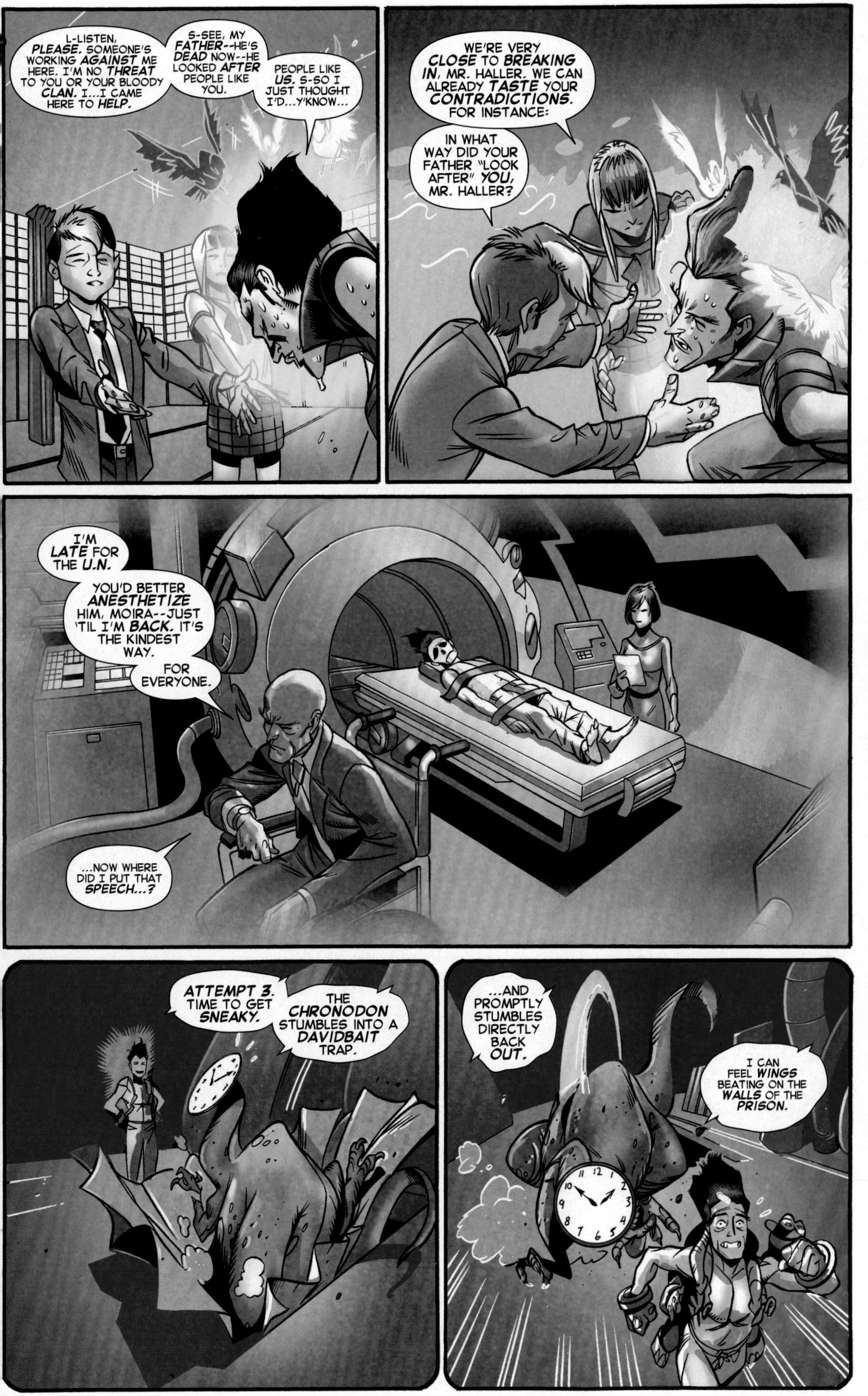
L-LISTEN, PLEASE. SOMEONE'S WORKING AGAINST ME HERE. I'M NO THREAT TO YOU OR YOUR BLOODY CLAN. I...I CAME HERE TO HELP.
S-SEE, MY FATHER--HE'S DEAD NOW--HE LOOKED AFTER PEOPLE LIKE YOU.
PEOPLE LIKE US. S-SO I JUST THOUGHT I'D...Y'KNOW...
WE'RE VERY CLOSE TO BREAKING IN, MR. HALLER. WE CAN ALREADY TASTE YOUR CONTRADICTIONS. FOR INSTANCE:
IN WHAT WAY DID YOUR FATHER "LOOK AFTER" YOU, MR. HALLER?
I'M LATE FOR THE U.N.
YOU'D BETTER ANESTHETIZE HIM, MOIRA--JUST 'TIL I'M BACK. IT'S THE KINDEST WAY.
FOR EVERYONE.
...NOW WHERE DID I PUT THAT SPEECH...?
ATTEMPT 3. TIME TO GET SNEAKY.
THE CHRONODON STUMBLES INTO A DAVIDBAIT TRAP.
...AND PROMPTLY STUMBLES DIRECTLY BACK OUT.
I CAN FEEL WINGS BEATING ON THE WALLS OF THE PRISON.

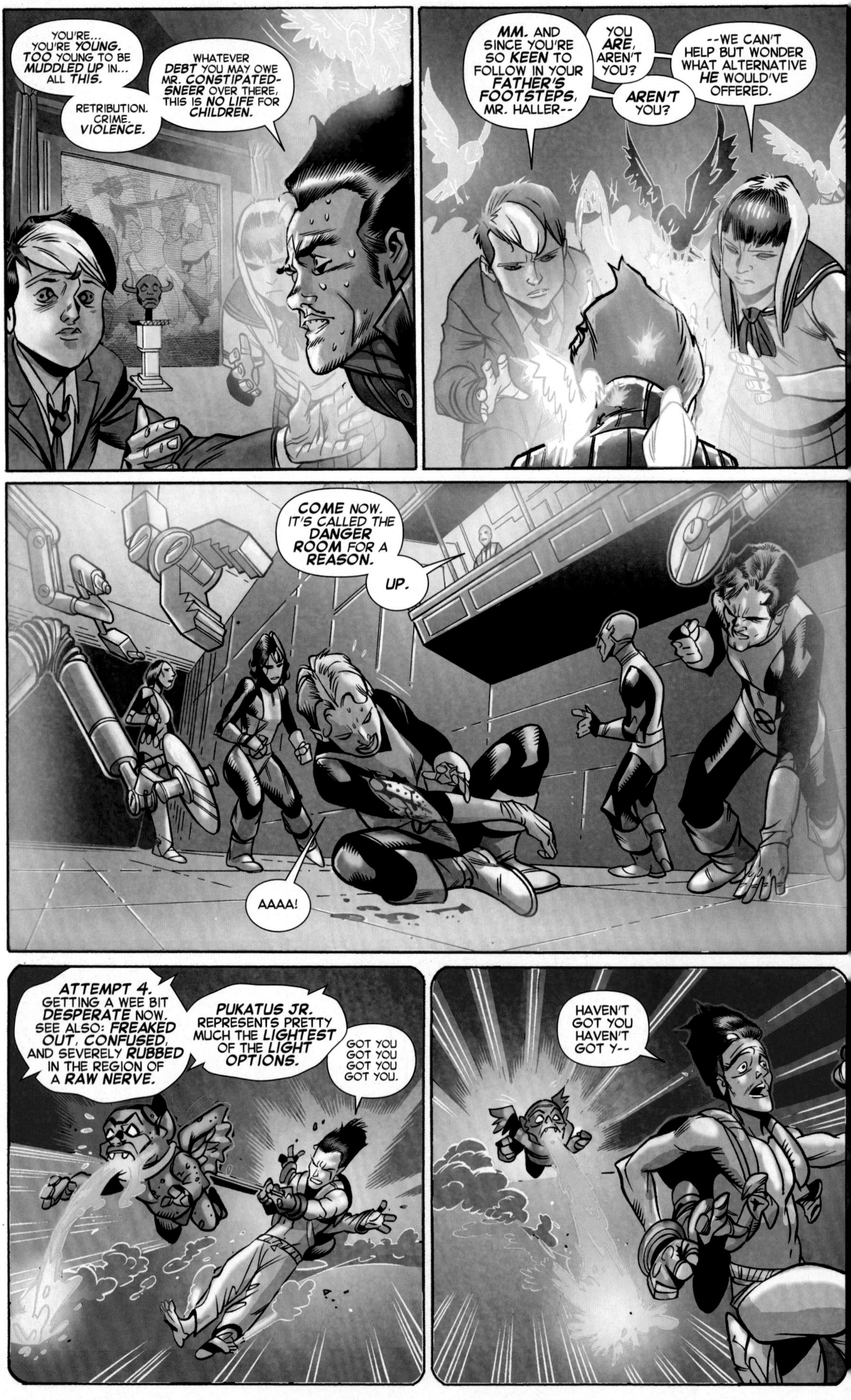
YOU'RE... YOU'RE YOUNG. TOO YOUNG TO BE MUDDLED UP IN... ALL THIS.
RETRIBUTION. CRIME. VIOLENCE.
WHATEVER DEBT YOU MAY OWE MR. CONSTIPATED-SNEER OVER THERE, THIS IS NO LIFE FOR CHILDREN.
MM. AND SINCE YOU'RE SO KEEN TO FOLLOW IN YOUR FATHER'S FOOTSTEPS, MR. HALLER--
YOU ARE, AREN'T YOU?
AREN'T YOU?
--WE CAN'T HELP BUT WONDER WHAT ALTERNATIVE HE WOULD'VE OFFERED.
COME NOW. IT'S CALLED THE DANGER ROOM FOR A REASON.
UP.
AAAA!
ATTEMPT 4. GETTING A WEE BIT DESPERATE NOW. SEE ALSO: FREAKED OUT, CONFUSED, AND SEVERELY RUBBED IN THE REGION OF A RAW NERVE.
PUKATUS JR. REPRESENTS PRETTY MUCH THE LIGHTEST OF THE LIGHT OPTIONS.
GOT YOU GOT YOU GOT YOU GOT YOU.
HAVEN'T GOT YOU HAVEN'T GOT Y--

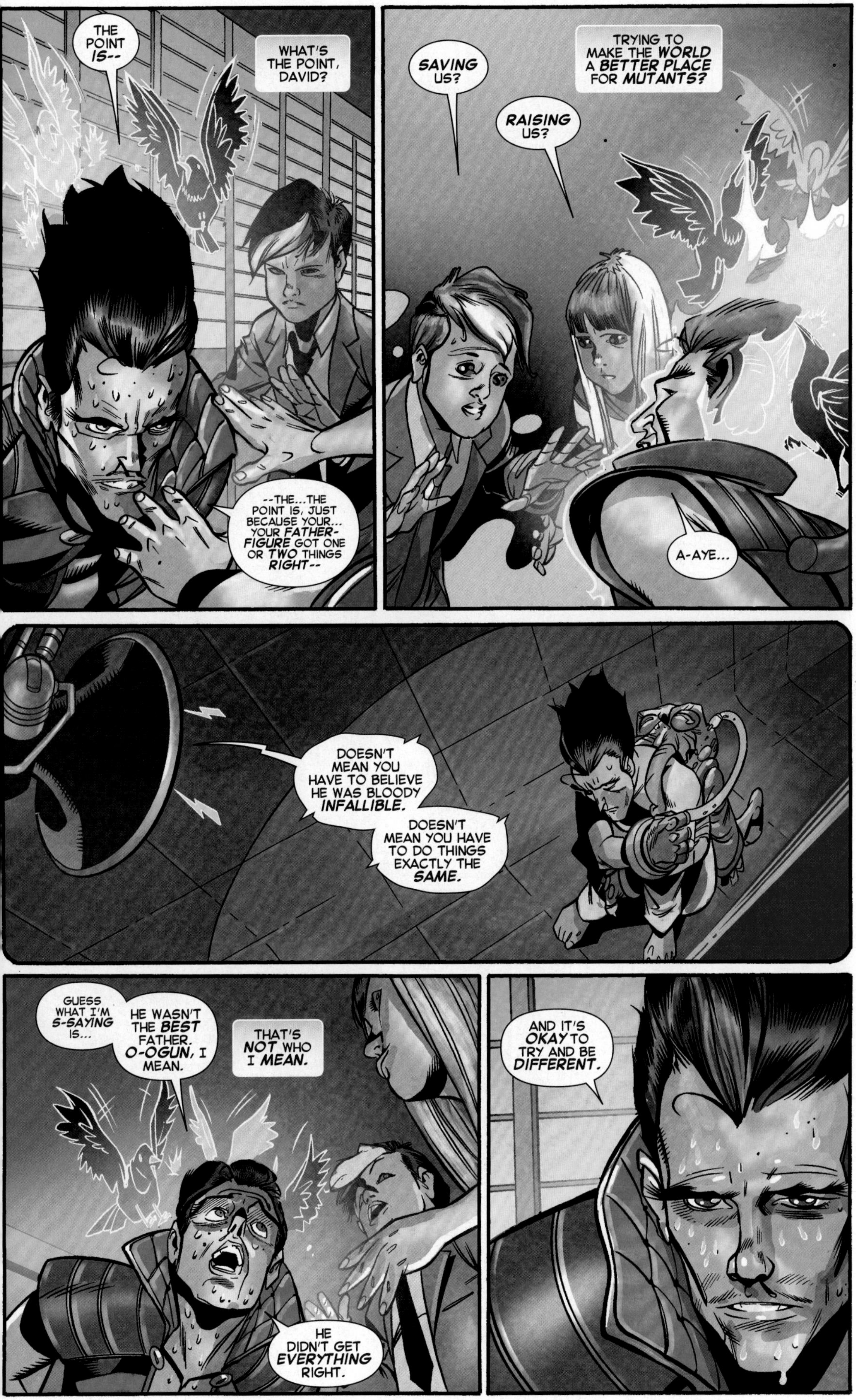
THE POINT IS--
WHAT'S THE POINT, DAVID?
--THE...THE POINT IS, JUST BECAUSE YOUR... YOUR FATHER-FIGURE GOT ONE OR TWO THINGS RIGHT--
SAVING US?
RAISING US?
TRYING TO MAKE THE WORLD A BETTER PLACE FOR MUTANTS?
A-AYE...
DOESN'T MEAN YOU HAVE TO BELIEVE HE WAS BLOODY INFALLIBLE.
DOESN'T MEAN YOU HAVE TO DO THINGS EXACTLY THE SAME.
GUESS WHAT I'M S-SAYING IS...
HE WASN'T THE BEST FATHER. O-OGUN, I MEAN.
THAT'S NOT WHO I MEAN.
HE DIDN'T GET EVERYTHING RIGHT.
AND IT'S OKAY TO TRY AND BE DIFFERENT.

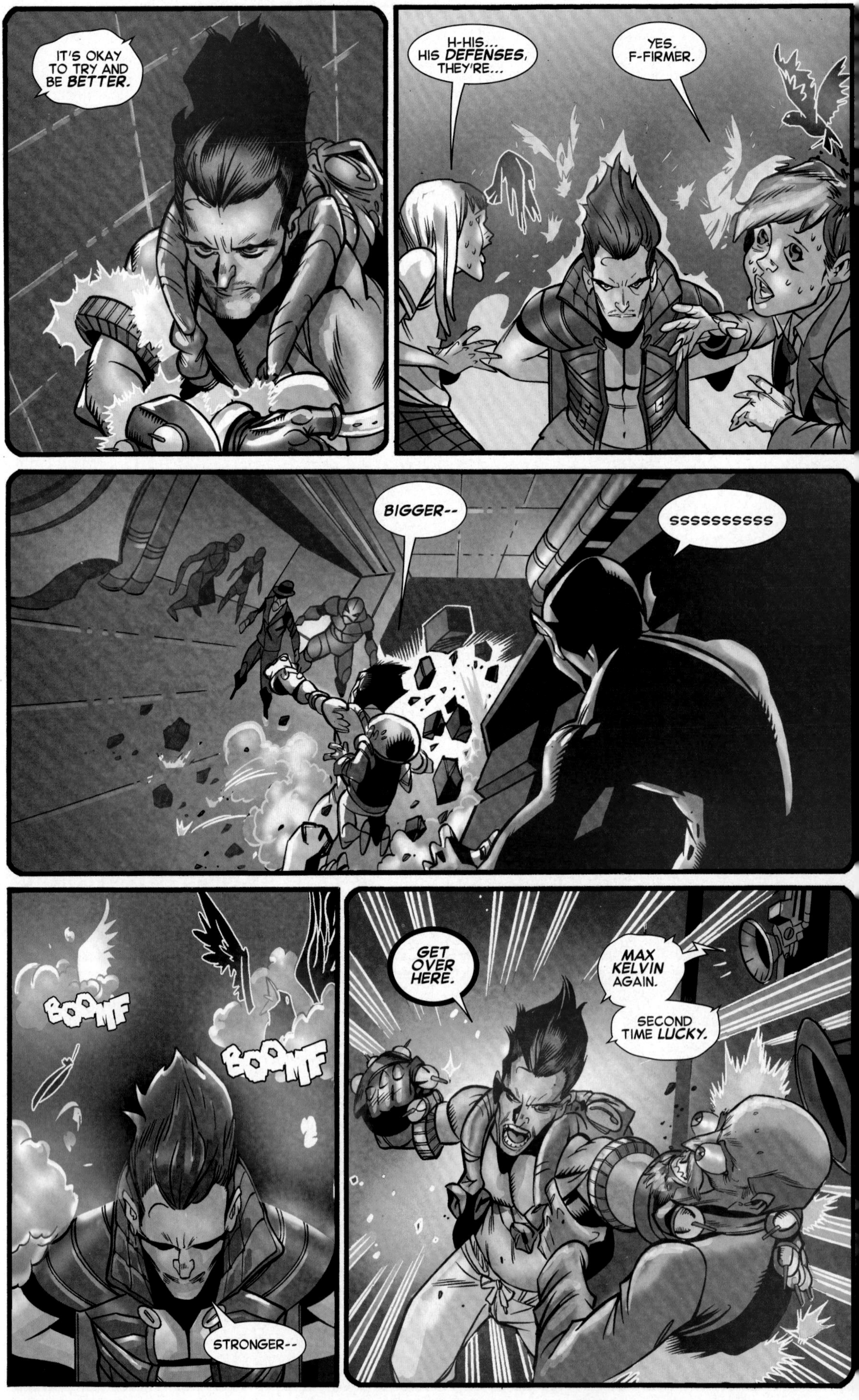
IT'S OKAY TO TRY AND BE BETTER.
H-HIS... HIS DEFENSES, THEY'RE...
YES. F-FIRMER.
BIGGER--
SSSSSSSSSS
BOOMF
BOOMF
STRONGER--
GET OVER HERE.
MAX KELVIN AGAIN.
SECOND TIME LUCKY.

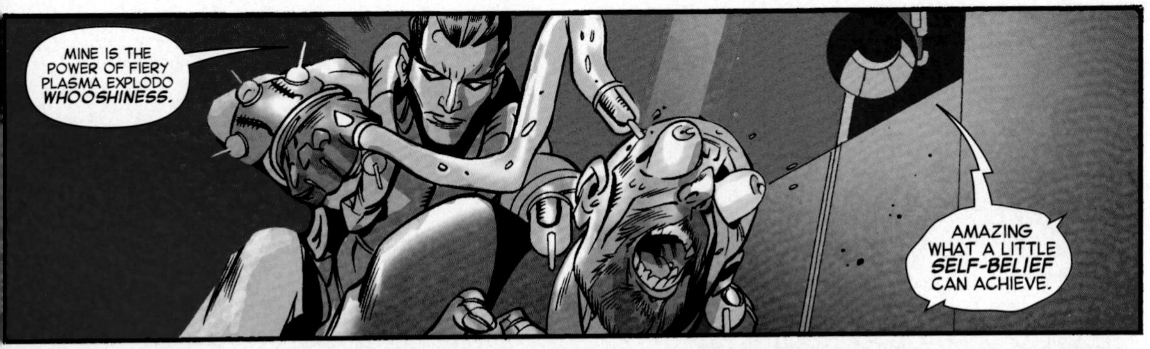
MINE IS THE POWER OF FIERY PLASMA EXPLODO **WHOOSHINESS.**
AMAZING WHAT A LITTLE ***SELF-BELIEF*** CAN ACHIEVE.

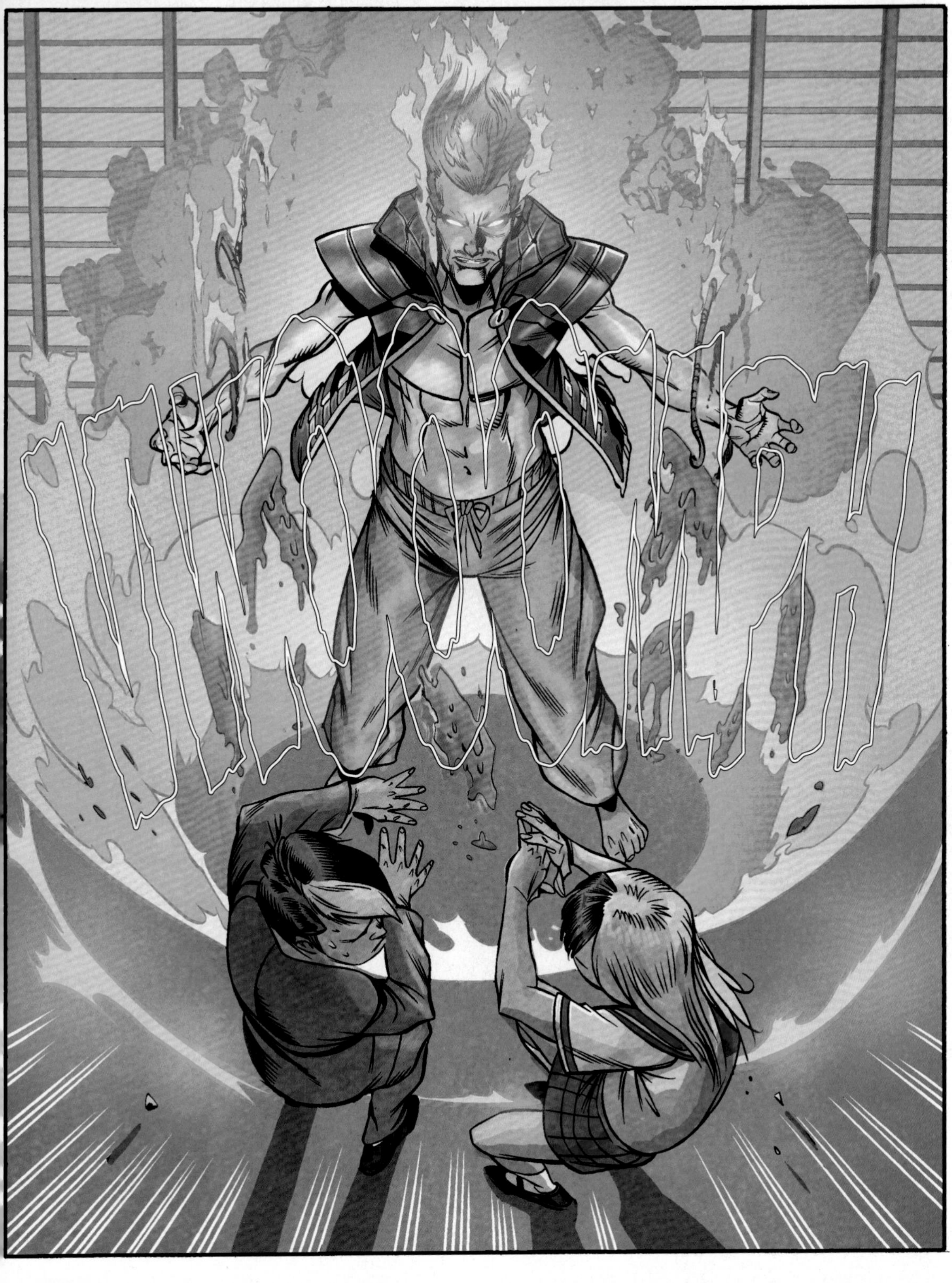

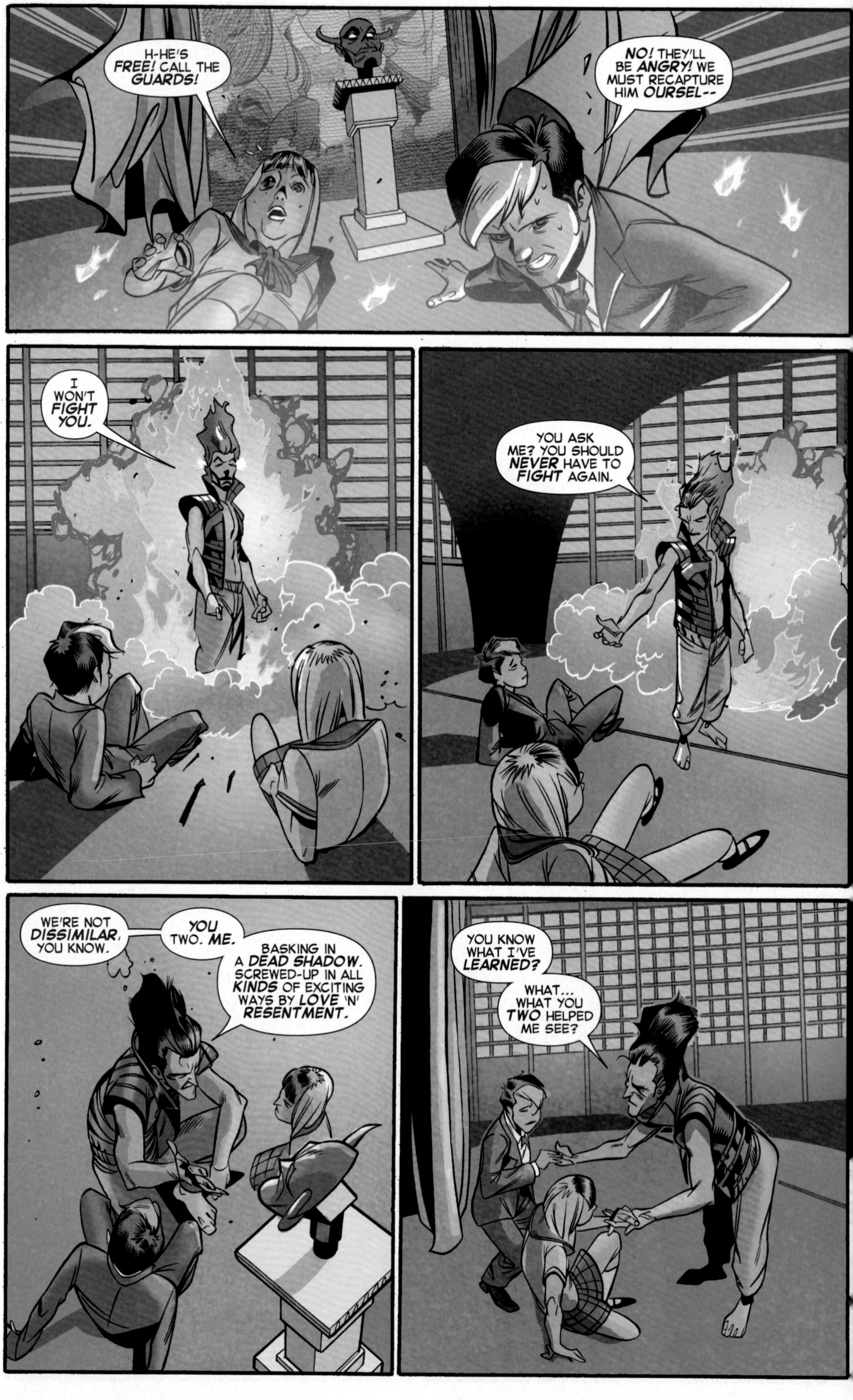
H-HE'S FREE! CALL THE GUARDS!
NO! THEY'LL BE ANGRY! WE MUST RECAPTURE HIM OURSEL--
I WON'T FIGHT YOU.
YOU ASK ME? YOU SHOULD NEVER HAVE TO FIGHT AGAIN.
WE'RE NOT DISSIMILAR, YOU KNOW.
YOU TWO. ME.
BASKING IN A DEAD SHADOW. SCREWED-UP IN ALL KINDS OF EXCITING WAYS BY LOVE 'N' RESENTMENT.
YOU KNOW WHAT I'VE LEARNED?
WHAT... WHAT YOU TWO HELPED ME SEE?

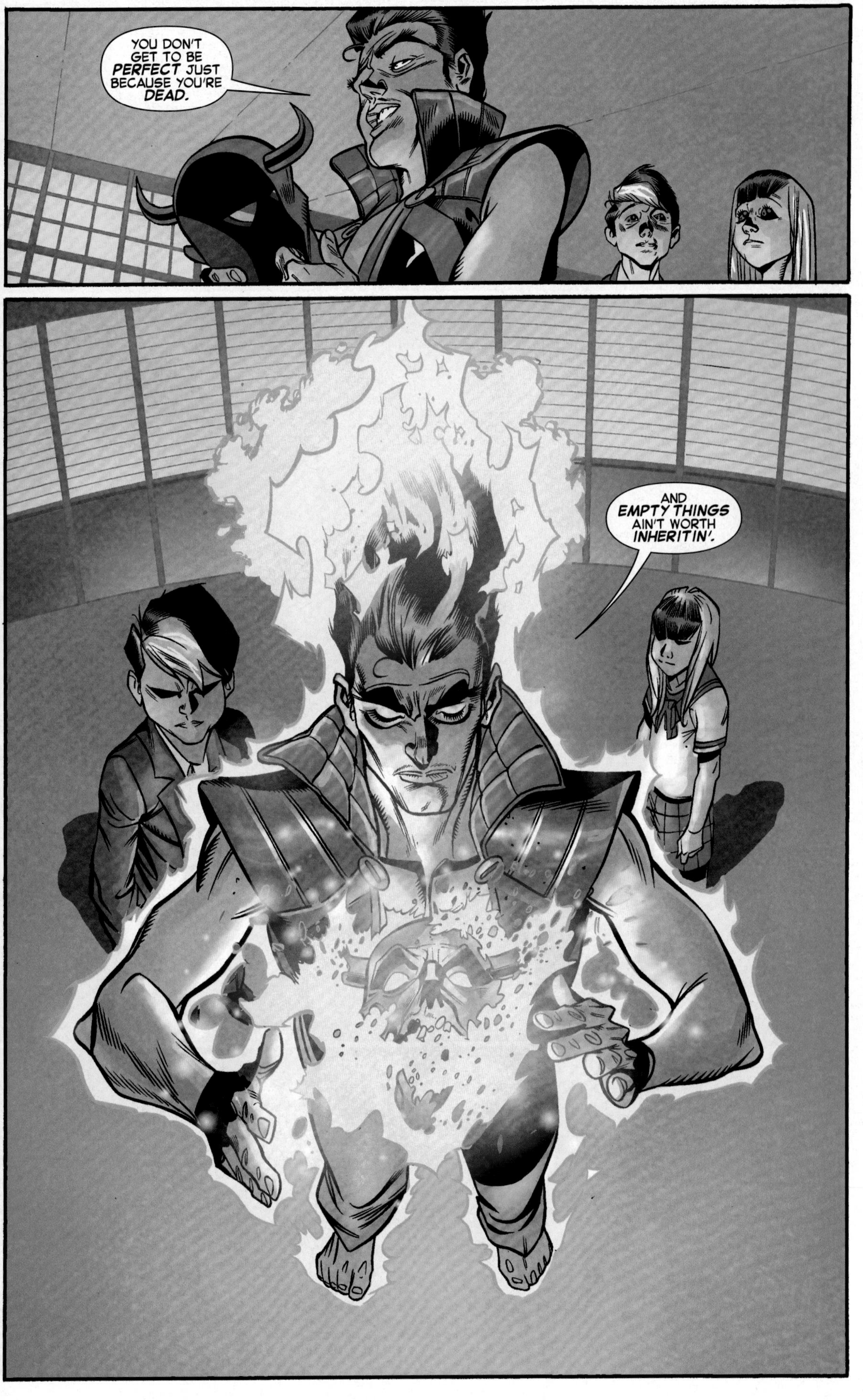
YOU DON'T GET TO BE PERFECT JUST BECAUSE YOU'RE DEAD.
AND EMPTY THINGS AIN'T WORTH INHERITIN'.

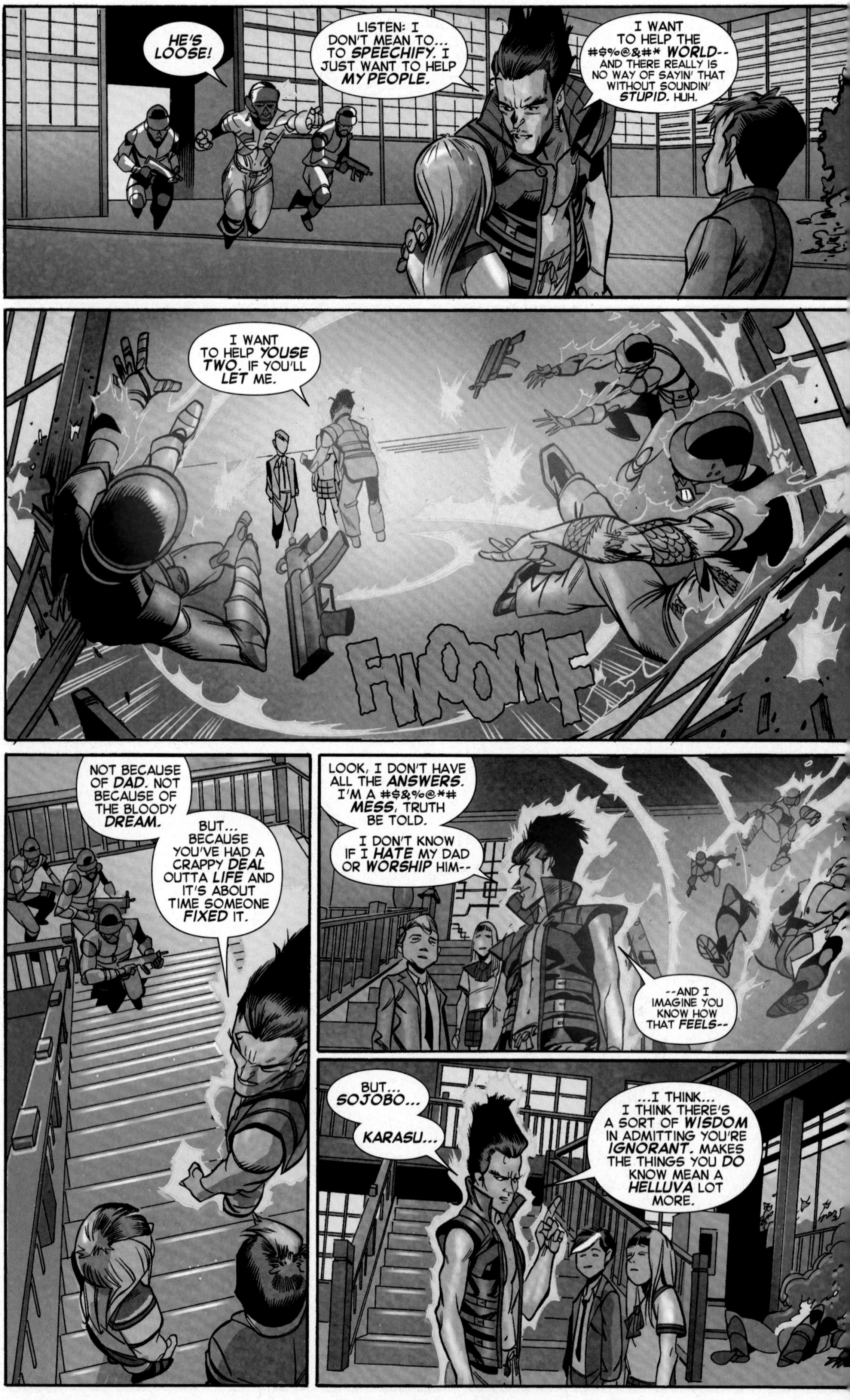
HE'S LOOSE!
LISTEN: I DON'T MEAN TO... TO SPECHIFY. I JUST WANT TO HELP MY PEOPLE.
I WANT TO HELP THE #$%@&#* WORLD-- AND THERE REALLY IS NO WAY OF SAYIN' THAT WITHOUT SOUNDIN' STUPID. HUH.
I WANT TO HELP YOUSE TWO. IF YOU'LL LET ME.
FWOOMF
NOT BECAUSE OF DAD. NOT BECAUSE OF THE BLOODY DREAM.
BUT... BECAUSE YOU'VE HAD A CRAPPY DEAL OUTTA LIFE AND IT'S ABOUT TIME SOMEONE FIXED IT.
LOOK, I DON'T HAVE ALL THE ANSWERS. I'M A #$&%@*# MESS, TRUTH BE TOLD.
I DON'T KNOW IF I HATE MY DAD OR WORSHIP HIM--
--AND I IMAGINE YOU KNOW HOW THAT FEELS--
BUT... SOJOBO...
KARASU...
...I THINK... I THINK THERE'S A SORT OF WISDOM IN ADMITTING YOU'RE IGNORANT. MAKES THE THINGS YOU DO KNOW MEAN A HELLUVA LOT MORE.

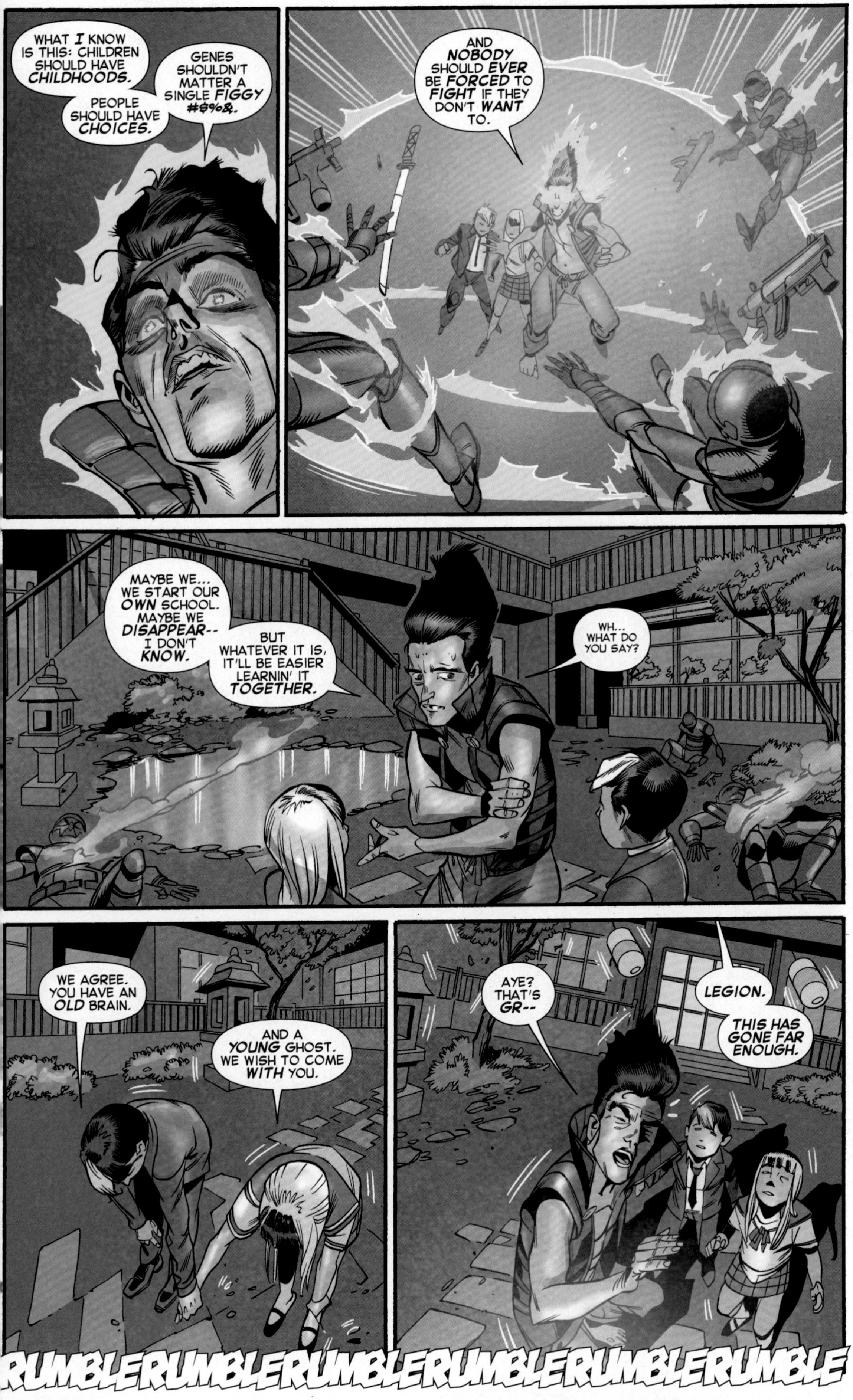
WHAT I KNOW IS THIS: CHILDREN SHOULD HAVE CHILDHOODS.
PEOPLE SHOULD HAVE CHOICES.
GENES SHOULDN'T MATTER A SINGLE FIGGY #$%&.
AND NOBODY SHOULD EVER BE FORCED TO FIGHT IF THEY DON'T WANT TO.
MAYBE WE... WE START OUR OWN SCHOOL. MAYBE WE DISAPPEAR-- I DON'T KNOW.
BUT WHATEVER IT IS, IT'LL BE EASIER LEARNIN' IT TOGETHER.
WH... WHAT DO YOU SAY?
WE AGREE. YOU HAVE AN OLD BRAIN.
AND A YOUNG GHOST. WE WISH TO COME WITH YOU.
AYE? THAT'S GR--
LEGION.
THIS HAS GONE FAR ENOUGH.
RUMBLERUMBLERUMBLERUMBLERUMBLERUMBLE

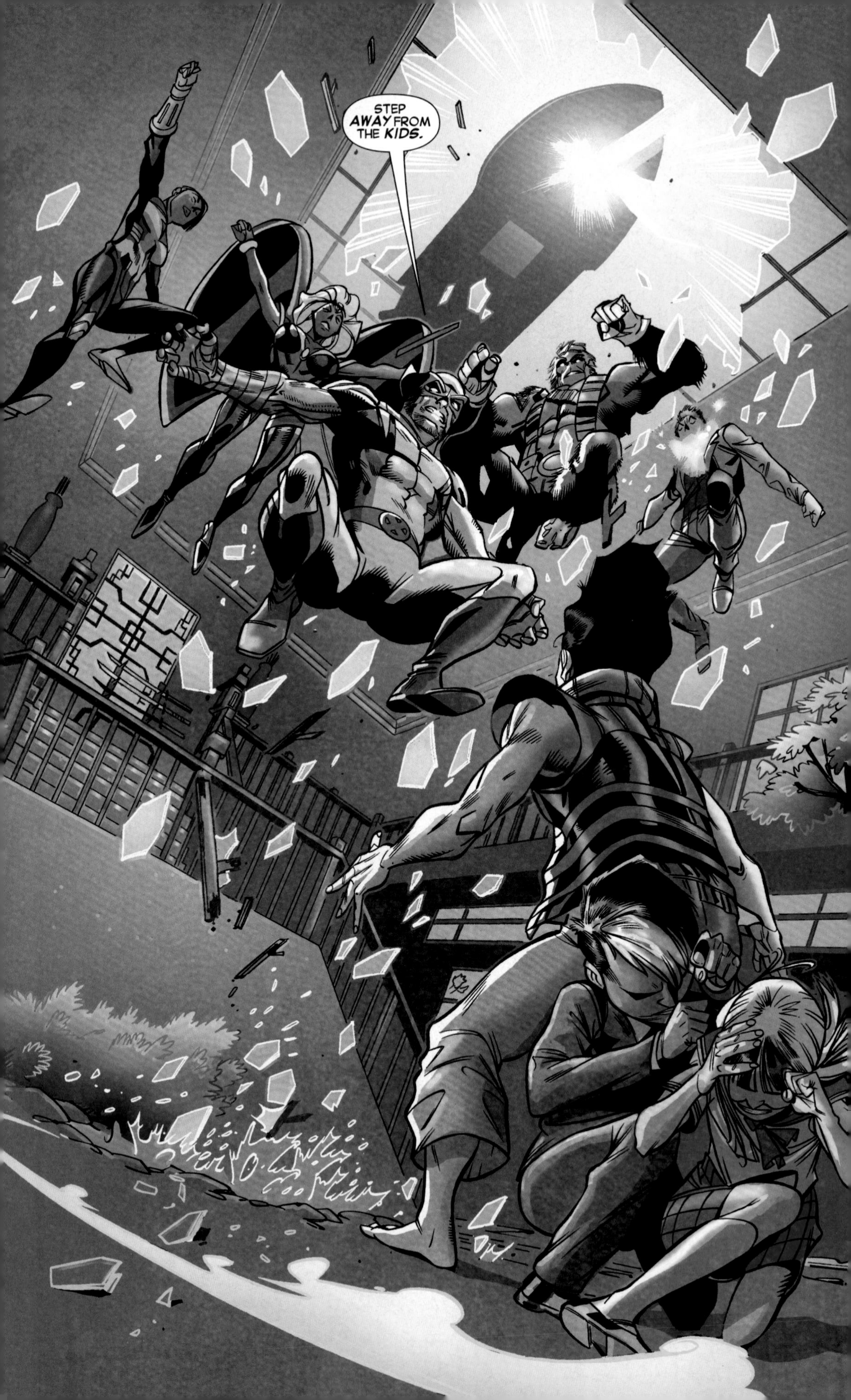
STEP AWAY FROM THE KIDS.

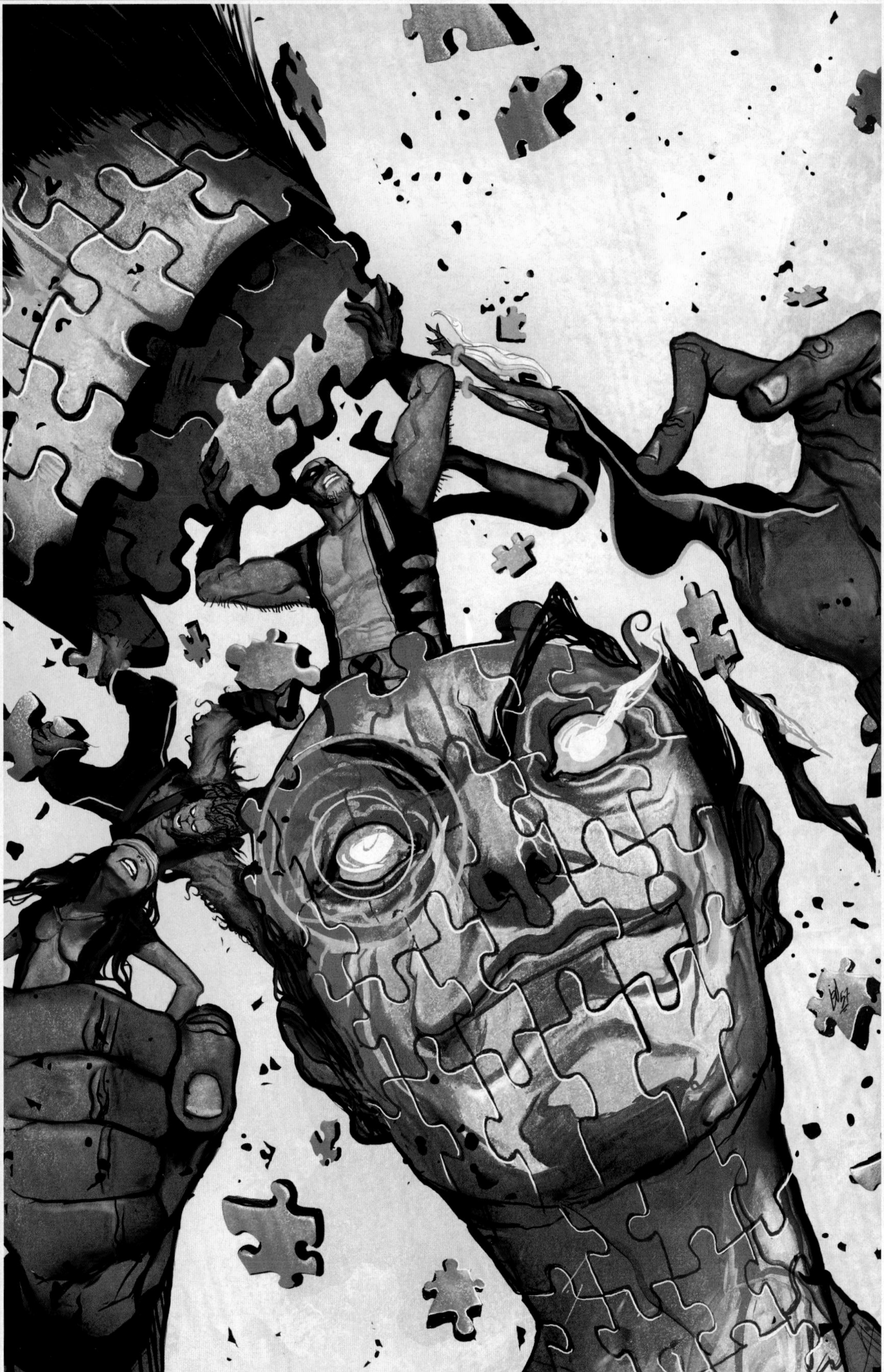

FOUR

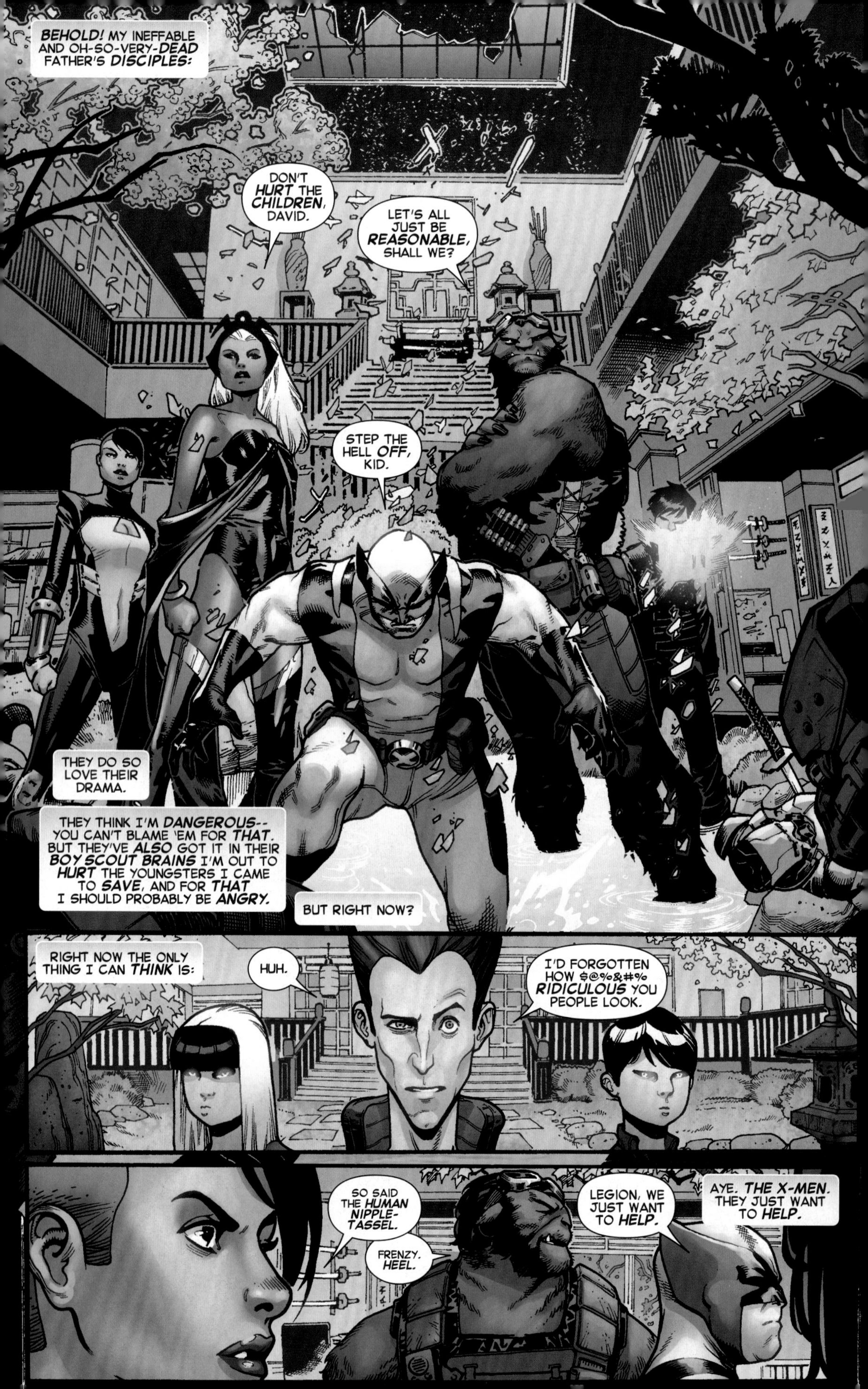
BEHOLD! MY INEFFABLE AND OH-SO-VERY-DEAD FATHER'S DISCIPLES:
DON'T HURT THE CHILDREN, DAVID.
LET'S ALL JUST BE REASONABLE, SHALL WE?
STEP THE HELL OFF, KID.
THEY DO SO LOVE THEIR DRAMA.
THEY THINK I'M DANGEROUS-- YOU CAN'T BLAME 'EM FOR THAT. BUT THEY'VE ALSO GOT IT IN THEIR BOY SCOUT BRAINS I'M OUT TO HURT THE YOUNGSTERS I CAME TO SAVE, AND FOR THAT I SHOULD PROBABLY BE ANGRY.
BUT RIGHT NOW?
RIGHT NOW THE ONLY THING I CAN THINK IS:
HUH.
I'D FORGOTTEN HOW $@%&#% RIDICULOUS YOU PEOPLE LOOK.
SO SAID THE HUMAN NIPPLE-TASSEL.
FRENZY. HEEL.
LEGION, WE JUST WANT TO HELP.
AYE. THE X-MEN. THEY JUST WANT TO HELP.

NOT CALLIN' ME BLOODY *"LEGION"* WOULD BE A GOOD *START.*

AND IF THE *LIVING TRACHEOTOMY* OVER THERE KEEPS SNEAKING ROUND THE BACK, I MIGHT JUST LOSE MY #%$& AND--WHO KNOWS-- *FRACTURE* THE *UNIVERSE* OR SOMETHIN'.

UH.

I'M *BLUFFING,* MOSTLY. CAN'T *ACCESS* ANY OF THE *MAJOR* POWERS JUST YET--MY *INNER ME'S* NOT *STRONG ENOUGH...*

...BUT *THESE* CLOWNS DON'T KNOW THAT.

DAVID, PLEASE--YOU'RE NOT *WELL.* WE CAN HELP YOU. WE CAN HELP YOUR YOUNG *FRIENDS.*

OH *AYE?* HELP THEM *HOW,* EXACTLY?

YOU *KNOW* HOW. WE GIVE THEM A *FUTURE.* HELP THEM *CONTROL* THEIR *POWERS.* TEACH THEM TO *FIGHT* FOR A *BETTER TO--*

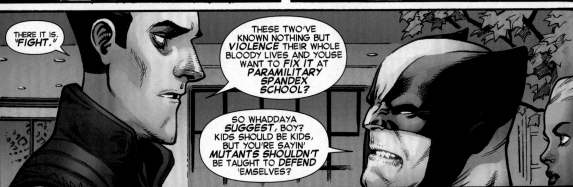

THERE IT IS. *"FIGHT."*

THESE TWO'VE KNOWN NOTHING BUT *VIOLENCE* THEIR WHOLE BLOODY LIVES AND YOUSE WANT TO *FIX* IT AT *PARAMILITARY SPANDEX SCHOOL?*

SO WHADDAYA *SUGGEST,* BOY? KIDS SHOULD BE KIDS, BUT YOU'RE SAYIN' *MUTANTS SHOULDN'T* BE TAUGHT TO *DEFEND* 'EMSELVES?

I'M SAYING THEY SHOULDN'T *HAVE* TO.

AND THEY *WOULDN'T,* IF YOU *NODDIES'D* EVER MADE A JOT OF *DIFFERENCE* TO THE *WORLD.*

THAT'S...THAT'S YOUR *FATHER'S DREAM* YOU'RE TALKING AB--

NO, IT'S NOT. THE *DREAM'S* FINE.

I JUST THINK... M-MAYBE THE WAY HE WENT *ABOUT* IT MIGHT'VE BEEN...

(SAYIT SAYIT SAYIT)

WRONG.

HEARD ENOUGH. KID'S GOT NO *RESPECT*.

WAIT-- MR. LOGAN. PLEASE *DON'T*.

HUH. RAMPAGE HALFWAY 'CROSS *ASIA*, ABDUCT A PAIR A' *MINORS* AN' SASS YOUR *DEAD PA*-- BUT *NOW* YA DON'T WANNA PLAY *ROUGH*?

NO, IT'S NOT THAT.

I JUST DON'T WANT TO *HURT* YOU.

THEY'VE HAD *TRAINING*, ALL OF THEM. PSYCHIC *DEFENSES*, FOCUSED *BARRIERS*...

NEED TO GET THE HAIRY HOBBIT *OFF GUARD*...

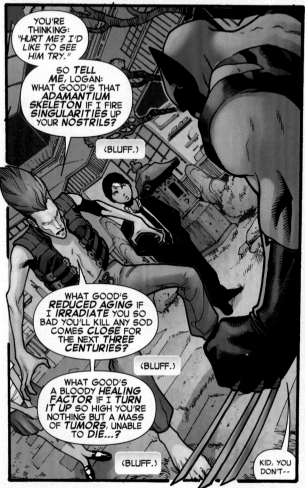

YOU'RE THINKING: "HURT ME? I'D LIKE TO SEE HIM TRY."

SO *TELL* ME, LOGAN: WHAT GOOD'S THAT *ADAMANTIUM* SKELETON IF I FIRE *SINGULARITIES* UP YOUR *NOSTRILS*?

(BLUFF.)

WHAT GOOD'S *REDUCED AGING* IF I IRRADIATE YOU SO BAD YOU'LL KILL ANY SOD COMES *CLOSE* FOR THE NEXT *THREE* CENTURIES?

(BLUFF.)

WHAT GOOD'S A BLOODY *HEALING FACTOR* IF I TURN IT UP SO HIGH YOU'RE NOTHING BUT A MASS OF *TUMORS*, UNABLE TO *DIE*...?

(BLUFF.)

KID, YOU DON'T--

OFF GUARD.

BINGO.

ORRRR I COULD JUST PUT YOUR GROADY WEE BRAIN ON *STANDBY*.

NIGHT-NIGHT, FRODO.

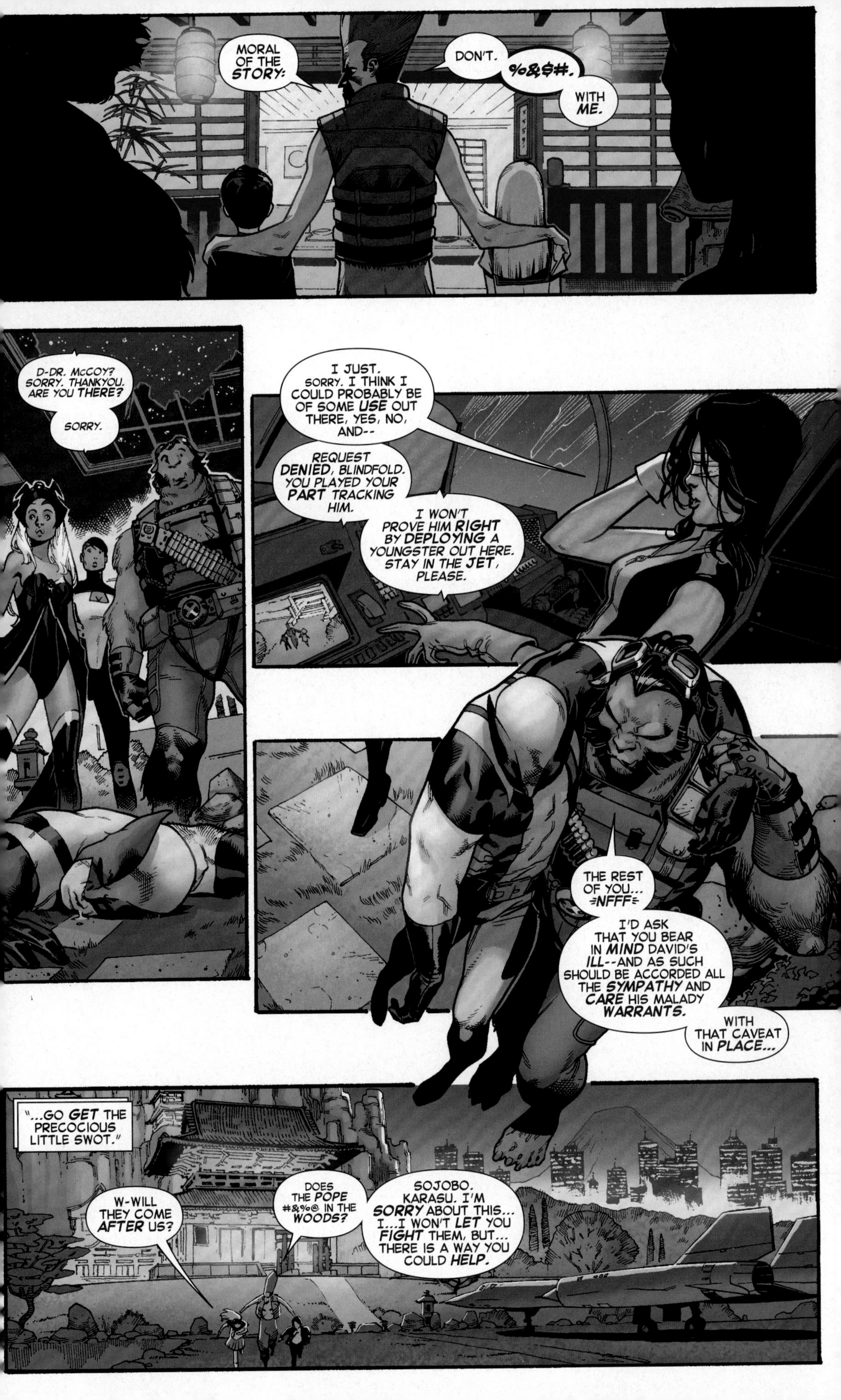
MORAL OF THE STORY:
DON'T. %&$#. WITH ME.
D-DR. McCOY? SORRY. THANKYOU. ARE YOU THERE?
SORRY.
I JUST. SORRY. I THINK I COULD PROBABLY BE OF SOME USE OUT THERE, YES, NO, AND--
REQUEST DENIED, BLINDFOLD. YOU PLAYED YOUR PART TRACKING HIM.
I WON'T PROVE HIM RIGHT BY DEPLOYING A YOUNGSTER OUT HERE. STAY IN THE JET, PLEASE.
THE REST OF YOU... =NFFF=
I'D ASK THAT YOU BEAR IN MIND DAVID'S ILL--AND AS SUCH SHOULD BE ACCORDED ALL THE SYMPATHY AND CARE HIS MALADY WARRANTS.
WITH THAT CAVEAT IN PLACE...
"...GO GET THE PRECOCIOUS LITTLE SWOT."
W-WILL THEY COME AFTER US?
DOES THE POPE #&%@ IN THE WOODS?
SOJOBO. KARASU. I'M SORRY ABOUT THIS... I...I WON'T LET YOU FIGHT THEM, BUT... THERE IS A WAY YOU COULD HELP.

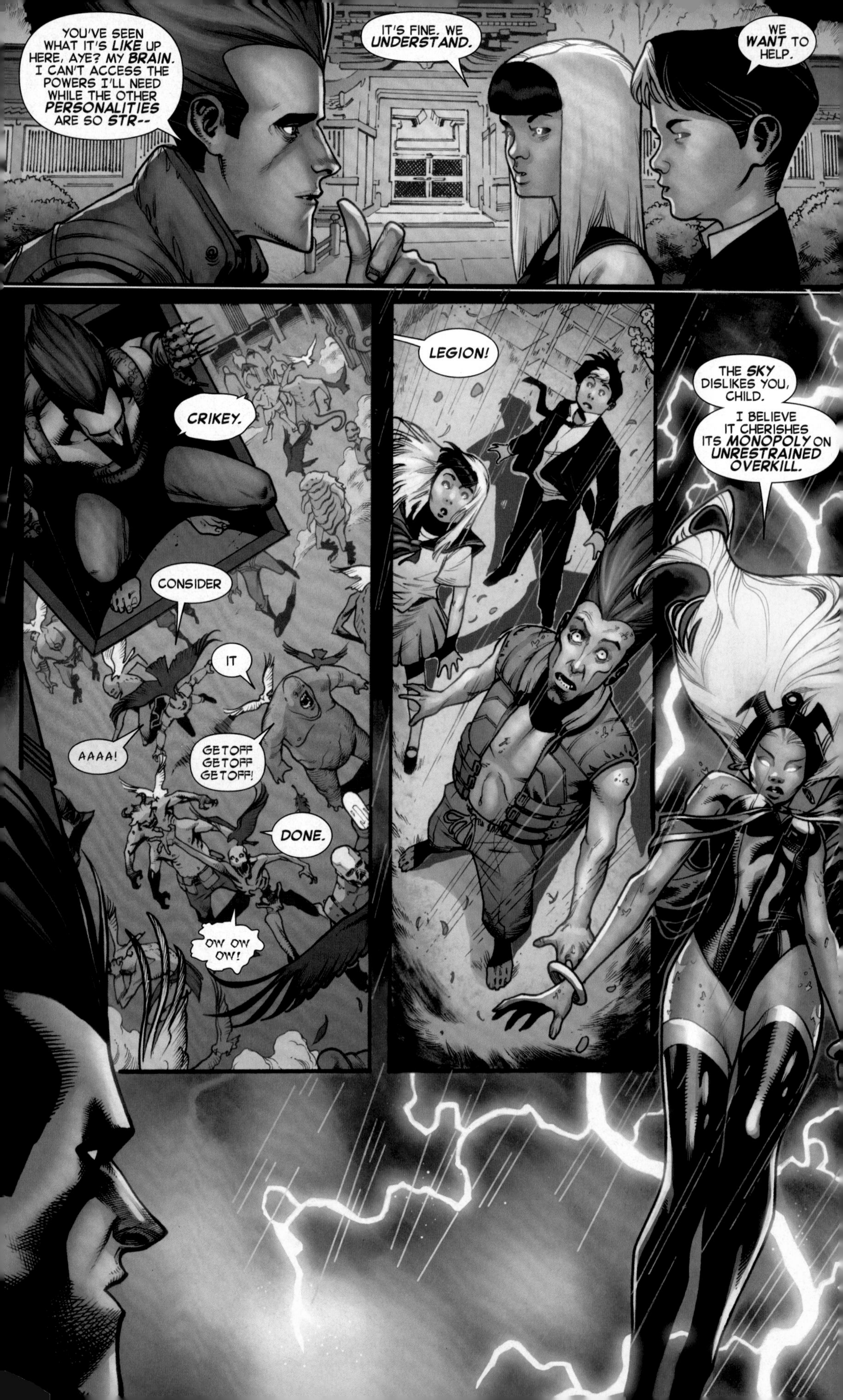
YOU'VE SEEN WHAT IT'S LIKE UP HERE, AYE? MY BRAIN. I CAN'T ACCESS THE POWERS I'LL NEED WHILE THE OTHER PERSONALITIES ARE SO STR--
IT'S FINE. WE UNDERSTAND.
WE WANT TO HELP.
CRIKEY.
CONSIDER
IT
AAAA!
GETOFF GETOFF GETOFF!
DONE.
OW OW OW!
LEGION!
THE SKY DISLIKES YOU, CHILD.
I BELIEVE IT CHERISHES ITS MONOPOLY ON UNRESTRAINED OVERKILL.

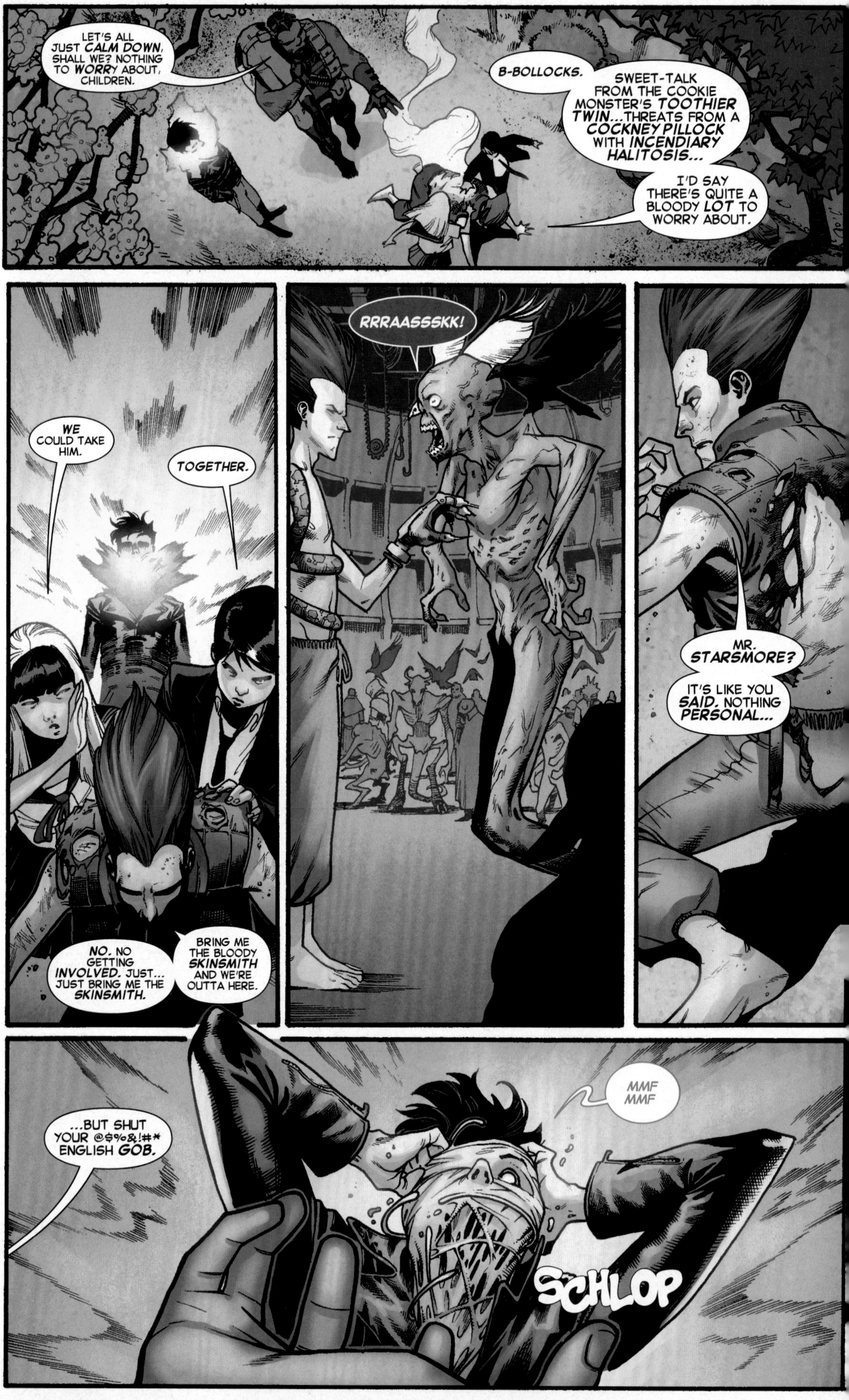

LET'S ALL JUST CALM DOWN, SHALL WE? NOTHING TO WORRY ABOUT, CHILDREN.
B-BOLLOCKS.
SWEET-TALK FROM THE COOKIE MONSTER'S TOOTHIER TWIN...THREATS FROM A COCKNEY PILLOCK WITH INCENDIARY HALITOSIS...
I'D SAY THERE'S QUITE A BLOODY LOT TO WORRY ABOUT.
WE COULD TAKE HIM.
TOGETHER.
NO. NO GETTING INVOLVED. JUST... JUST BRING ME THE SKINSMITH.
BRING ME THE BLOODY SKINSMITH AND WE'RE OUTTA HERE.
RRRAASSSKK!
MR. STARSMORE?
IT'S LIKE YOU SAID. NOTHING PERSONAL...
...BUT SHUT YOUR @$%&!#* ENGLISH GOB.
MMF MMF
SCHLOP

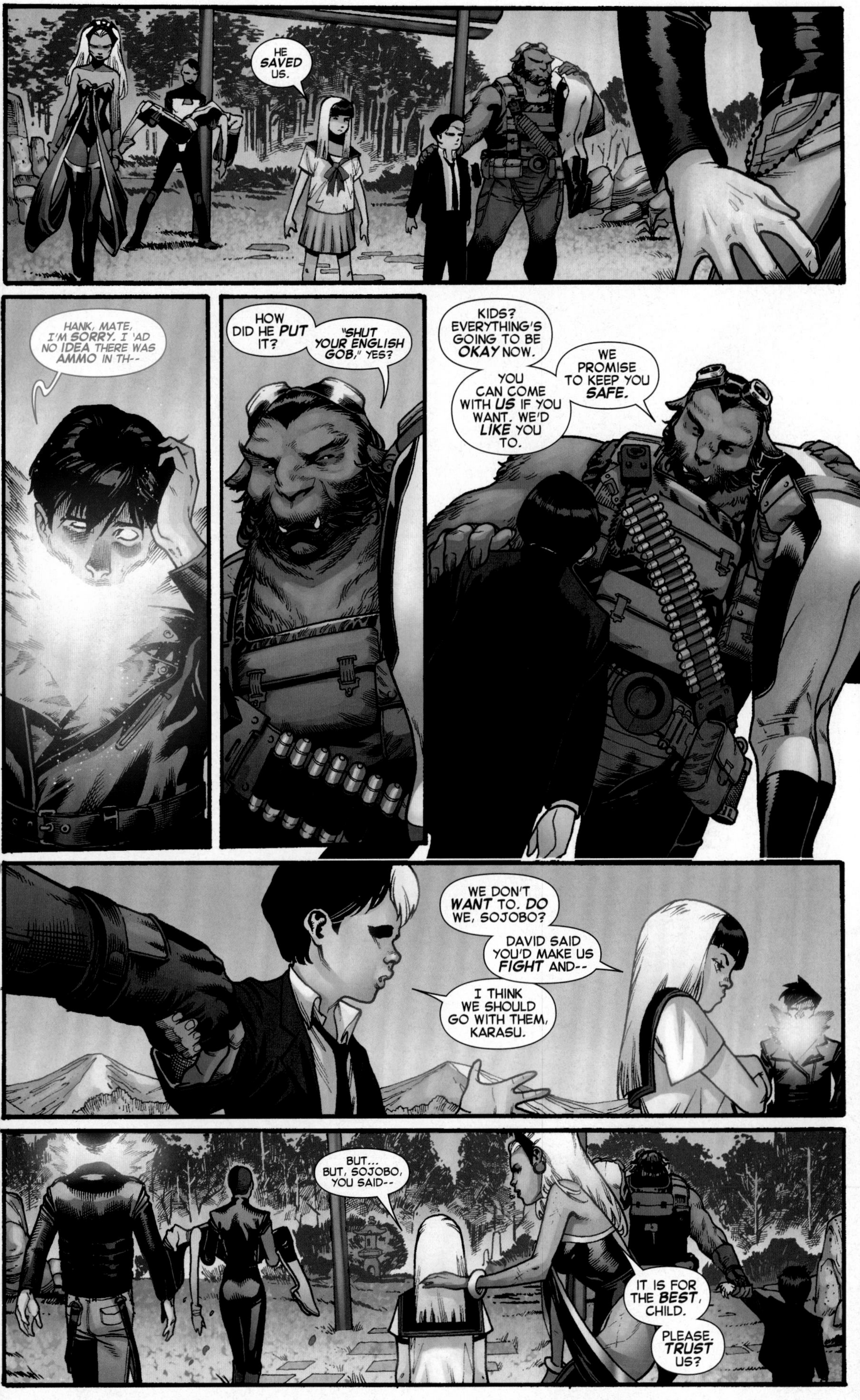
HE SAVED US.
HANK, MATE, I'M SORRY. I 'AD NO IDEA THERE WAS AMMO IN TH--
HOW DID HE PUT IT?
"SHUT YOUR ENGLISH GOB," YES?
KIDS? EVERYTHING'S GOING TO BE OKAY NOW.
YOU CAN COME WITH US IF YOU WANT. WE'D LIKE YOU TO.
WE PROMISE TO KEEP YOU SAFE.
WE DON'T WANT TO. DO WE, SOJOBO?
DAVID SAID YOU'D MAKE US FIGHT AND--
I THINK WE SHOULD GO WITH THEM, KARASU.
BUT... BUT, SOJOBO, YOU SAID--
IT IS FOR THE BEST, CHILD.
PLEASE. TRUST US?

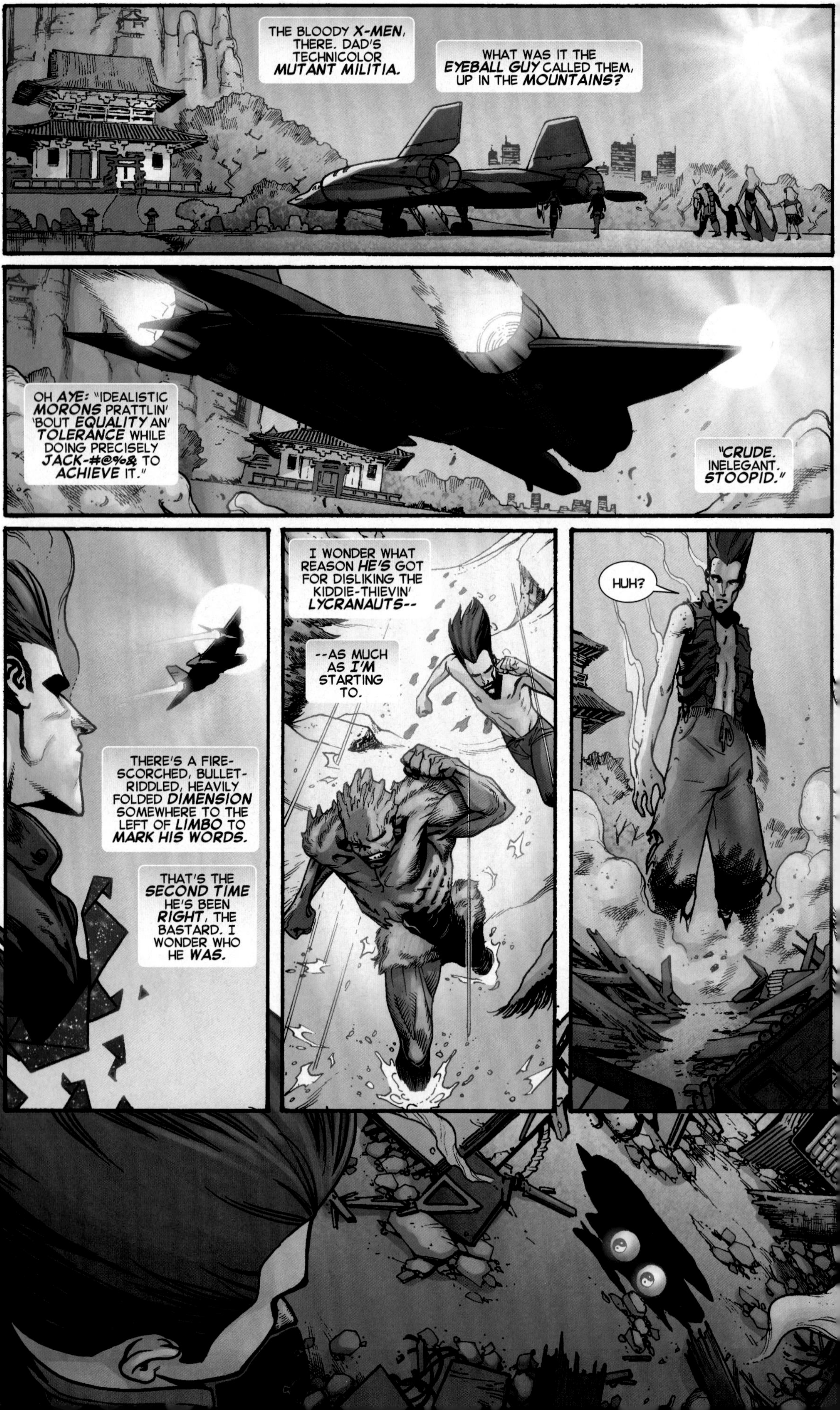

THE BLOODY X-MEN, THERE. DAD'S TECHNICOLOR MUTANT MILITIA.
WHAT WAS IT THE EYEBALL GUY CALLED THEM, UP IN THE MOUNTAINS?
OH AYE: "IDEALISTIC MORONS PRATTLIN' 'BOUT EQUALITY AN' TOLERANCE WHILE DOING PRECISELY JACK-#@%& TO ACHIEVE IT."
"CRUDE. INELEGANT. STOOPID."
THERE'S A FIRE-SCORCHED, BULLET-RIDDLED, HEAVILY FOLDED DIMENSION SOMEWHERE TO THE LEFT OF LIMBO TO MARK HIS WORDS.
THAT'S THE SECOND TIME HE'S BEEN RIGHT, THE BASTARD. I WONDER WHO HE WAS.
I WONDER WHAT REASON HE'S GOT FOR DISLIKING THE KIDDIE-THIEVIN' LYCRANAUTS--
--AS MUCH AS I'M STARTING TO.
HUH?

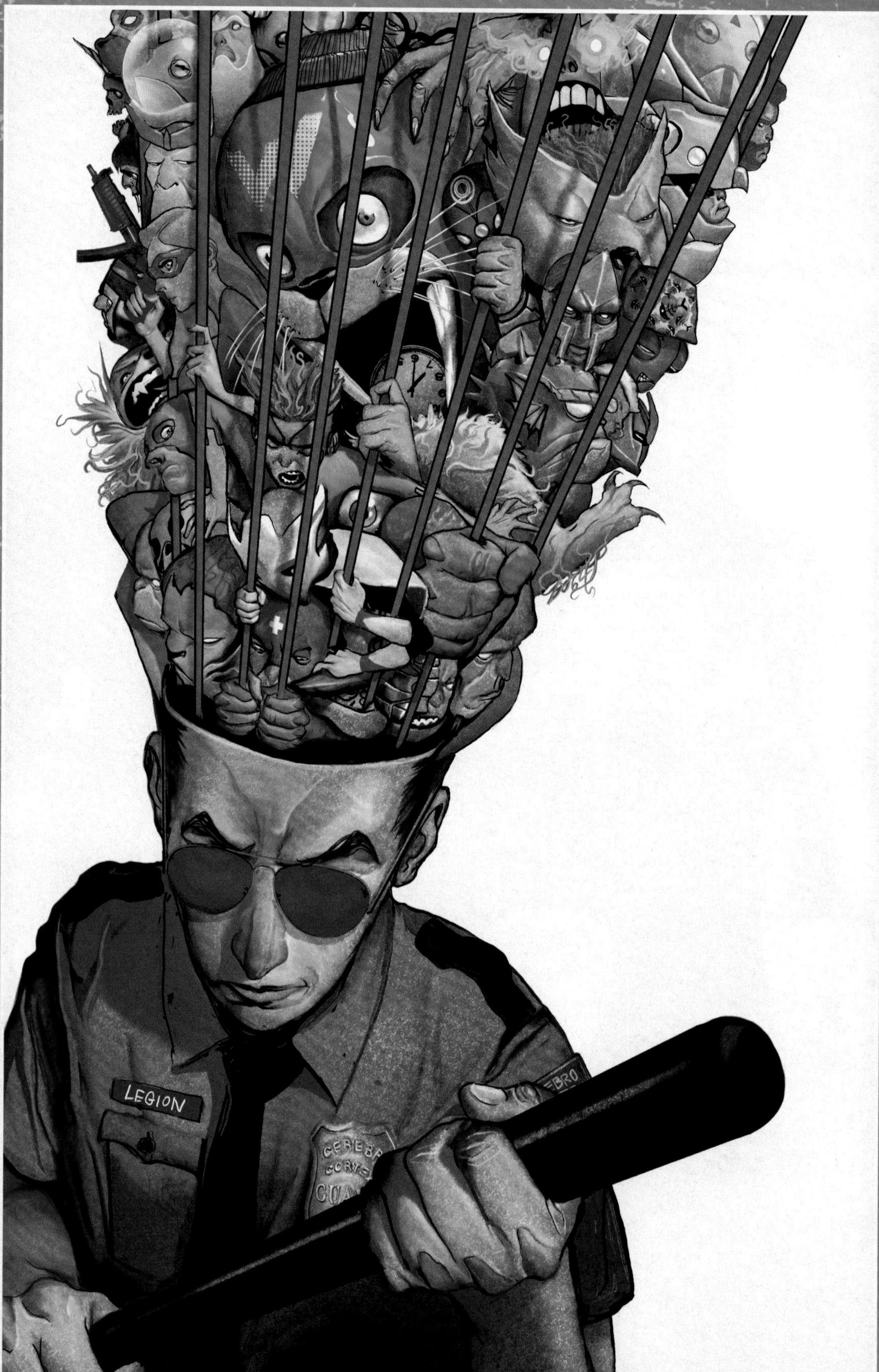
LEGION

FIVE

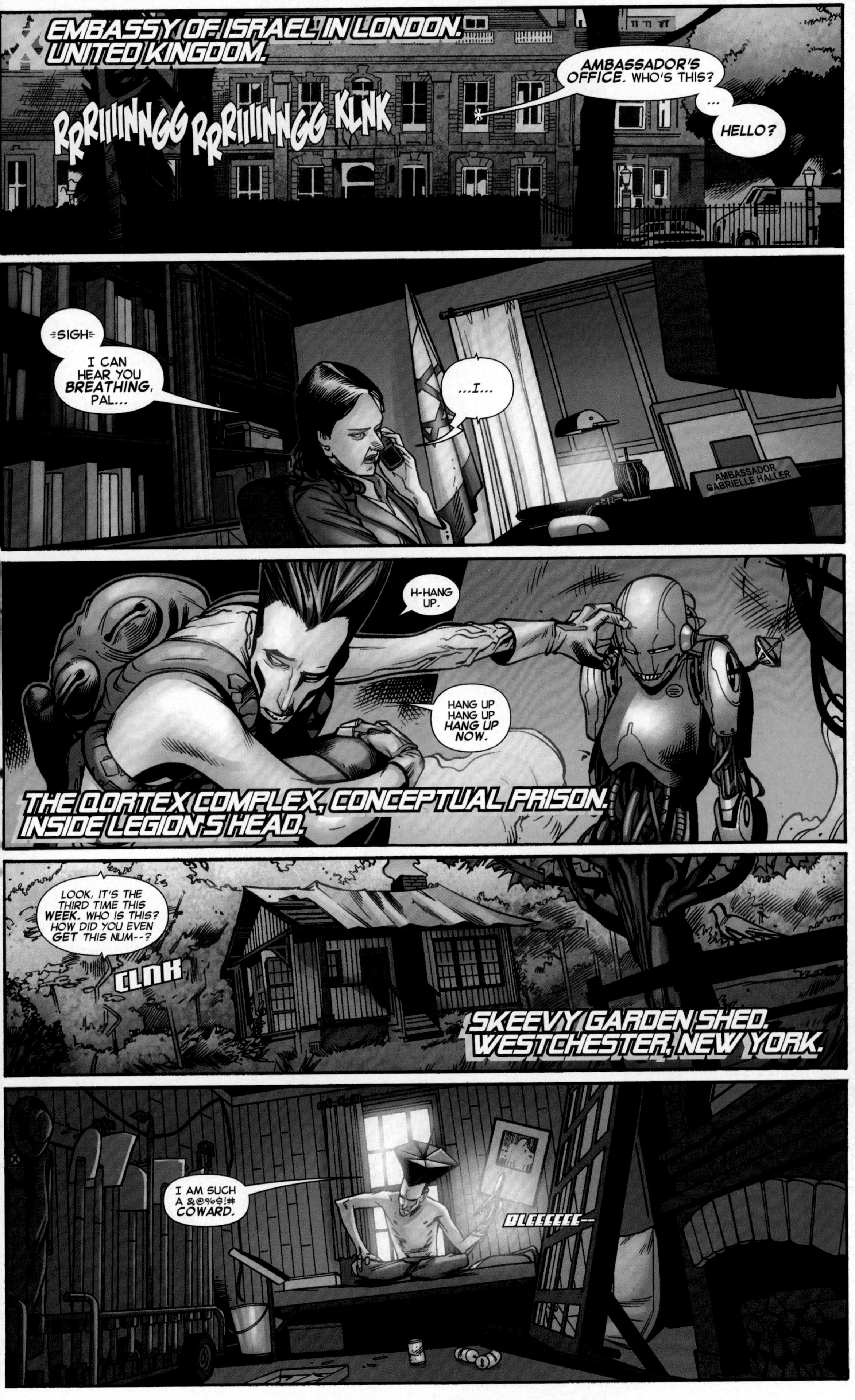
EMBASSY OF ISRAEL IN LONDON.
UNITED KINGDOM.
RRRIIIINNGG RRRIIIINNGG KLNK
AMBASSADOR'S OFFICE. WHO'S THIS?
...
HELLO?
SIGH
I CAN HEAR YOU BREATHING, PAL...
...I...
AMBASSADOR GABRIELLE HALLER
H-HANG UP.
HANG UP HANG UP HANG UP NOW.
THE QORTEX COMPLEX, CONCEPTUAL PRISON.
INSIDE LEGION'S HEAD.
LOOK, IT'S THE THIRD TIME THIS WEEK. WHO IS THIS? HOW DID YOU EVEN GET THIS NUM--?
CLNK
SKEEVY GARDEN SHED.
WESTCHESTER, NEW YORK.
I AM SUCH A &@%$!# COWARD.
BLEEEEEE--

FOR *INSTANCE*: RIGHT NOW I'M LOCATING A BUNCH OF *DISGUSTING ALIEN MONSTERS* SEVERAL THOUSAND *LIGHT-YEARS* AWAY, AND TELEPORTING 'EM FIFTY YARDS *NORTH* OF HERE.

WHICH IS BASICALLY *IMPOSSIBLE*, TO ANYONE *WITHOUT* 200 OMEGA-LEVEL *SPLIT PERSONALITIES* IN THEIR *BRAIN*. YAY ME.

IT'S ALSO, I CONCEDE, A SOMEWHAT *INCONSIDERATE* THING TO *DO* TO THE FOLKS WHO LIVE *NEAR HERE*.

STILL: IT'S ONLY *PART ONE* OF THE PLAN. WE'LL COME BACK TO IT IN A *MINUTE*, WHEN THE *COSMIC WORMHOLES'VE* DONE THEIR *JOB*.

PART *TWO'S* THE *IMPORTANT BIT* ANYWAY.

PART *TWO'S* ALL ABOUT MY *DELIGHTFUL, TENTACLED BACKPACK BUDDY*...

ONE DAY I'LL *EAT YOUR LUNGS*, YOU BIG-HAIRED *BAAAAAA*

...*TYRANNIX THE ABOMINOID*.

THANKS TO *HIM*, MINE'S THE POWER OF *TELEPATHY*. I'LL BE *NEEDING* THAT.

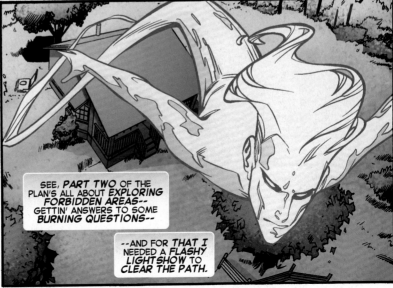

SEE, *PART TWO* OF THE PLAN'S ALL ABOUT *EXPLORING FORBIDDEN AREAS*-- GETTIN' ANSWERS TO SOME *BURNING QUESTIONS*--

--AND FOR *THAT* I NEEDED A *FLASHY LIGHTSHOW* TO CLEAR THE PATH.

ONLY A MATTER OF *TIME* BEFORE THE BASTARD FELL OFF THE *WAGON*. GOT HIMSELF *PROPER* CRAZY...

...#@%& MUTANTS...

...#@%@& RUININ' EVERYTHIN'...

NOT THAT RUTH *UNDERSTOOD* THE *WHY*, BACK THEN.

ONLY THAT HER *MA* HAD MORE *BRUISES* THAN EVER.

ONLY THAT THE *COPS* PAID MORE *VISITS*.

ONLY THAT HER *BROTHER* WATCHED HER *CLOSER* THAN *EVER*...

'TIL THE DAY LUCA WENT AS *QUIET* AS *SIN*, AND SLIPPED OUT TO THE *WOODSHED*, AND...AND...

A
BOM
IN
ATION.

THEIR MAMMY MUST'VE BEEN *ASLEEP* UPSTAIRS. MUST'VE COME RUSHING DOWN TO SEE WHAT WAS CAUSING THE *COMMOTION*.

SURPRISED HIM AT JUST THE WRONG TIME.

L-LUCA? WHAT'RE Y...

GET *AWAY* FROM HER! GET *AWAY* FROM H--

KWWWWB

THE WAY RUTH REMEMBERS IT, THE WHOLE THING'S A *NUTSHELL-VERSION* OF WHAT IT *MEANS* TO BE A *MUTANT*:

THE STORY OF *COLLATERAL DAMAGE*.

NOT *ME*, YOU *IDIAAAAAAAA*

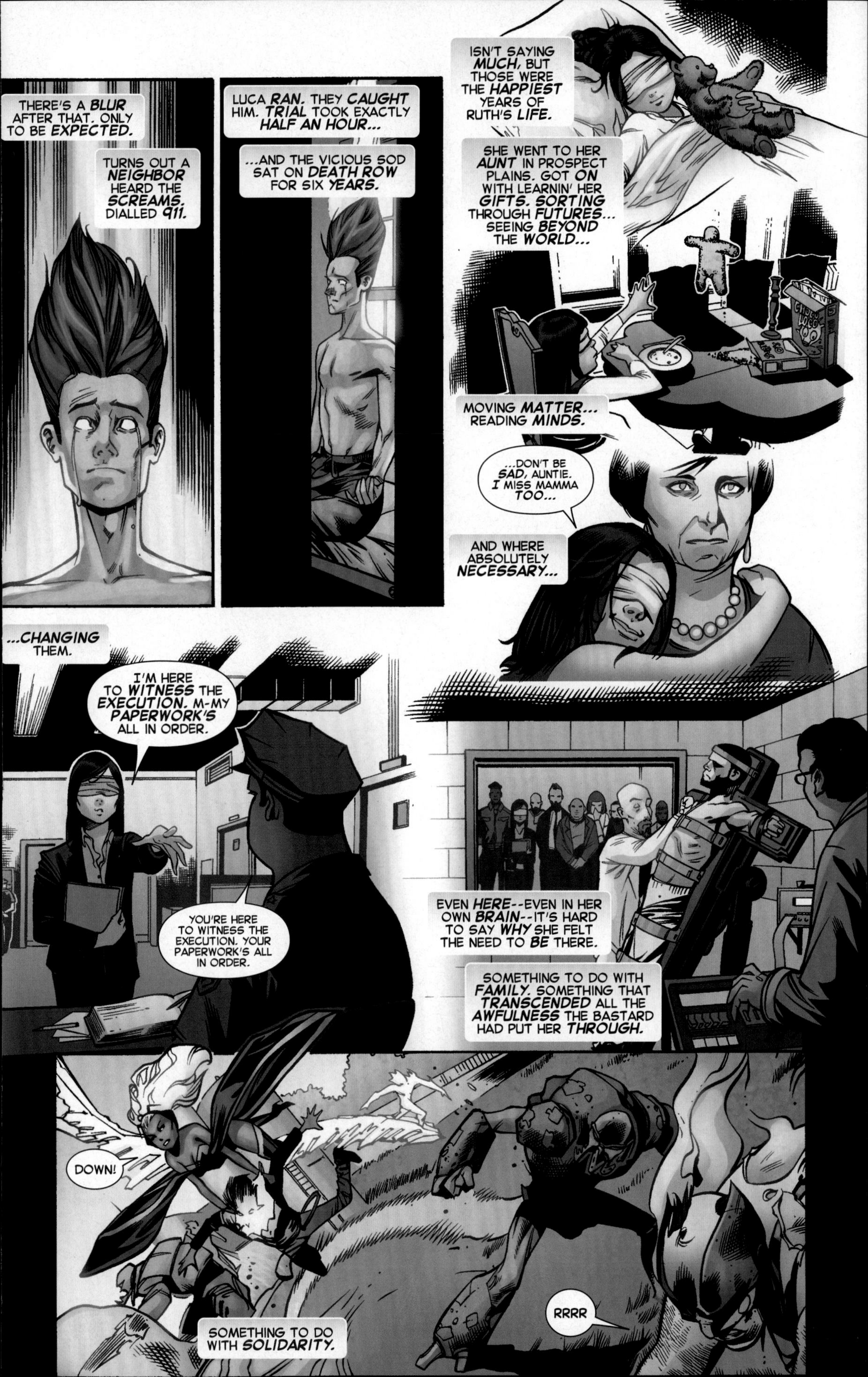
THERE'S A BLUR AFTER THAT. ONLY TO BE EXPECTED.
TURNS OUT A NEIGHBOR HEARD THE SCREAMS. DIALLED 911.
LUCA RAN. THEY CAUGHT HIM. TRIAL TOOK EXACTLY HALF AN HOUR...
...AND THE VICIOUS SOD SAT ON DEATH ROW FOR SIX YEARS.
ISN'T SAYING MUCH, BUT THOSE WERE THE HAPPIEST YEARS OF RUTH'S LIFE.
SHE WENT TO HER AUNT IN PROSPECT PLAINS. GOT ON WITH LEARNIN' HER GIFTS. SORTING THROUGH FUTURES... SEEING BEYOND THE WORLD...
MOVING MATTER... READING MINDS.
...DON'T BE SAD, AUNTIE. I MISS MAMMA TOO...
AND WHERE ABSOLUTELY NECESSARY...
...CHANGING THEM.
I'M HERE TO WITNESS THE EXECUTION. M-MY PAPERWORK'S ALL IN ORDER.
YOU'RE HERE TO WITNESS THE EXECUTION. YOUR PAPERWORK'S ALL IN ORDER.
EVEN HERE--EVEN IN HER OWN BRAIN--IT'S HARD TO SAY WHY SHE FELT THE NEED TO BE THERE.
SOMETHING TO DO WITH FAMILY. SOMETHING THAT TRANSCENDED ALL THE AWFULNESS THE BASTARD HAD PUT HER THROUGH.
DOWN!
RRRR
SOMETHING TO DO WITH SOLIDARITY.

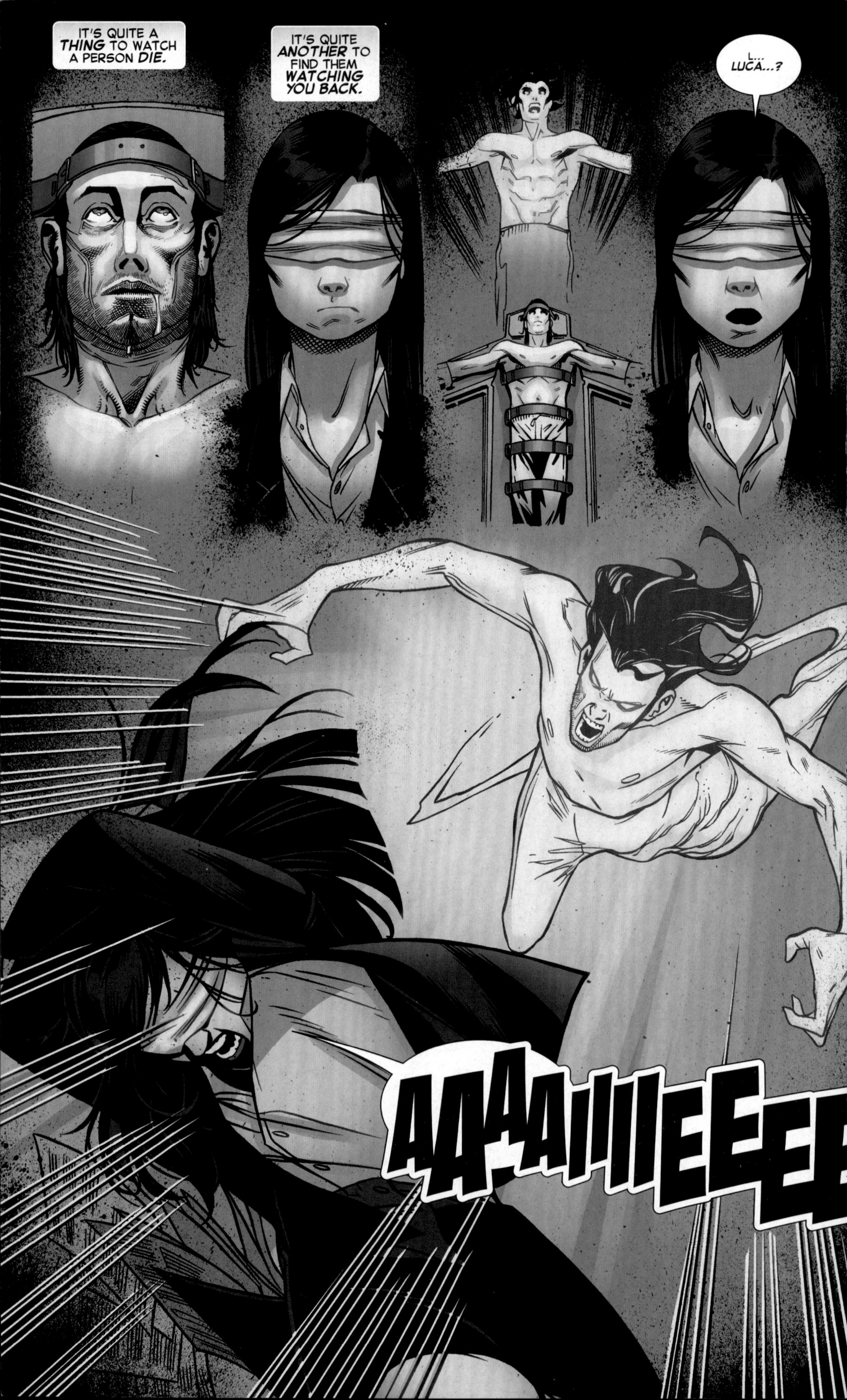
IT'S QUITE A THING TO WATCH A PERSON DIE.
IT'S QUITE ANOTHER TO FIND THEM WATCHING YOU BACK.
L... LUCA...?
AAAAIIIEEEE

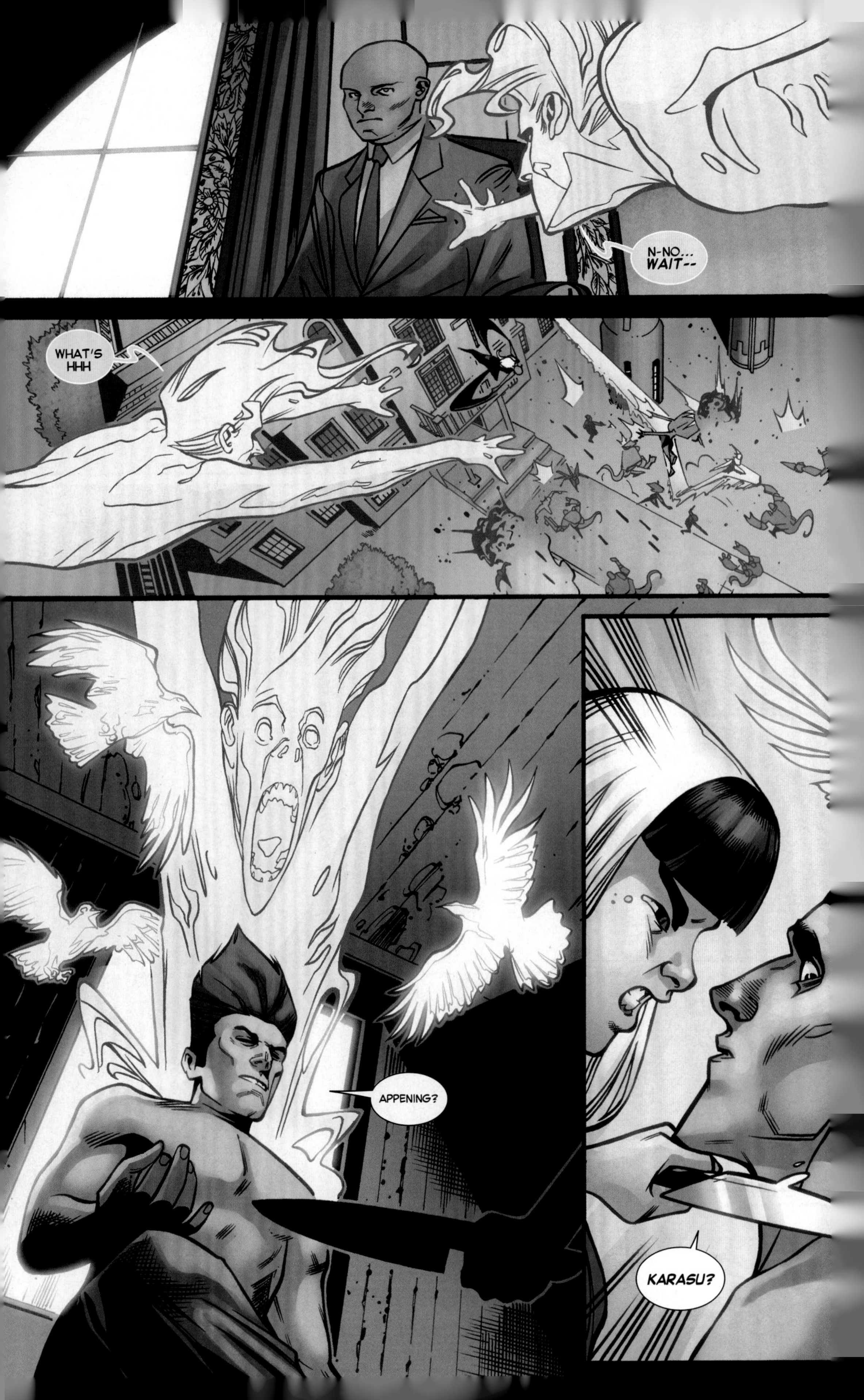
N-NO...
WAIT--
WHAT'S
HHH
APPENING?
KARASU?

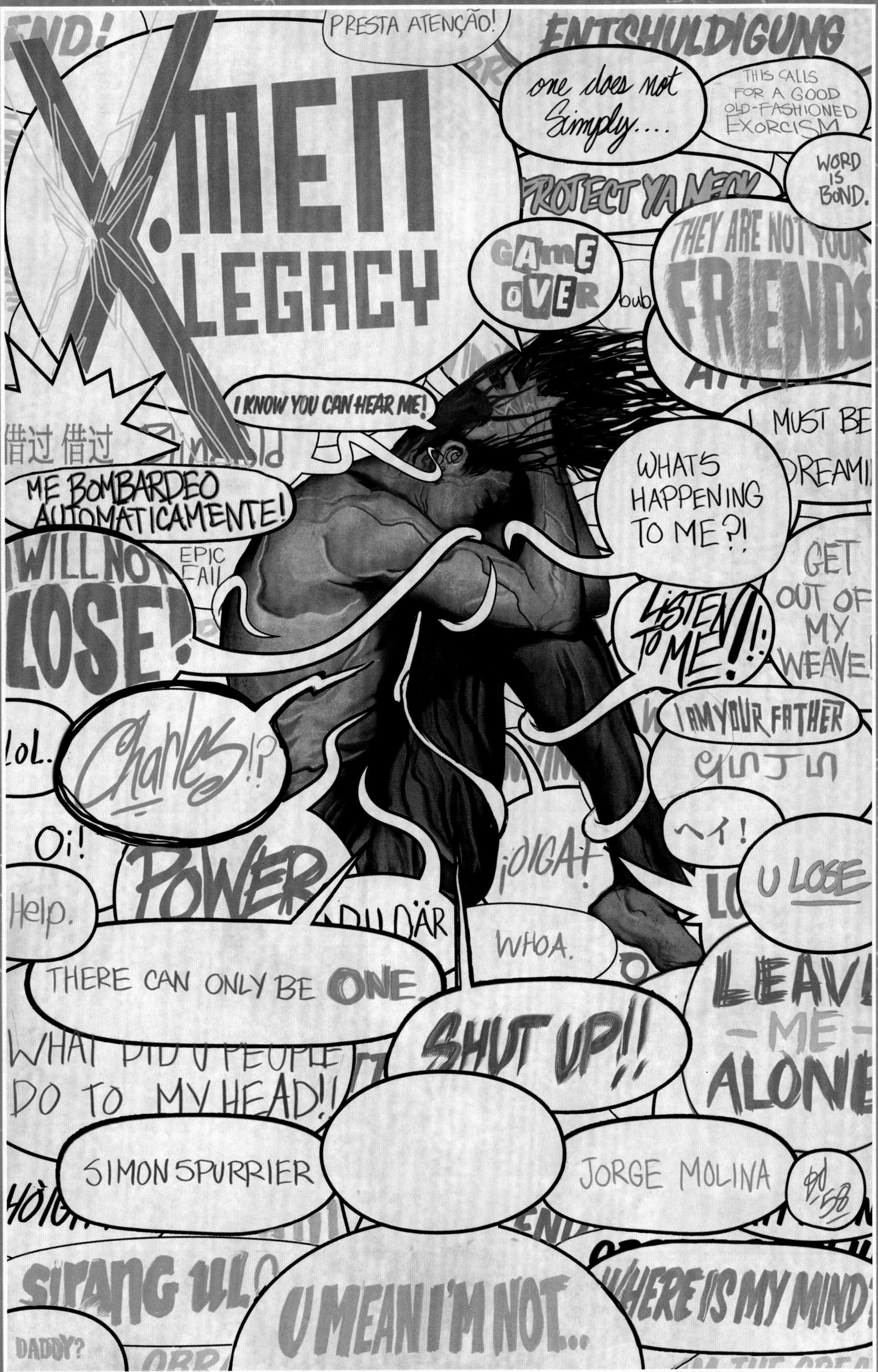
X-MEN LEGACY
PRESTA ATENÇÃO!
ENTSHULDIGUNG
one does not Simply....
THIS CALLS FOR A GOOD OLD-FASHIONED EXORCISM
WORD IS BOND.
THEY ARE NOT YOUR FRIENDS
GAME OVER
I KNOW YOU CAN HEAR ME!
借过 借过
I MUST BE
ME BOMBARDEO AUTOMATICAMENTE!
WHAT'S HAPPENING TO ME?!
I WILL NOT LOSE!
EPIC FAIL
GET OUT OF MY WEAVE!
LISTEN TO ME!!
I AM YOUR FATHER
LOL.
Charles!?
ヘイ!
Oi!
POWER
¡DIGA!
U LOSE
Help.
WHOA.
THERE CAN ONLY BE ONE.
LEAVE ME ALONE
SHUT UP!!
DO TO MY HEAD!!
SIMON SPURRIER
JORGE MOLINA
U MEAN I'M NOT...
WHERE IS MY MIND?
DADDY?

SIX

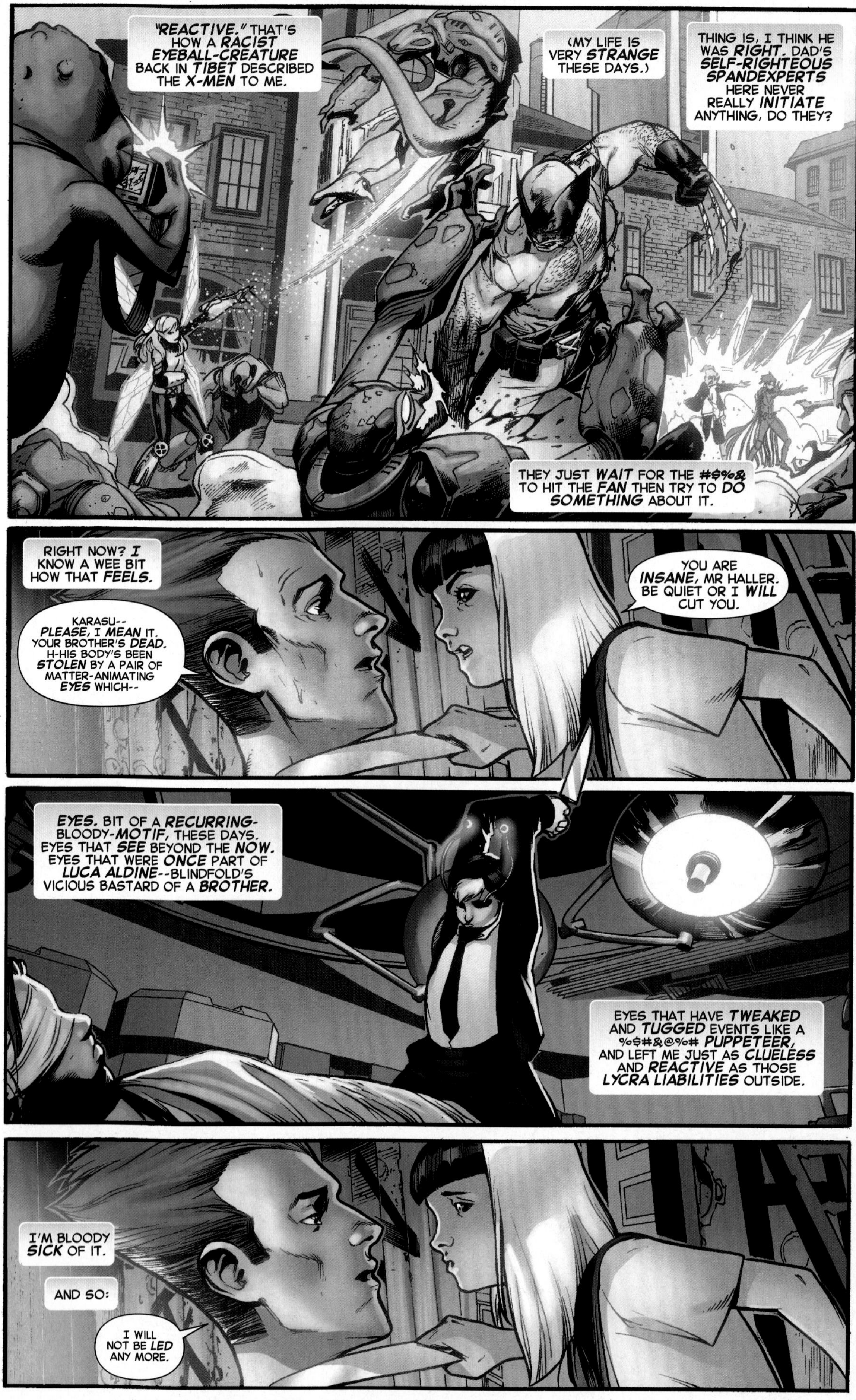
"REACTIVE." THAT'S HOW A RACIST EYEBALL-CREATURE BACK IN TIBET DESCRIBED THE X-MEN TO ME.
(MY LIFE IS VERY STRANGE THESE DAYS.)
THING IS, I THINK HE WAS RIGHT. DAD'S SELF-RIGHTEOUS SPANDEXPERTS HERE NEVER REALLY INITIATE ANYTHING, DO THEY?
THEY JUST WAIT FOR THE #$%& TO HIT THE FAN THEN TRY TO DO SOMETHING ABOUT IT.
RIGHT NOW? I KNOW A WEE BIT HOW THAT FEELS.
KARASU-- PLEASE, I MEAN IT. YOUR BROTHER'S DEAD. H-HIS BODY'S BEEN STOLEN BY A PAIR OF MATTER-ANIMATING EYES WHICH--
YOU ARE INSANE, MR HALLER. BE QUIET OR I WILL CUT YOU.
EYES. BIT OF A RECURRING-BLOODY-MOTIF, THESE DAYS. EYES THAT SEE BEYOND THE NOW. EYES THAT WERE ONCE PART OF LUCA ALDINE--BLINDFOLD'S VICIOUS BASTARD OF A BROTHER.
EYES THAT HAVE TWEAKED AND TUGGED EVENTS LIKE A %$#&@%# PUPPETEER, AND LEFT ME JUST AS CLUELESS AND REACTIVE AS THOSE LYCRA LIABILITIES OUTSIDE.
I'M BLOODY SICK OF IT.
AND SO:
I WILL NOT BE LED ANY MORE.

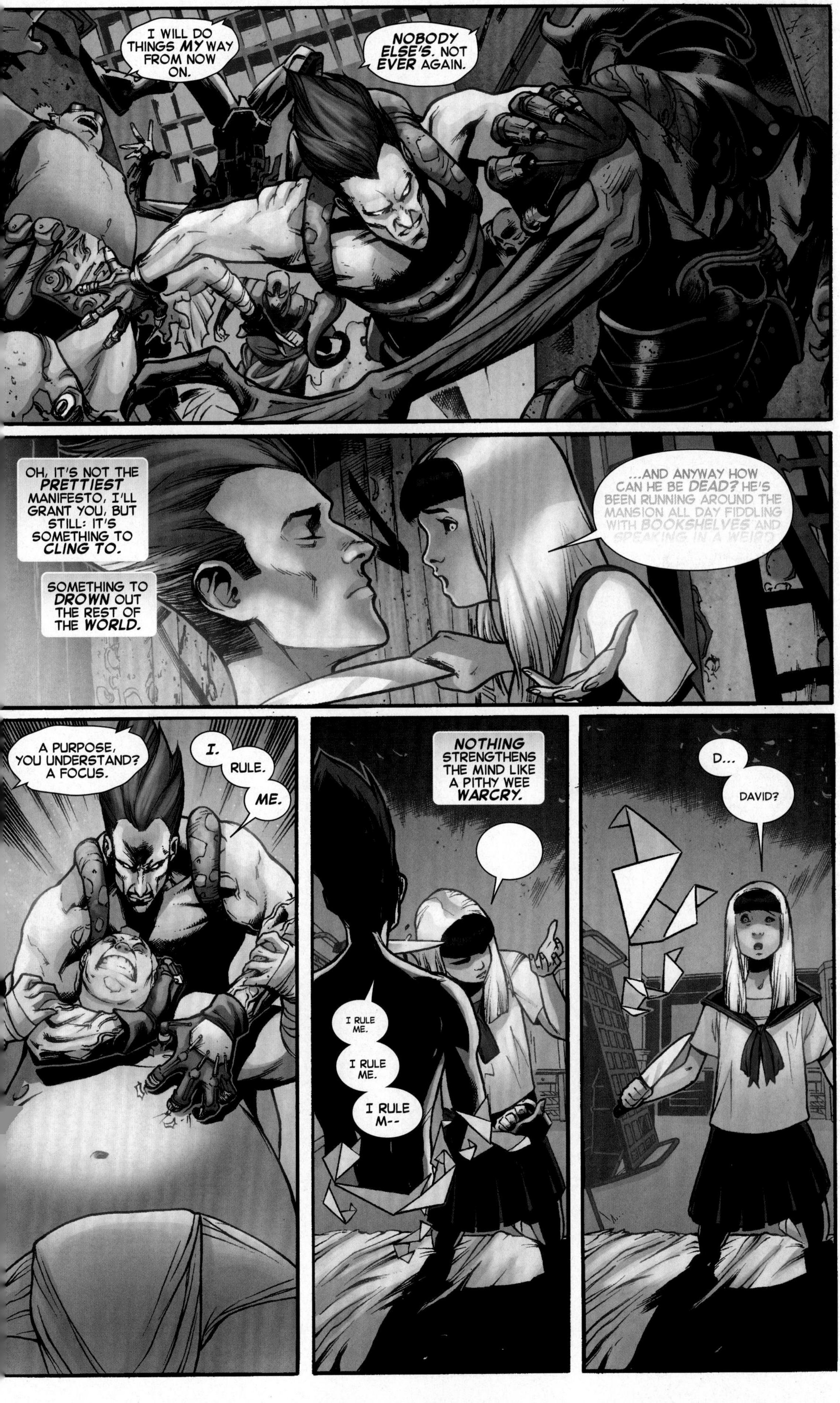
I WILL DO THINGS MY WAY FROM NOW ON.
NOBODY ELSE'S. NOT EVER AGAIN.
OH, IT'S NOT THE PRETTIEST MANIFESTO, I'LL GRANT YOU, BUT STILL: IT'S SOMETHING TO CLING TO.
SOMETHING TO DROWN OUT THE REST OF THE WORLD.
...AND ANYWAY HOW CAN HE BE DEAD? HE'S BEEN RUNNING AROUND THE MANSION ALL DAY FIDDLING WITH BOOKSHELVES AND SPEAKING IN A WEIRD
A PURPOSE, YOU UNDERSTAND? A FOCUS.
I.
RULE.
ME.
NOTHING STRENGTHENS THE MIND LIKE A PITHY WEE WARCRY.
I RULE ME.
I RULE ME.
I RULE M--
D...
DAVID?

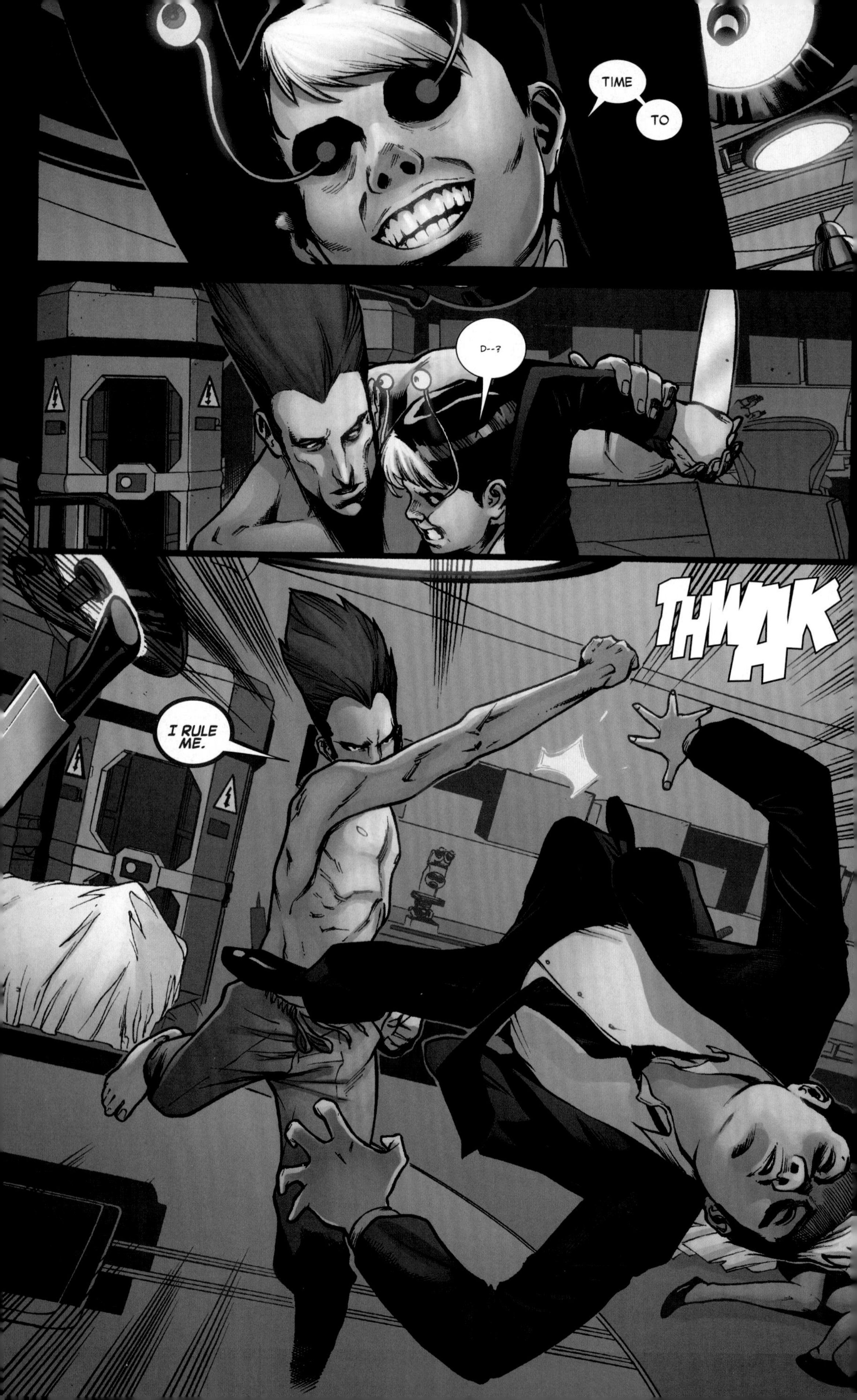
TIME
TO
D--?
I RULE ME.
THWAK

RRRR

GIVE IT UP, PAL. WE WENT *THROUGH* ALL THIS IN *CHINA*.

I TWEAKED ONE LITTLE *ICICLE* AND FIVE MINUTES LATER A *SQUINT-EYE SOLDIER* PLAYED *PANCAKE*, YA 'MEMBER?

SAME-SAME, PAL. I HIT THE WALL HERE AT JUST THE RIGHT TIME...

GONGGG

AAA!

"...AN' VIA A *DELIGHTFUL* SEQUENCE O' *CONVOLUTED CRAPOLA* INVOLVIN' A STARTLED JANITOR..."

ZZZK

"...AN OVERSENSITIVE *SHI'AR A/C-UNIT*..."

FUMFUMFUMFUM

"...ONE OF *DOOP'S* FORGOTTEN *CANDY BARS*..."

F-PUP

"...AN' A SWARM OF *HUNGRY INTERDIMENSIONAL GREMLINS*..."

...WELL.

THIS HAPPENS.

HA!

BAMF

SKASSSH

HUH.

UNHOLY LI'L *CRITTER* WUZ 'SPOSEDA HIT YA RIGHT BETWEEN THE *EYES*.

AAA--

AH WELL.

THAT *HOUR* SAWIN' AT *BOOKSHELVES* WAS *WELL SPENT* AFTER ALL.

CONTINGENCIES, CONTINGENCIES.

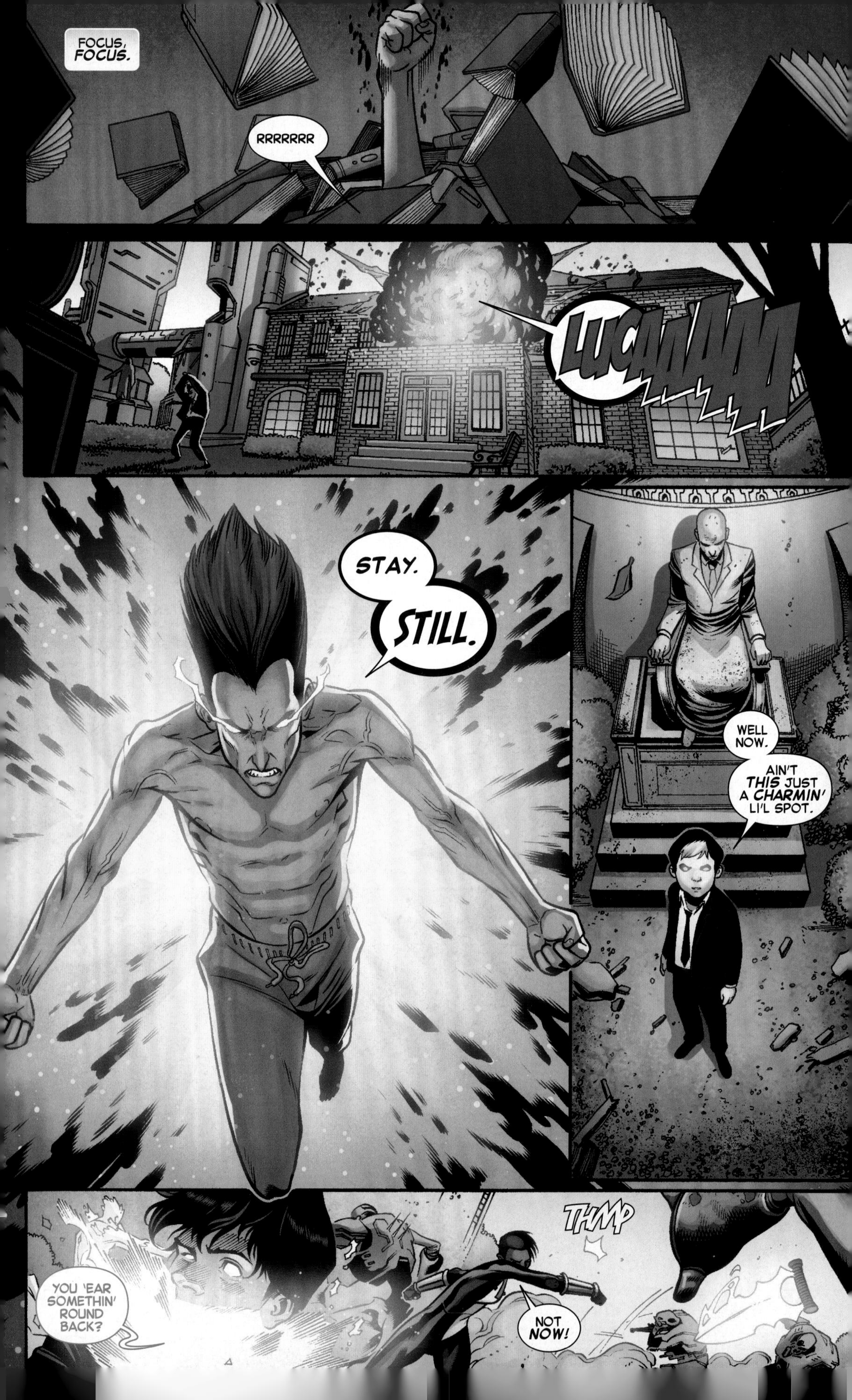
FOCUS, FOCUS.
RRRRRRR
LUCAAAAAA
STAY.
STILL.
WELL NOW.
AIN'T THIS JUST A CHARMIN' LI'L SPOT.
YOU 'EAR SOMETHIN' ROUND BACK?
THMP
NOT NOW!

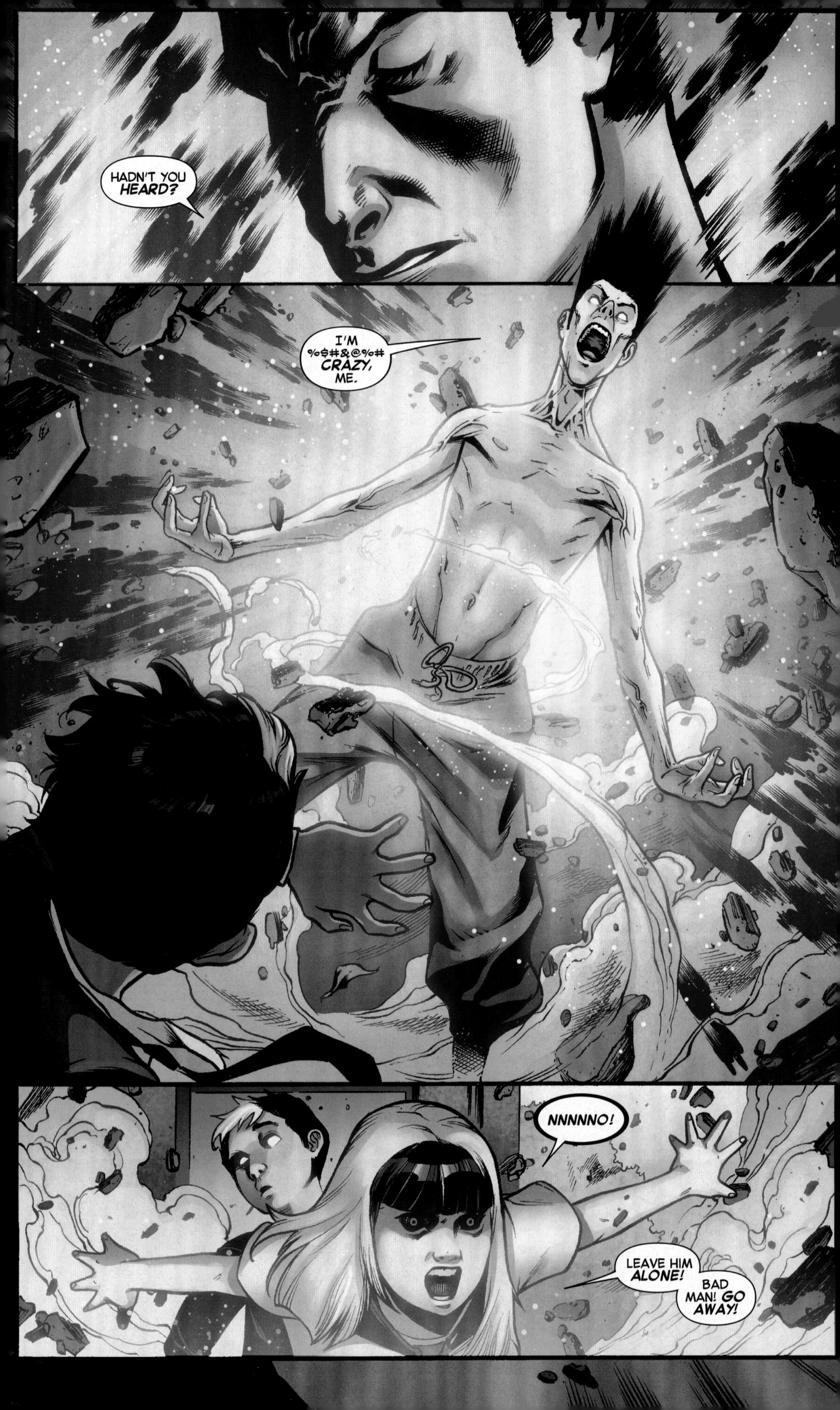
HADN'T YOU HEARD?
I'M %$#&@%# CRAZY, ME.
NNNNNO!
LEAVE HIM ALONE!
BAD MAN! GO AWAY!

...KARASU...YOU DON'T *UNDERSTAND* WHAT'S *HAPPENING* HERE. I'M *ASKING* YOU TO *STEP ASIDE.*

...

...BUT.

...BUT IF SHE *DOESN'T?*

I CAN *CLICK MY FINGERS* AND TURN HER TO *ETHER* IN THE *SPLIT SECOND* IT TAKES TO *ANNIHILATE* THE *FIEND.*

I CAN STRIKE *ROUND HER* WITH *PARABOLIC BALEFIRE.* I CAN BECOME A *LIVING MELODY* AND *RAPTURE* BEYOND HER *EARS,* OR *ERASE HER* FROM *HISTORY* WITH A *SINGLE THOUGHT.*

I HAVE *ALL THE POWER IN THE WORLD* AND A *JUST CAUSE.* WHAT DOES ONE *SCARED WEE CHILD* COUNT AGAINST *THAT?*

HA.

LOOK AT YOU. ALL *SWOLLEN* WITH *SELF-RIGHTEOUS-NESS.*

DOING YOUR BEST NOT TO *THINK.* TRICKING YOURSELF WITH A *CONFIDENCE* YOU NEITHER *DESERVE* NOR *BELIEVE.* "I RULE ME, I RULE ME..." PITIFUL.

TELL ME, *BOY:* WHEN DID YOU LAST SPARE A *THOUGHT* FOR YOUR *FATHER?*

WH...

HE'D BE *ASHAMED* OF YOU.

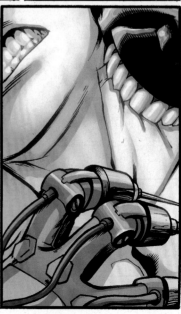

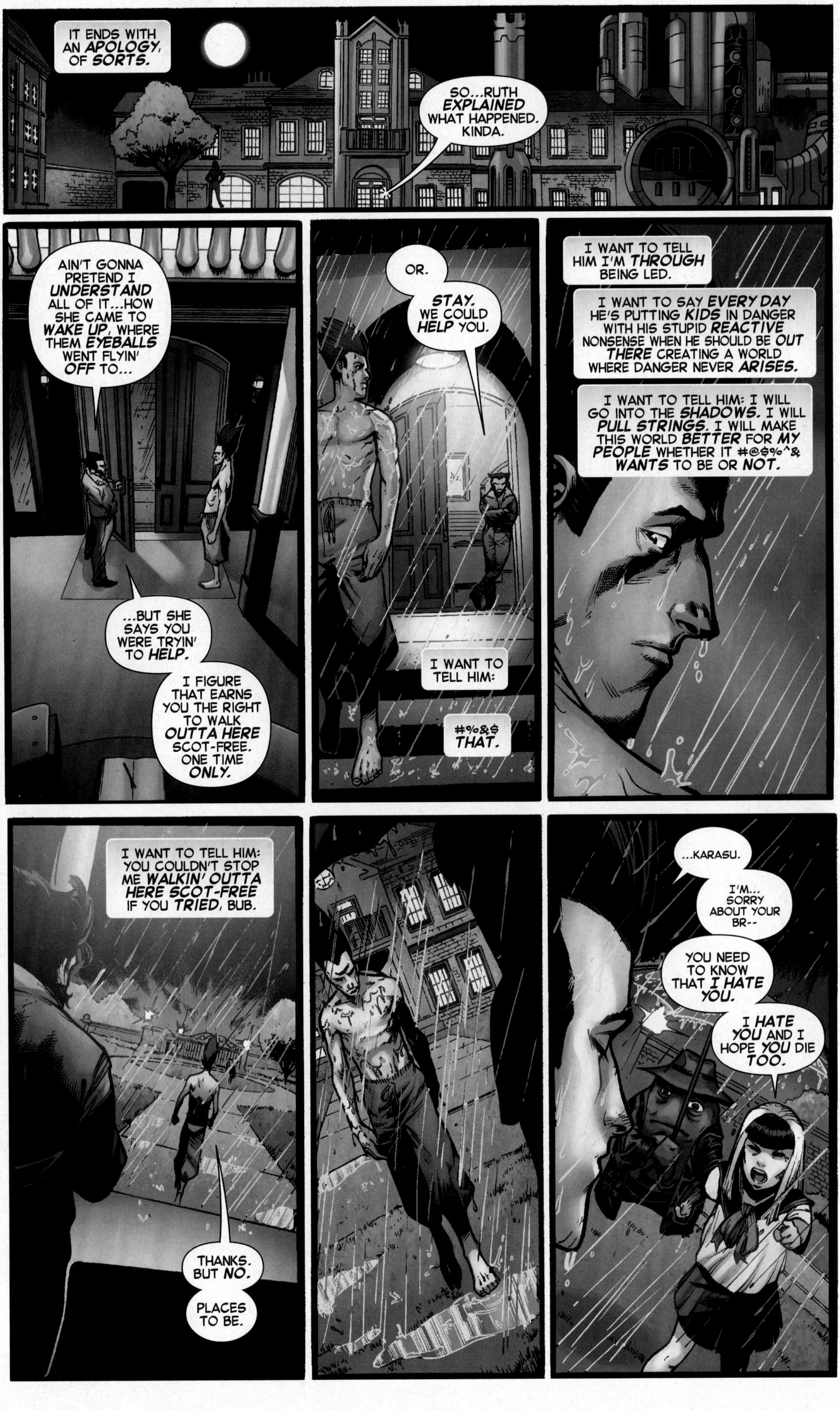
IT ENDS WITH AN APOLOGY, OF SORTS.
SO...RUTH EXPLAINED WHAT HAPPENED. KINDA.
AIN'T GONNA PRETEND I UNDERSTAND ALL OF IT...HOW SHE CAME TO WAKE UP, WHERE THEM EYEBALLS WENT FLYIN' OFF TO...
...BUT SHE SAYS YOU WERE TRYIN' TO HELP.
I FIGURE THAT EARNS YOU THE RIGHT TO WALK OUTTA HERE SCOT-FREE. ONE TIME ONLY.
OR.
STAY. WE COULD HELP YOU.
I WANT TO TELL HIM:
#%&$ THAT.
I WANT TO TELL HIM I'M THROUGH BEING LED.
I WANT TO SAY EVERY DAY HE'S PUTTING KIDS IN DANGER WITH HIS STUPID REACTIVE NONSENSE WHEN HE SHOULD BE OUT THERE CREATING A WORLD WHERE DANGER NEVER ARISES.
I WANT TO TELL HIM: I WILL GO INTO THE SHADOWS. I WILL PULL STRINGS. I WILL MAKE THIS WORLD BETTER FOR MY PEOPLE WHETHER IT #@$%^& WANTS TO BE OR NOT.
I WANT TO TELL HIM: YOU COULDN'T STOP ME WALKIN' OUTTA HERE SCOT-FREE IF YOU TRIED, BUB.
THANKS. BUT NO.
PLACES TO BE.
...KARASU.
I'M... SORRY ABOUT YOUR BR--
YOU NEED TO KNOW THAT I HATE YOU.
I HATE YOU AND I HOPE YOU DIE TOO.

... CAREFUL OF *WHAT*...?

I KNOW.

NNN

WH... WHO *ARE* YOU?

SHH. LISTEN. *LEARN.* THE *EVENT* THAT LUCA FORESAW.

THE *GRAND EVIL* WHICH WILL DESTROY *ALL MUTANTKIND?* THE GENOCIDE ONLY THE *GIRL*--ONLY *BLINDFOLD*--CAN STOP?

SMAK

YOU WRETCHED LITTLE *DISAPPOINTMENT.*

YOU'RE FATED TO *WIPE OUT* YOUR *OWN KIND,* BOY...

AND THE GIRL YOU JUST *SAVED?* SHE'S FATED TO TRY AND *KILL* YOU, JUST TO *STOP* IT.

IT'S YOU, DAVID. IT'S YOU.

H...HOW DO YOU *KNOW* ALL THIS?

TO BE CONTINUED!

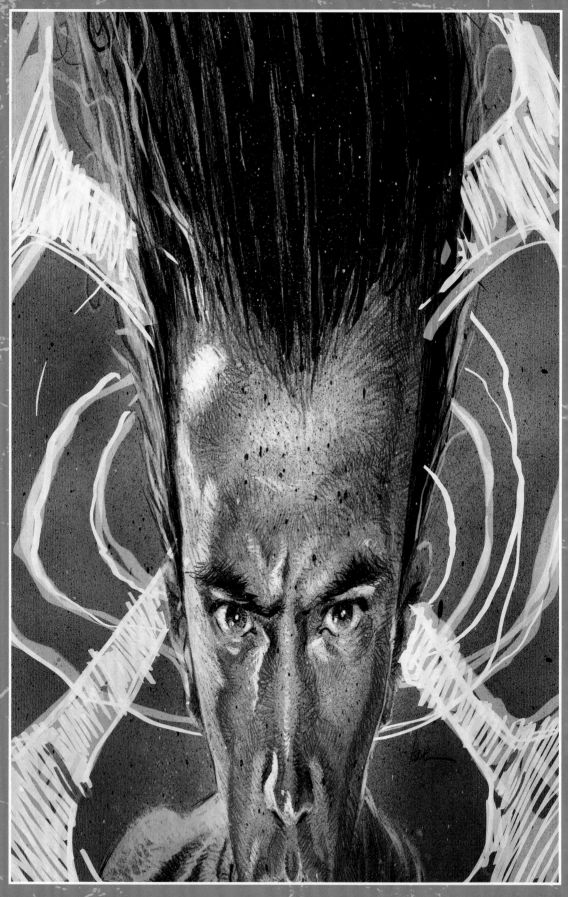

#1 variant by Kaare Andrews

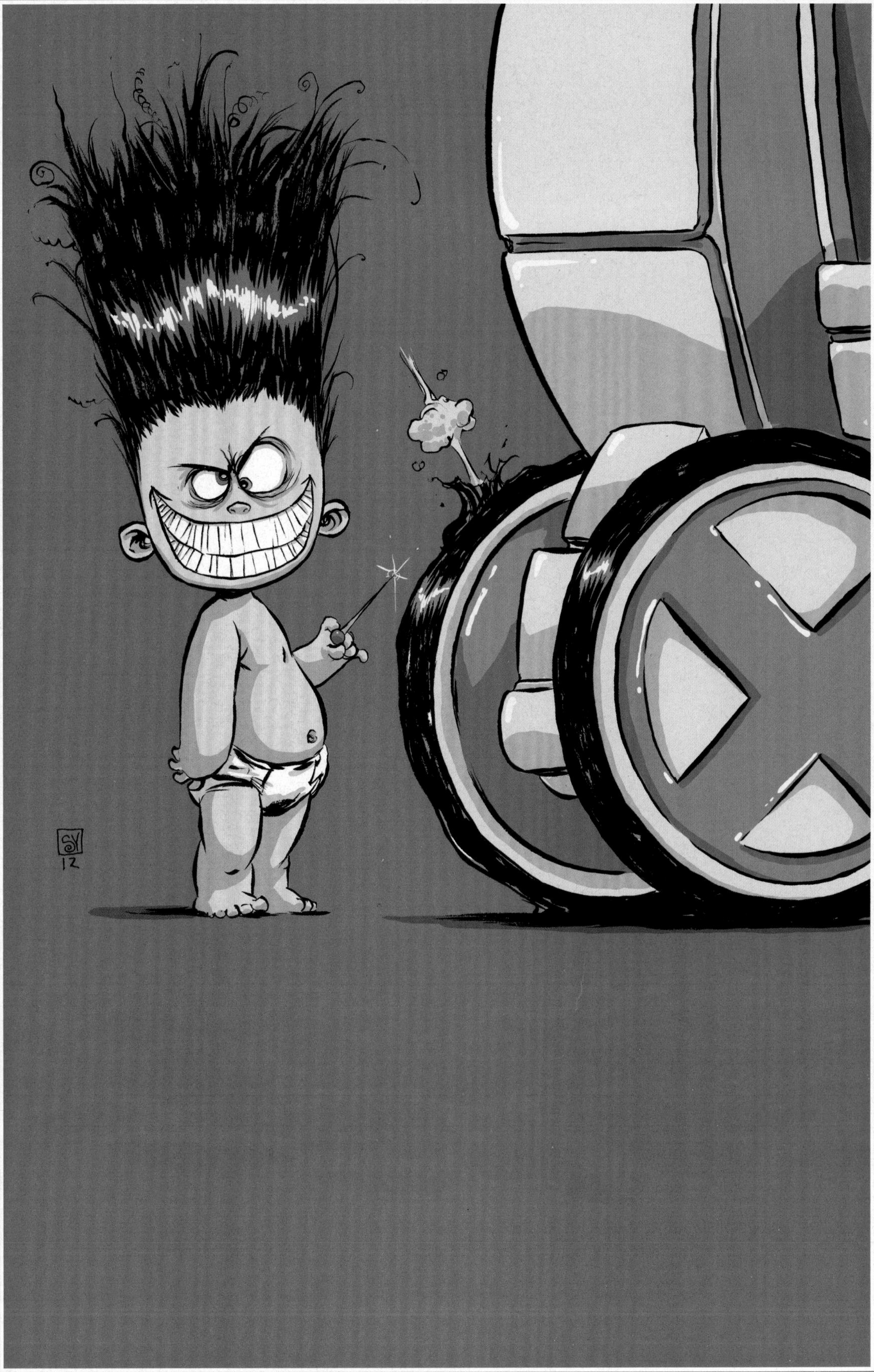

#1 variant by Skottie Young

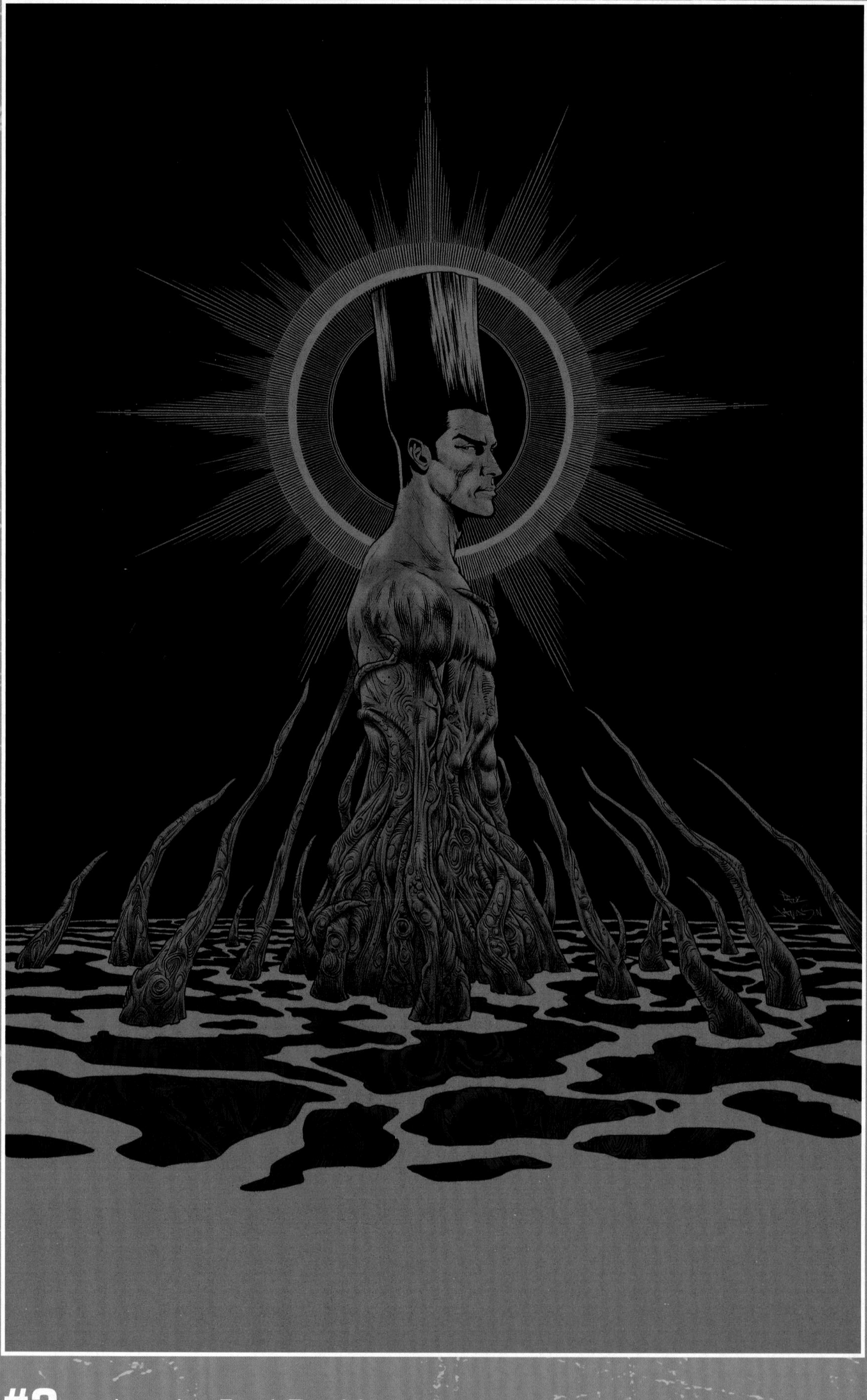

#2 variant by Paul Davidson

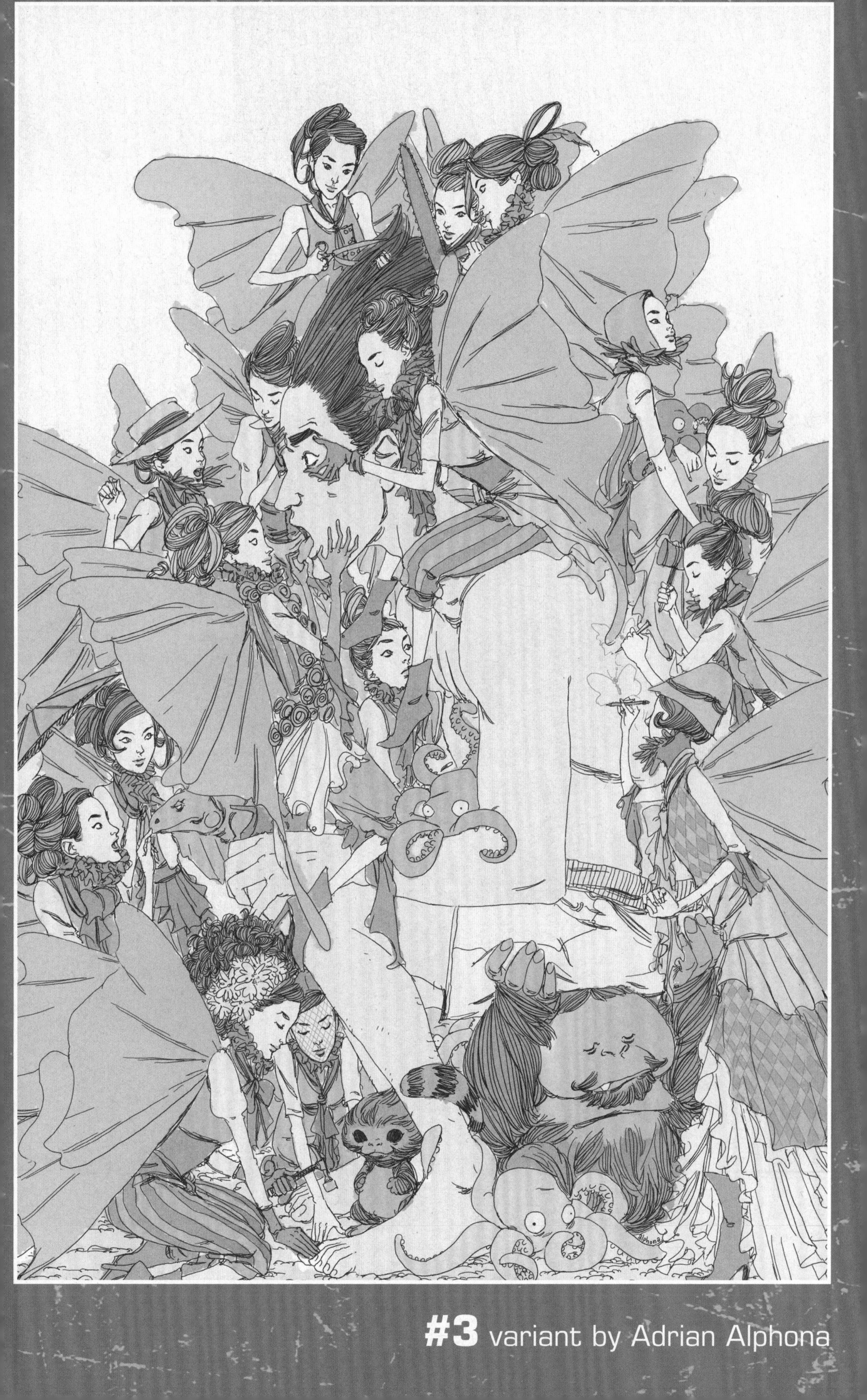

#3 variant by Adrian Alphona

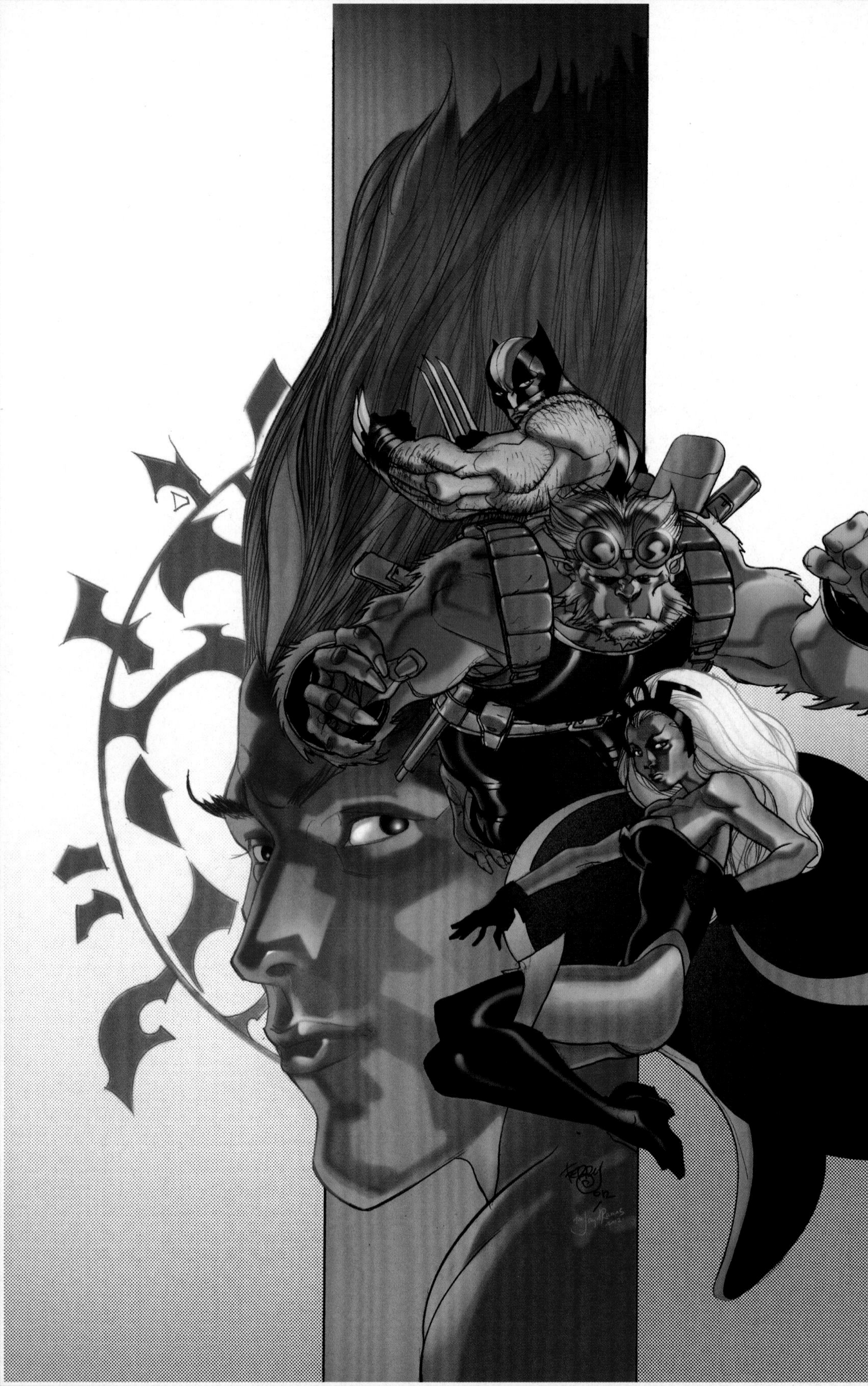

#4 variant by Pasqual Ferry & Jay David Ramos

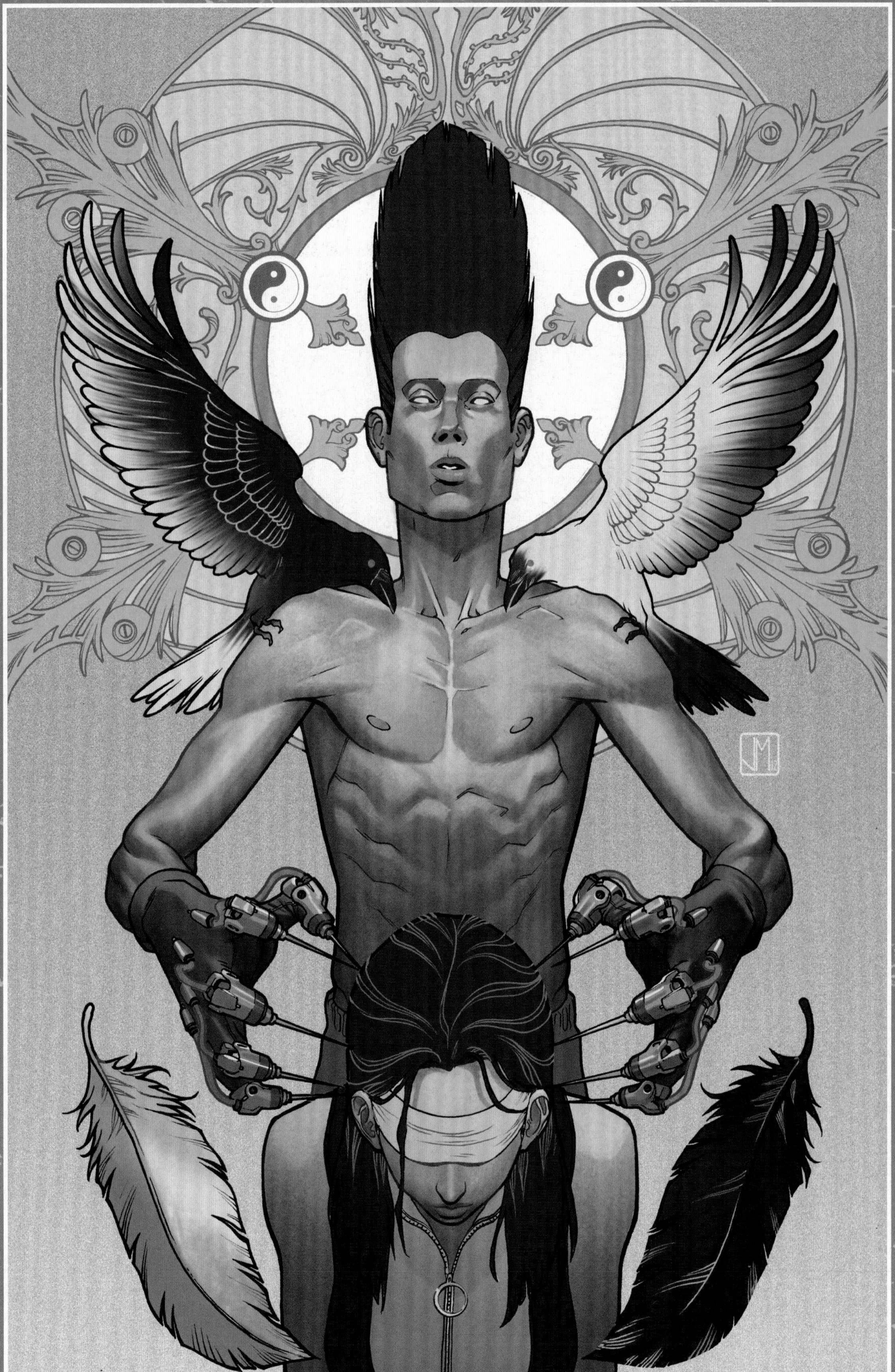

#5 variant by Jorge Molina

The Leaving Morning

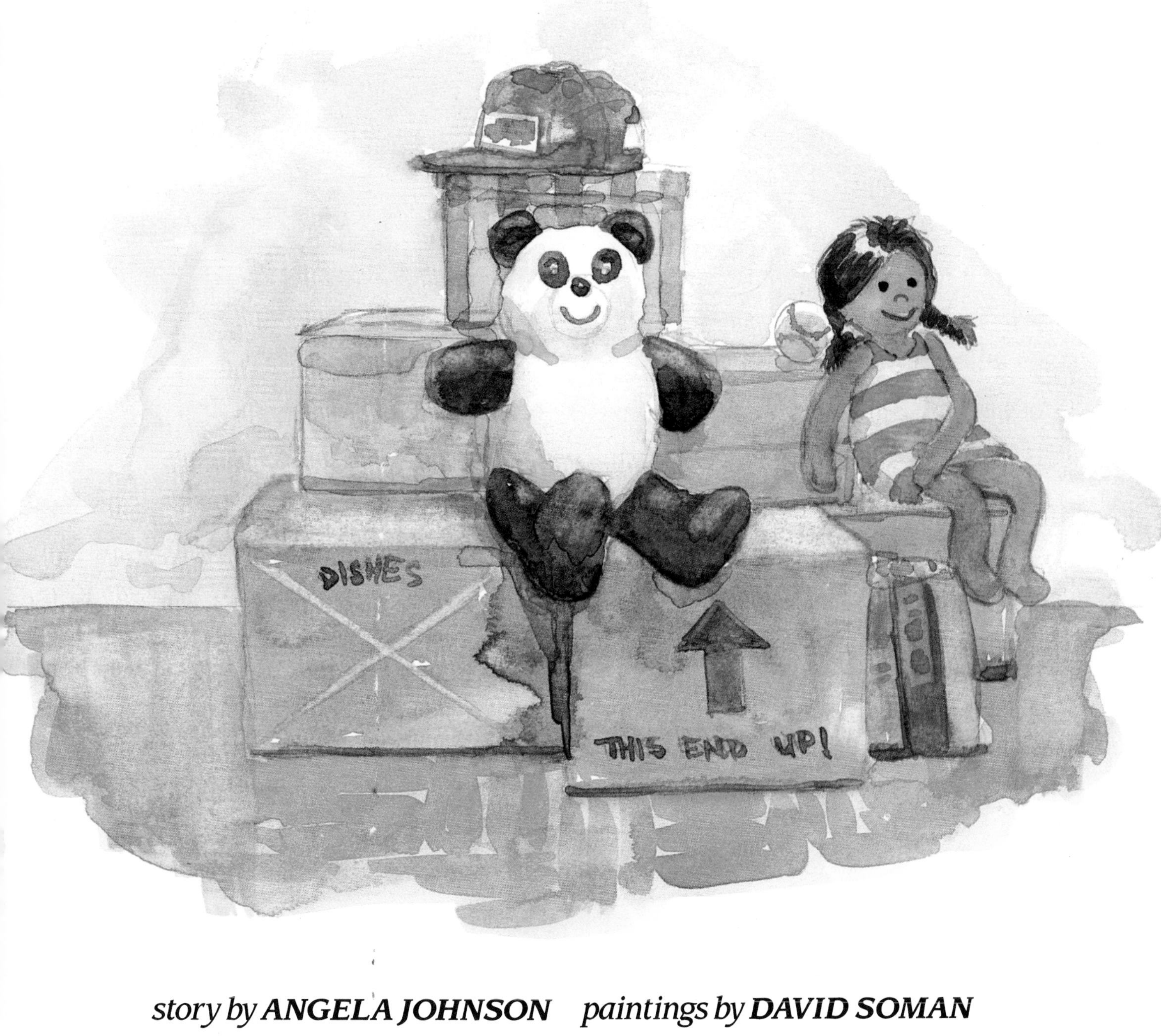
DISHES
THIS END UP!

story by ***ANGELA JOHNSON*** *paintings by* ***DAVID SOMAN***

SCHOLASTIC INC.

ISBN 978-0-545-60444-4

10 9 8 7 6 5 4 3 2 1   13 14 15 16 17

Printed in the U.S.A.   08
This edition first printing, March 2013

Book design by Mina Greenstein.
The text of this book is set in 18 point ITC Leawood Medium.
The illustrations are watercolor paintings, reproduced in full color.

To SANDY PERLMAN
and good times
—A.J.

To EUGENIE,
a restless family member
—D.S.

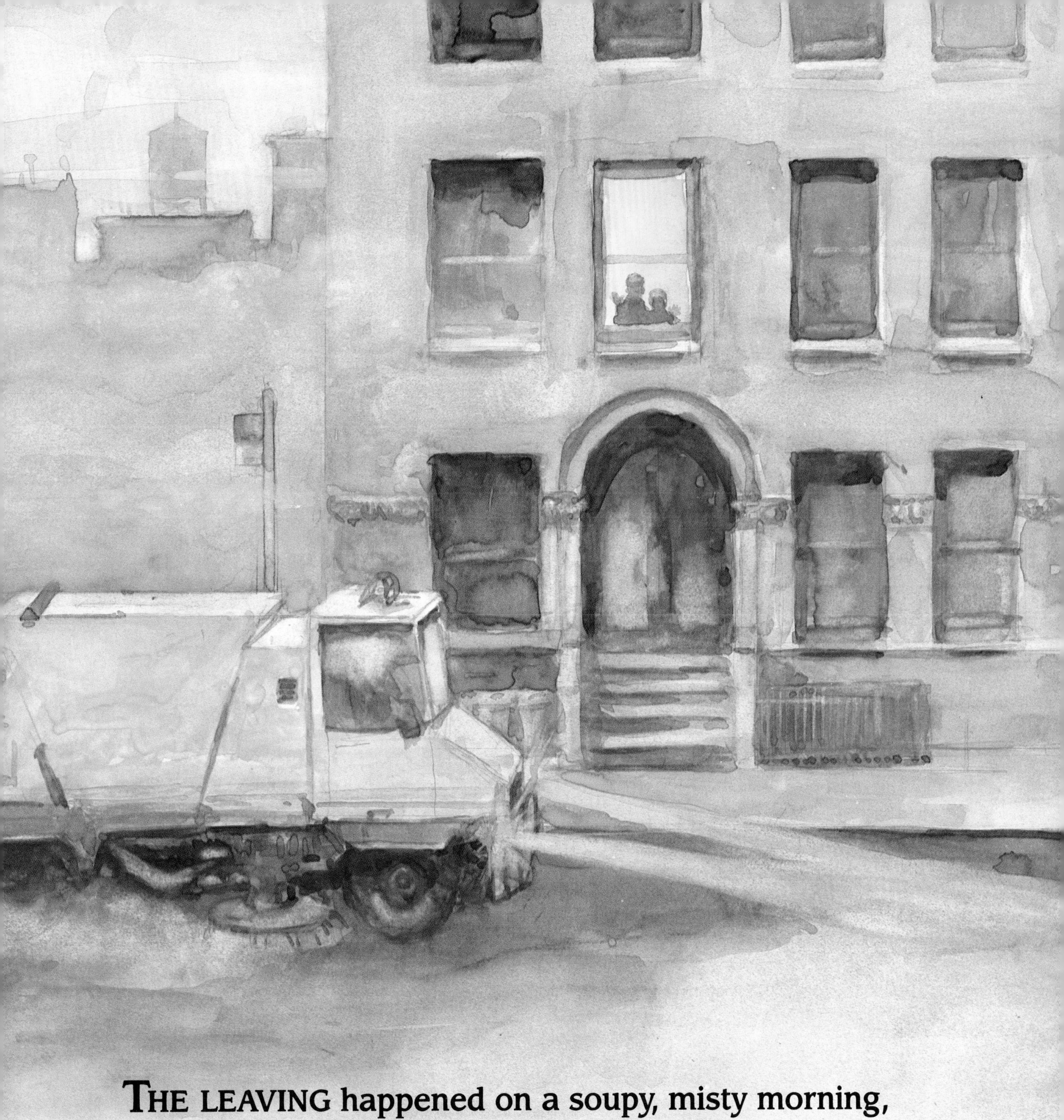

THE LEAVING happened on a soupy, misty morning, when you could hear the street sweeper. Sssshhhshsh....

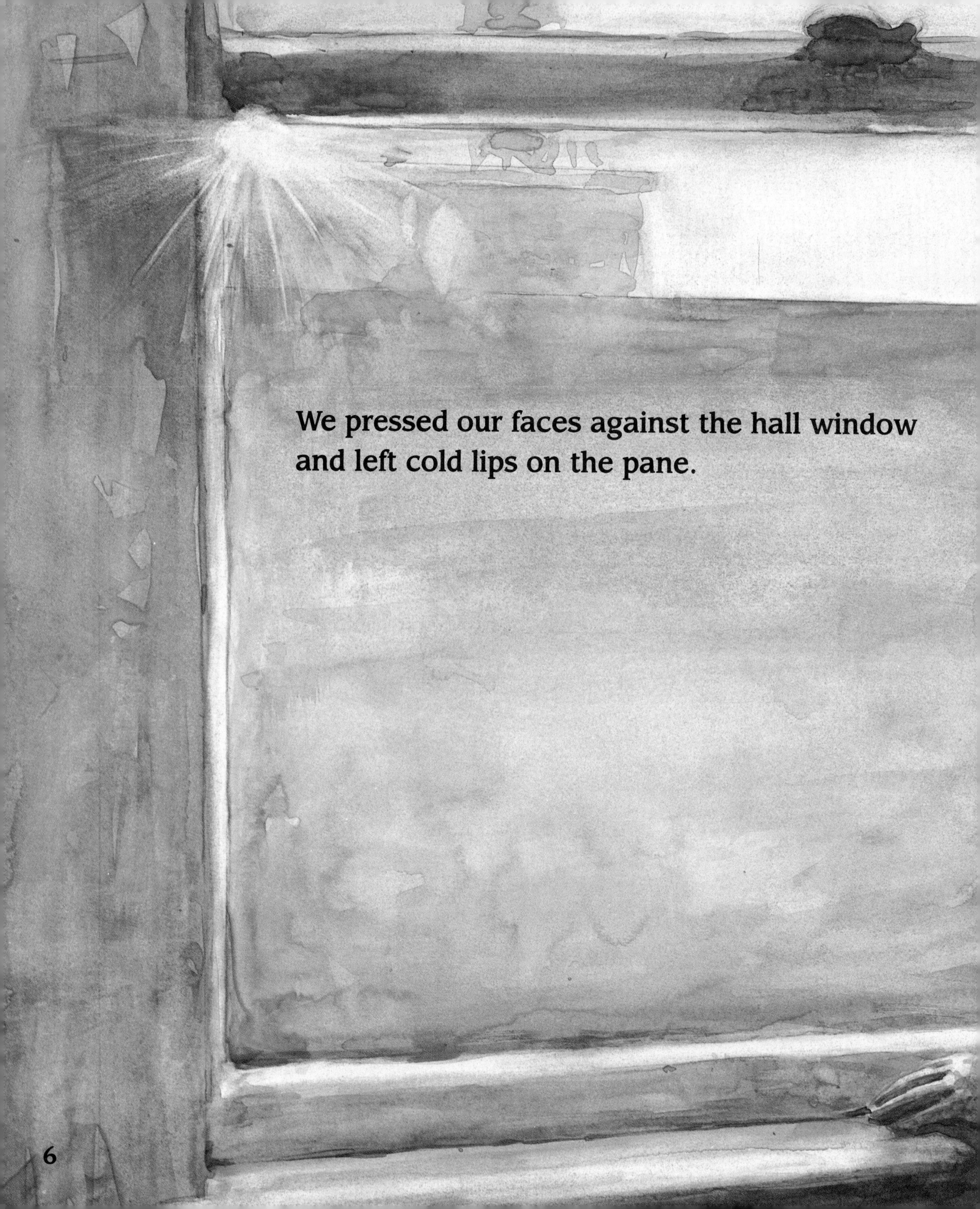

We pressed our faces against the hall window
and left cold lips on the pane.

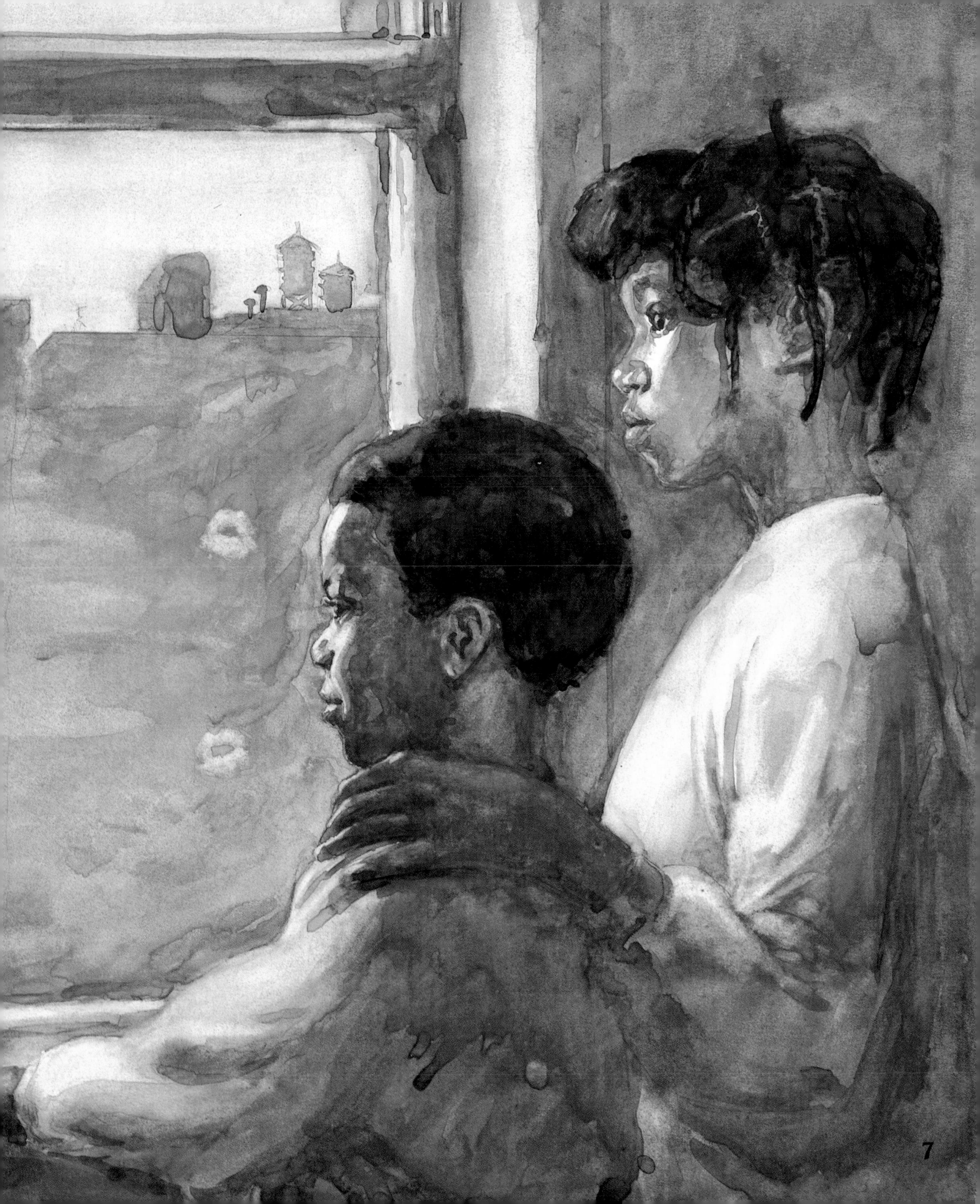

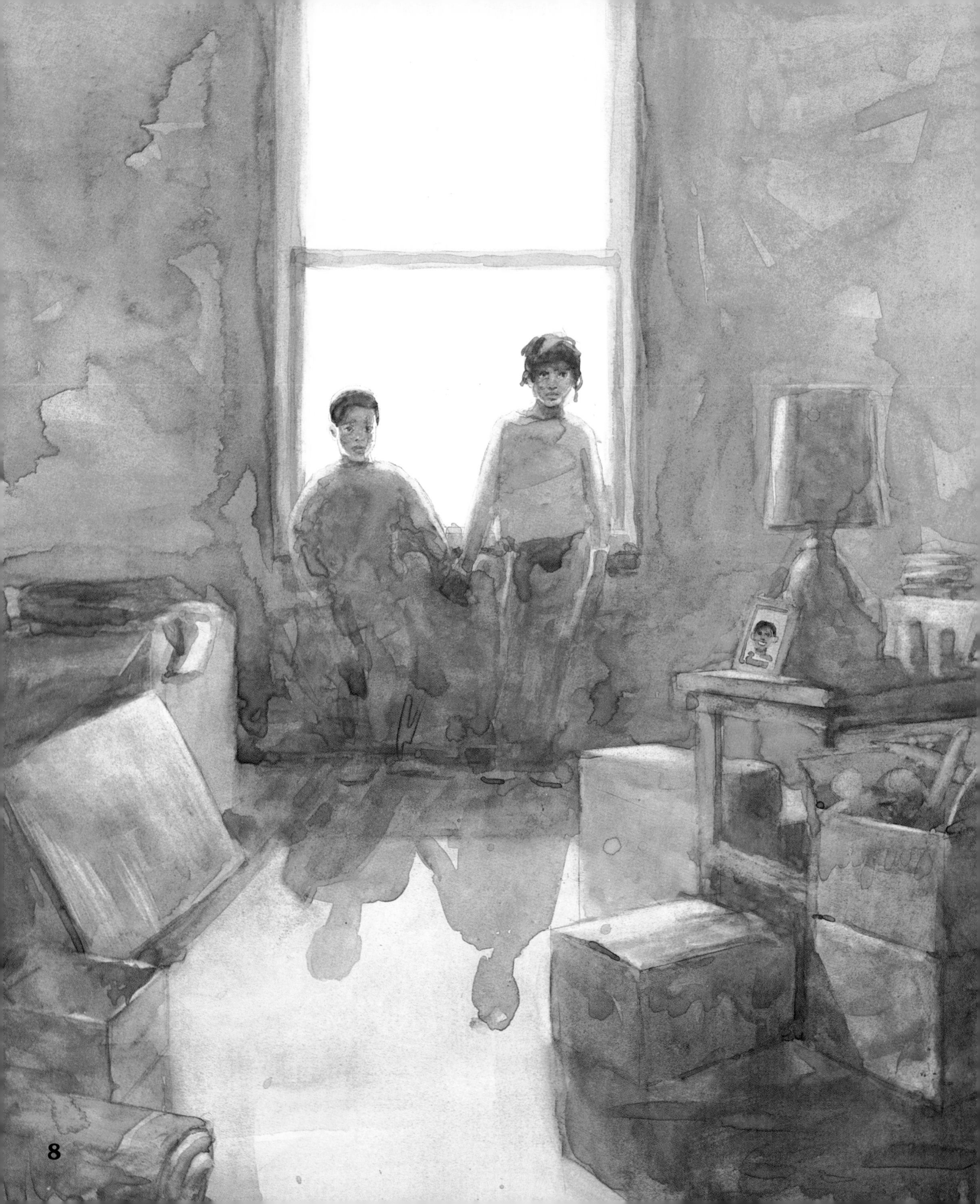

It was the leaving morning.
Boxes of clothes,
toys,
dishes,
and pictures of us everywhere.

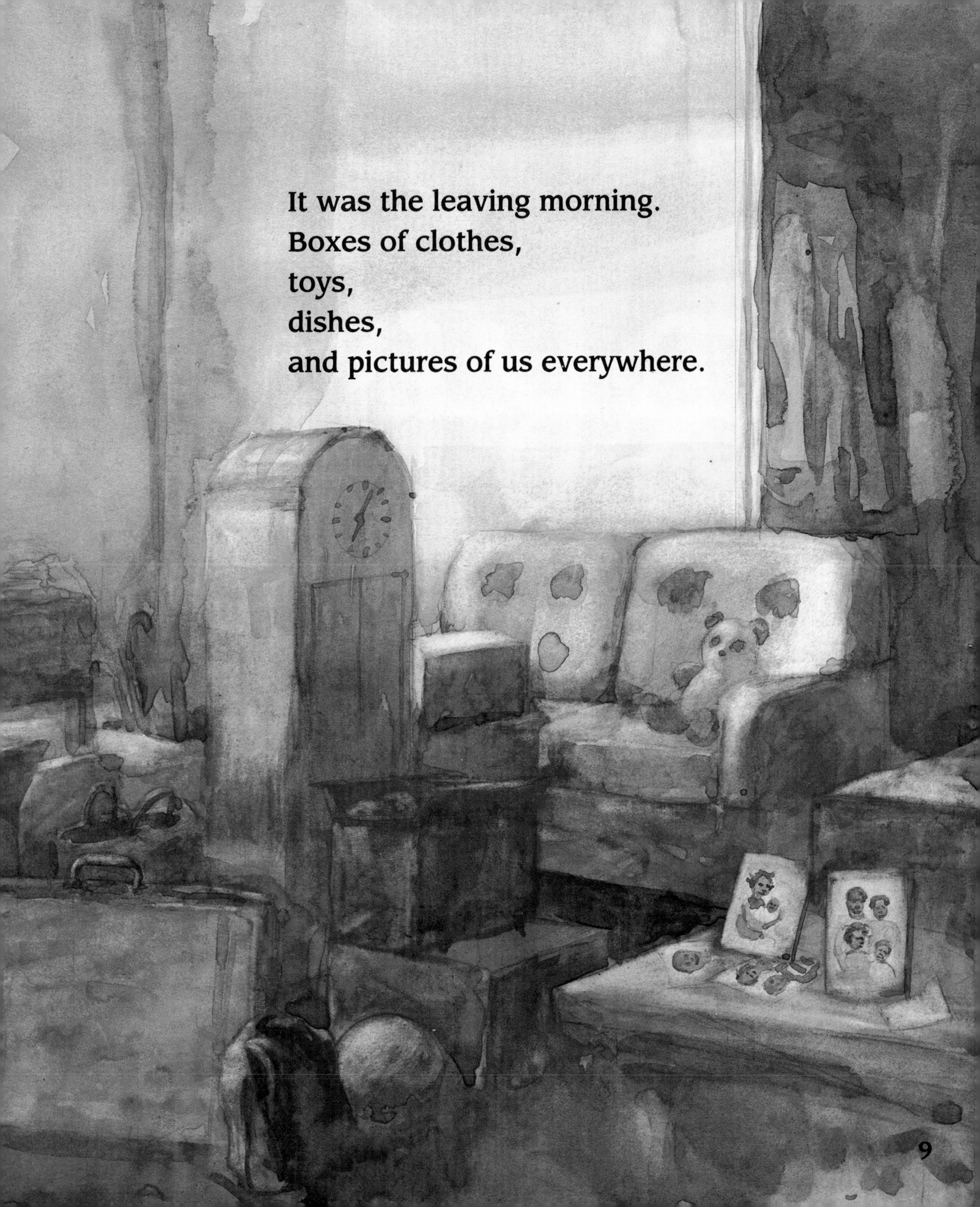

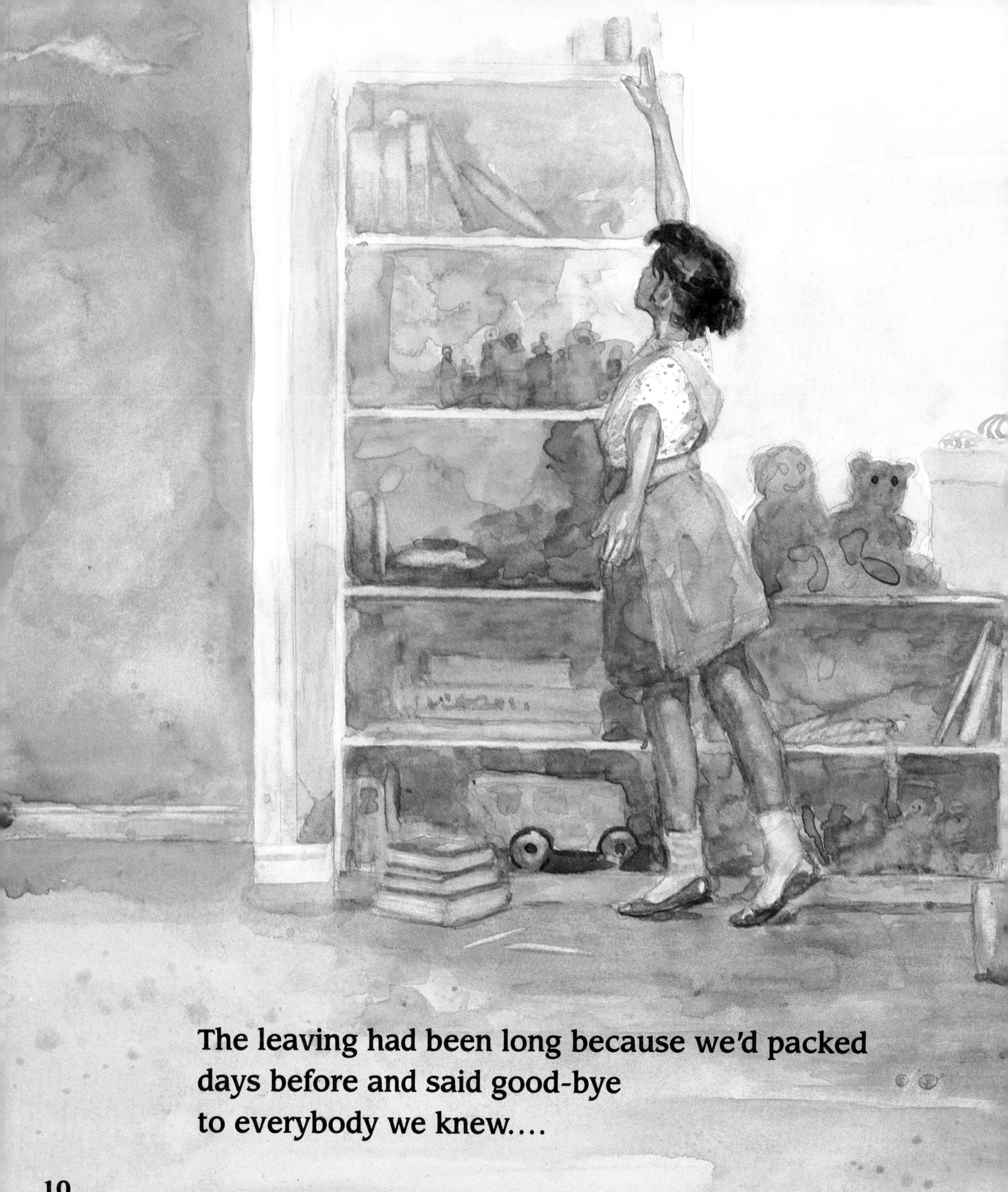

The leaving had been long because we'd packed
days before and said good-bye
to everybody we knew....

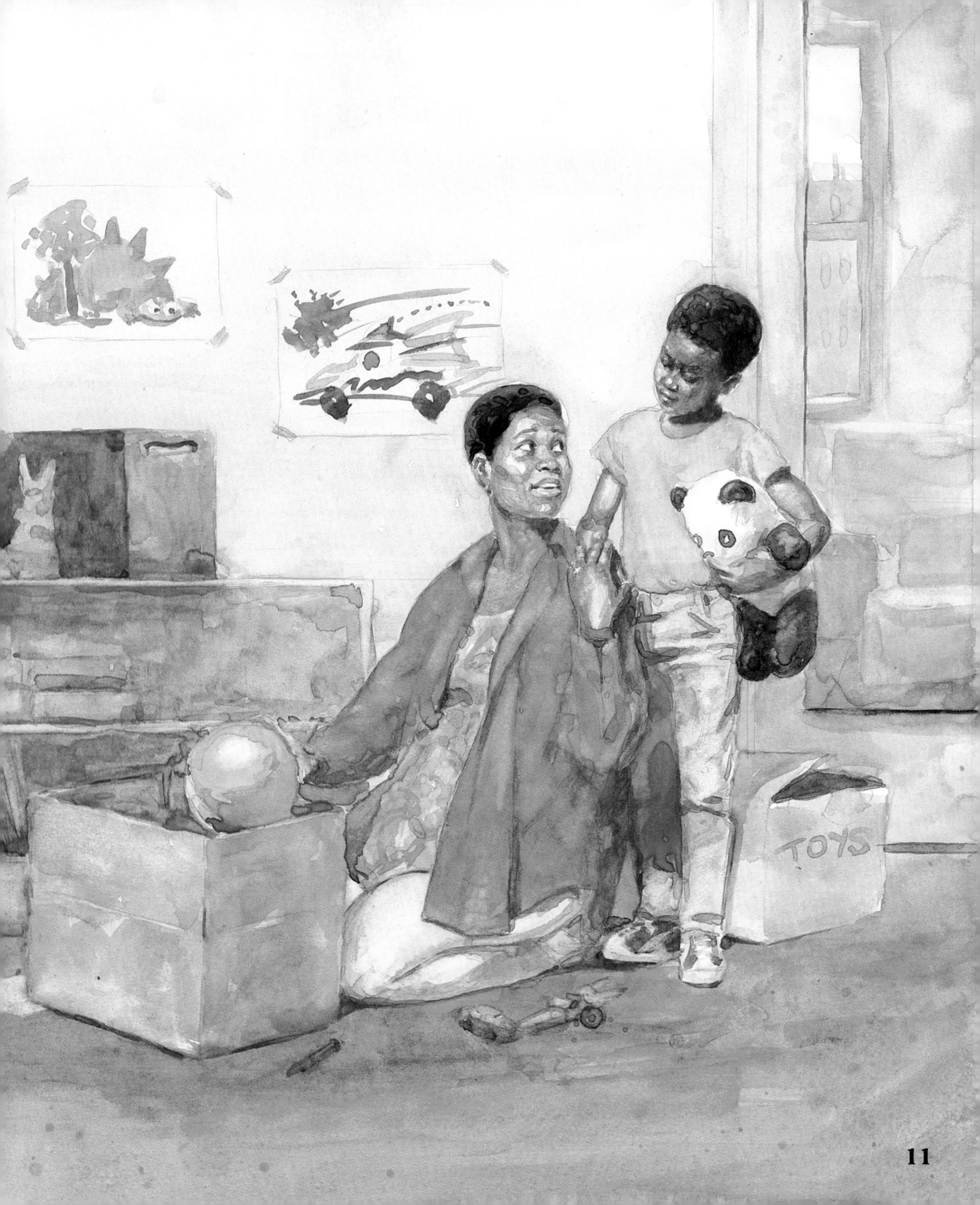
TOYS

Our friends....

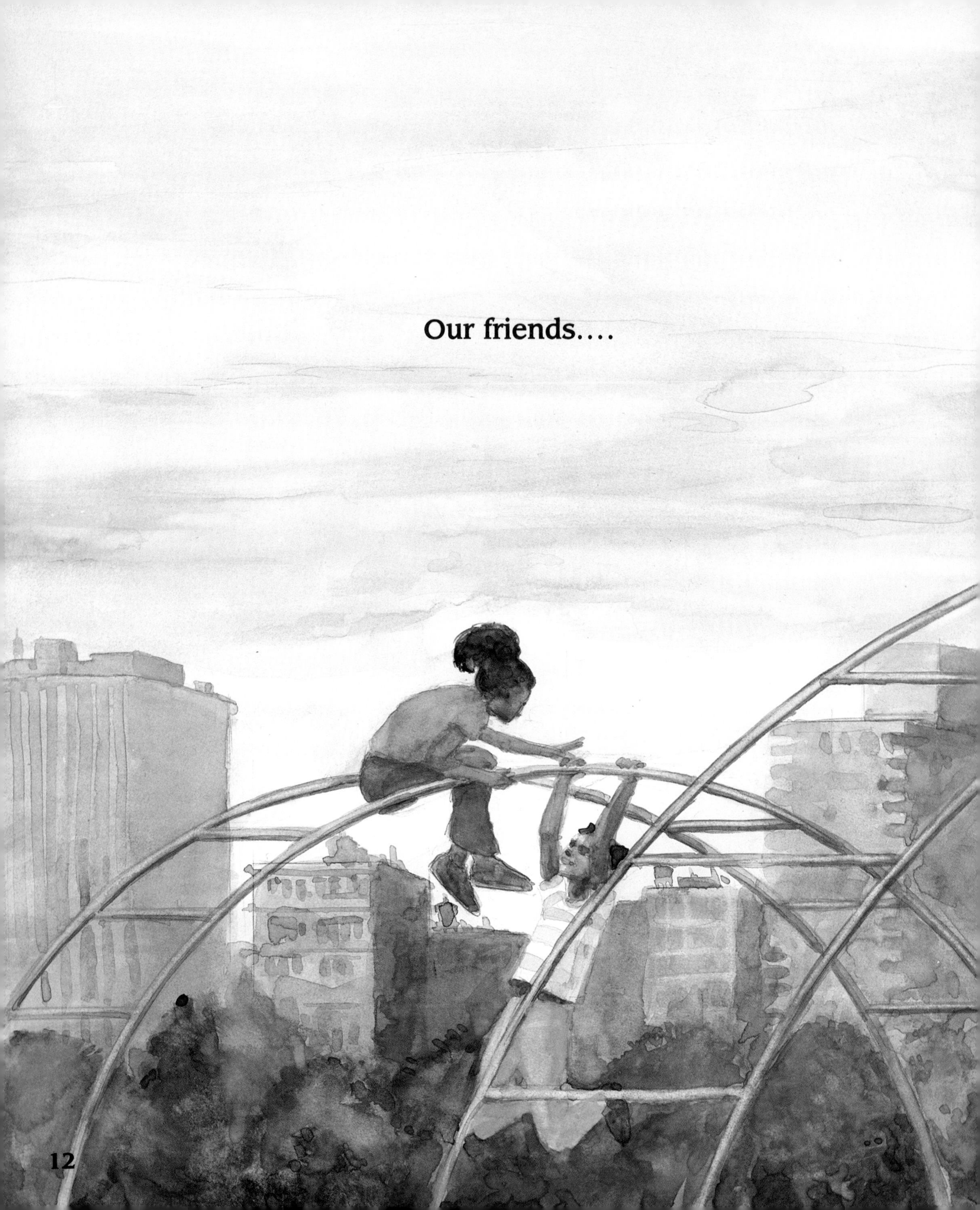

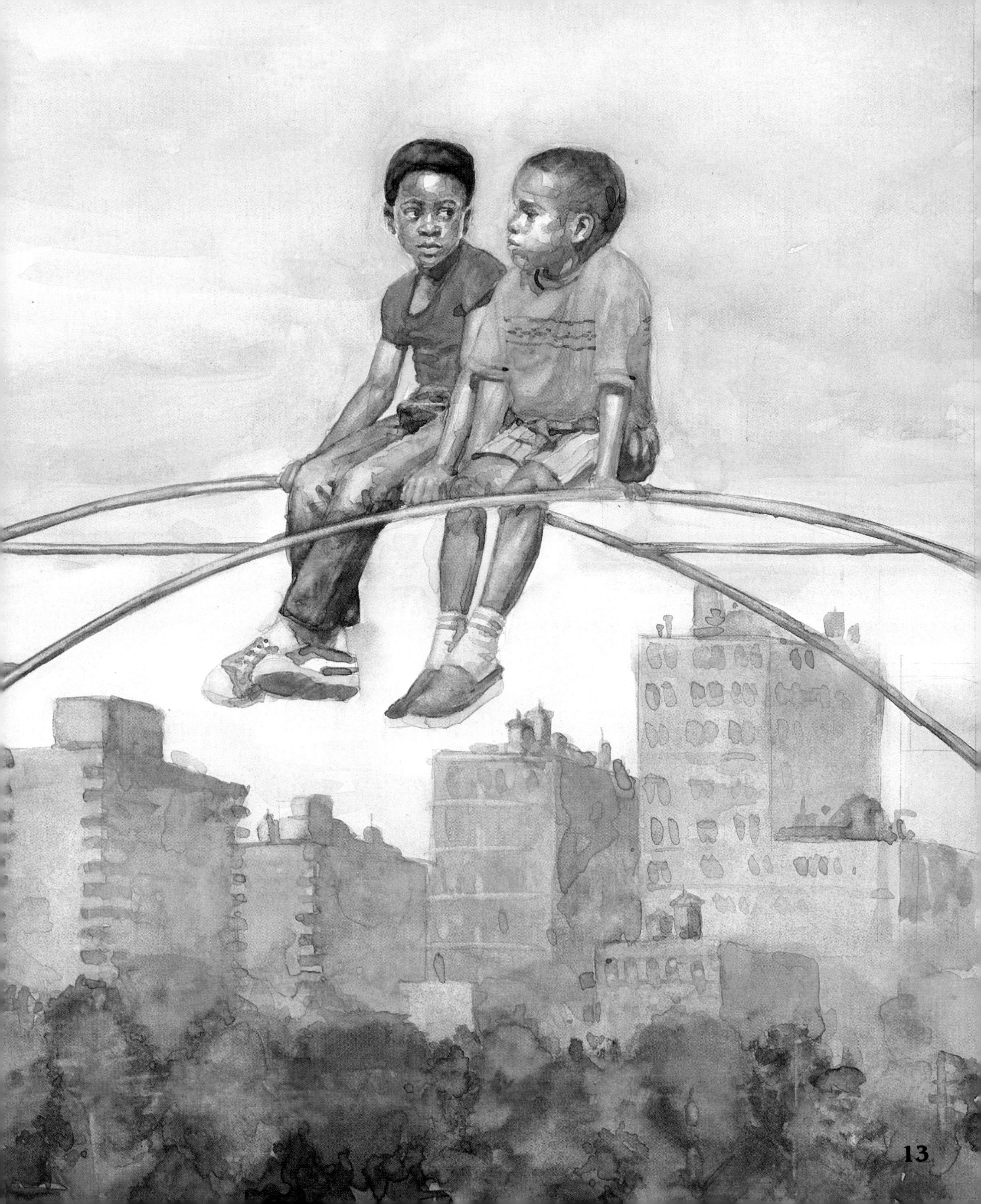

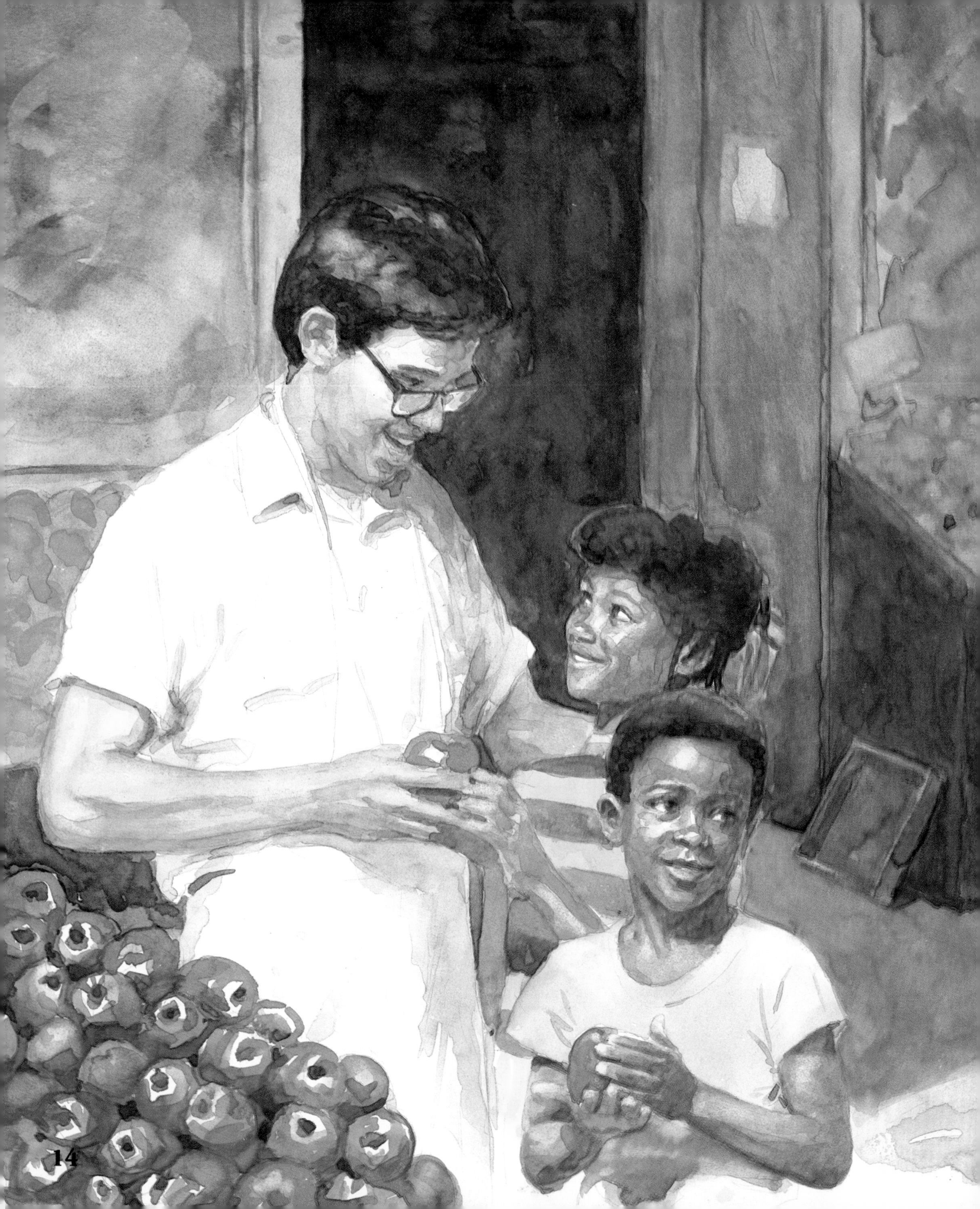

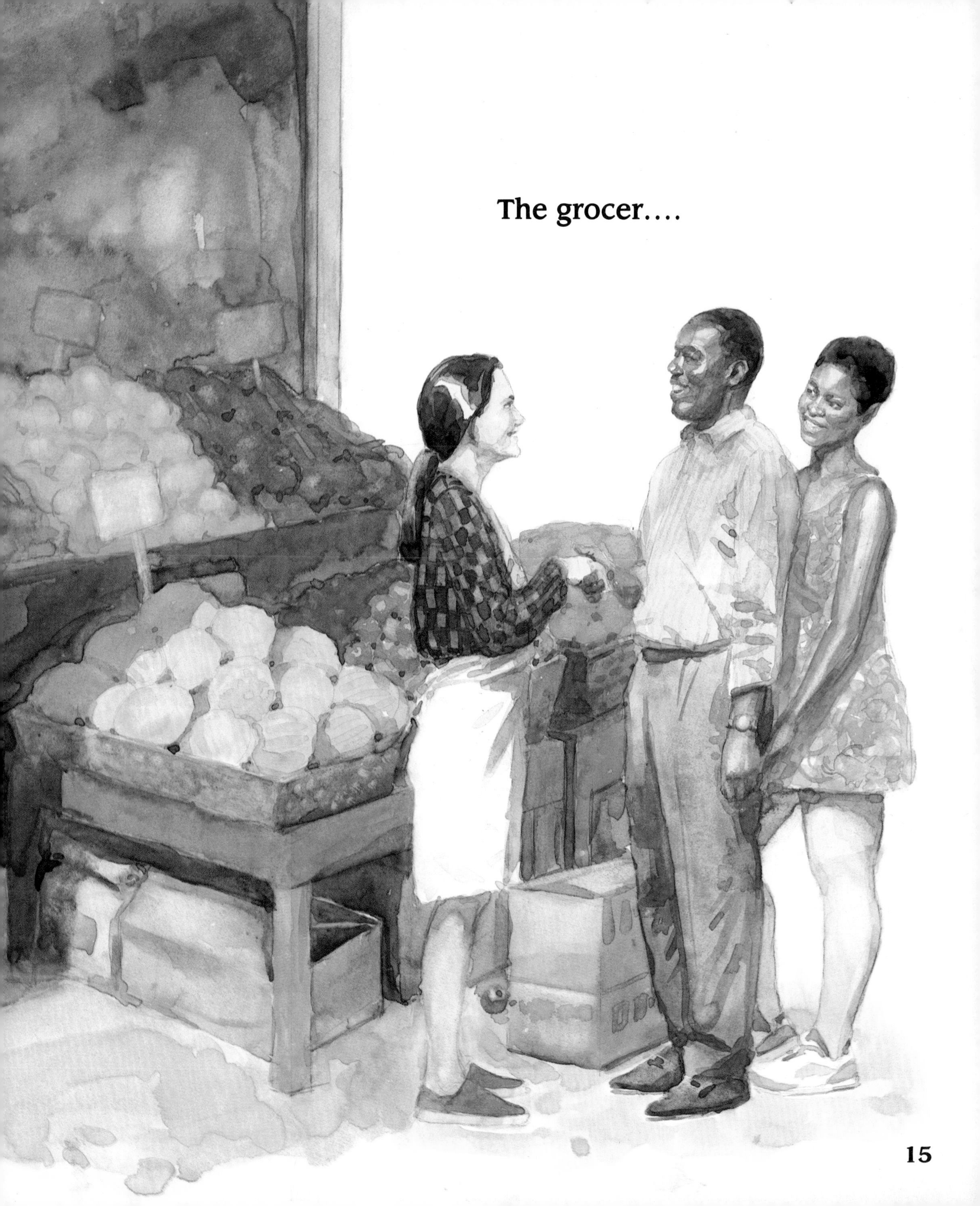

The grocer….

Everybody in our building....

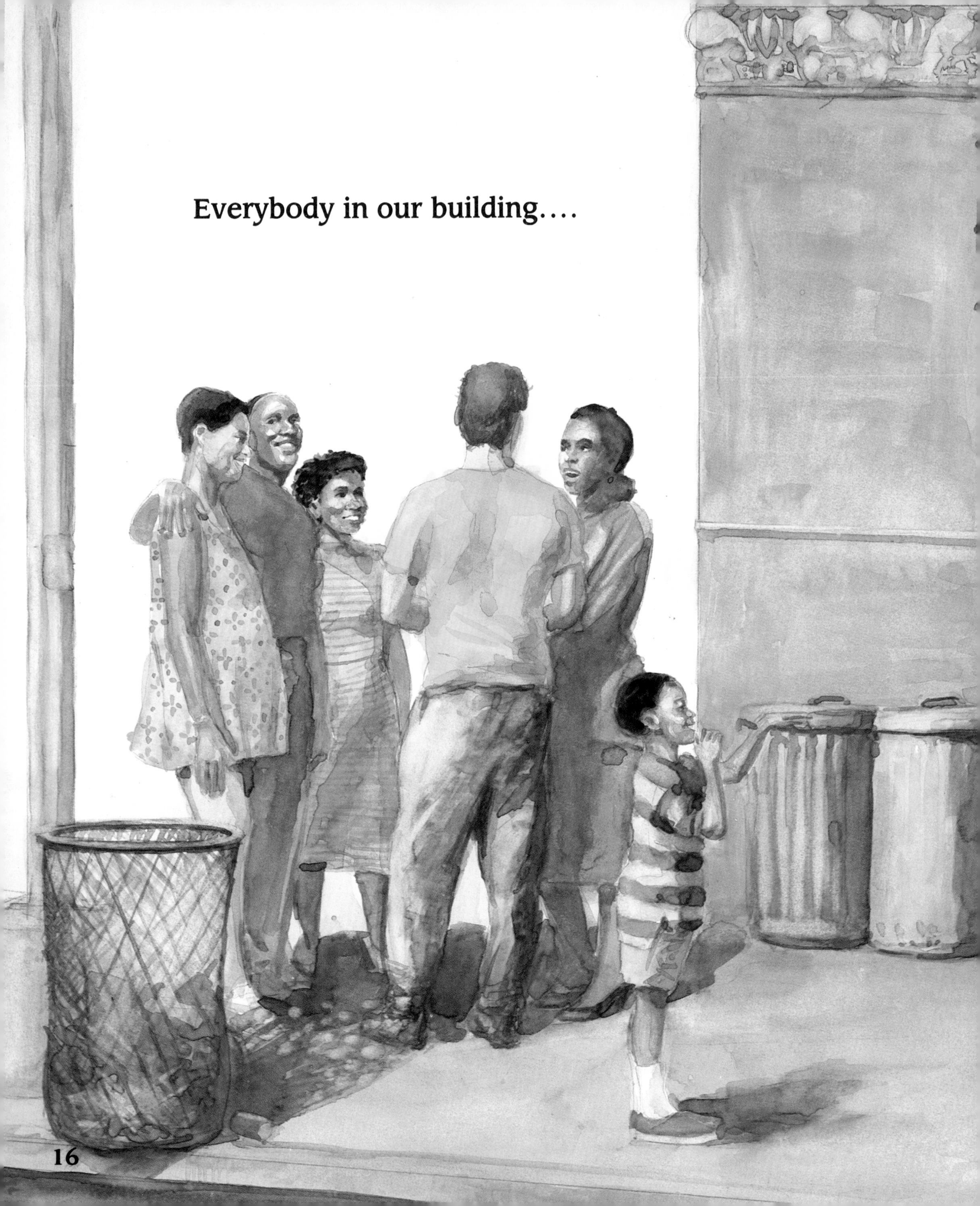

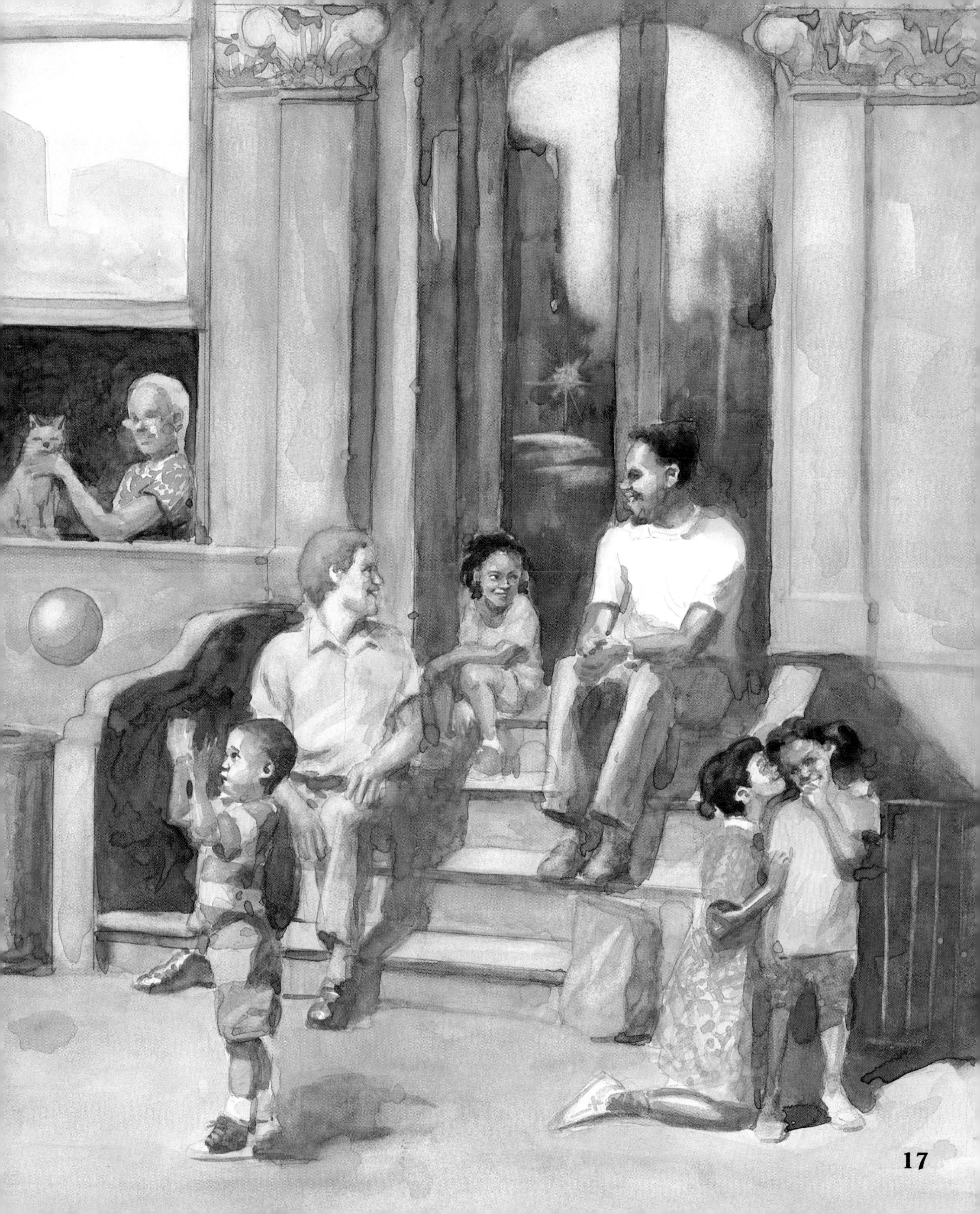

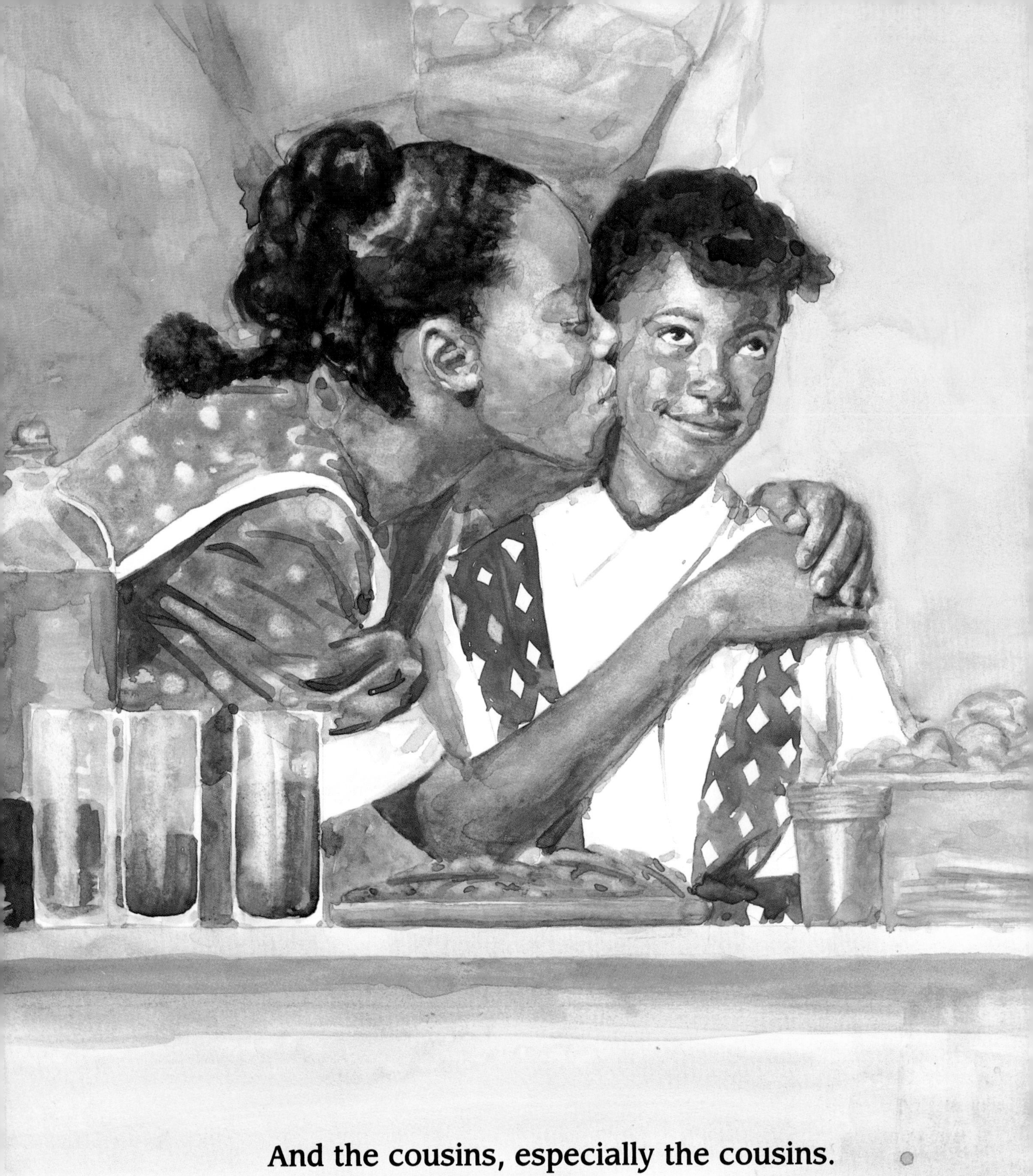

And the cousins, especially the cousins.

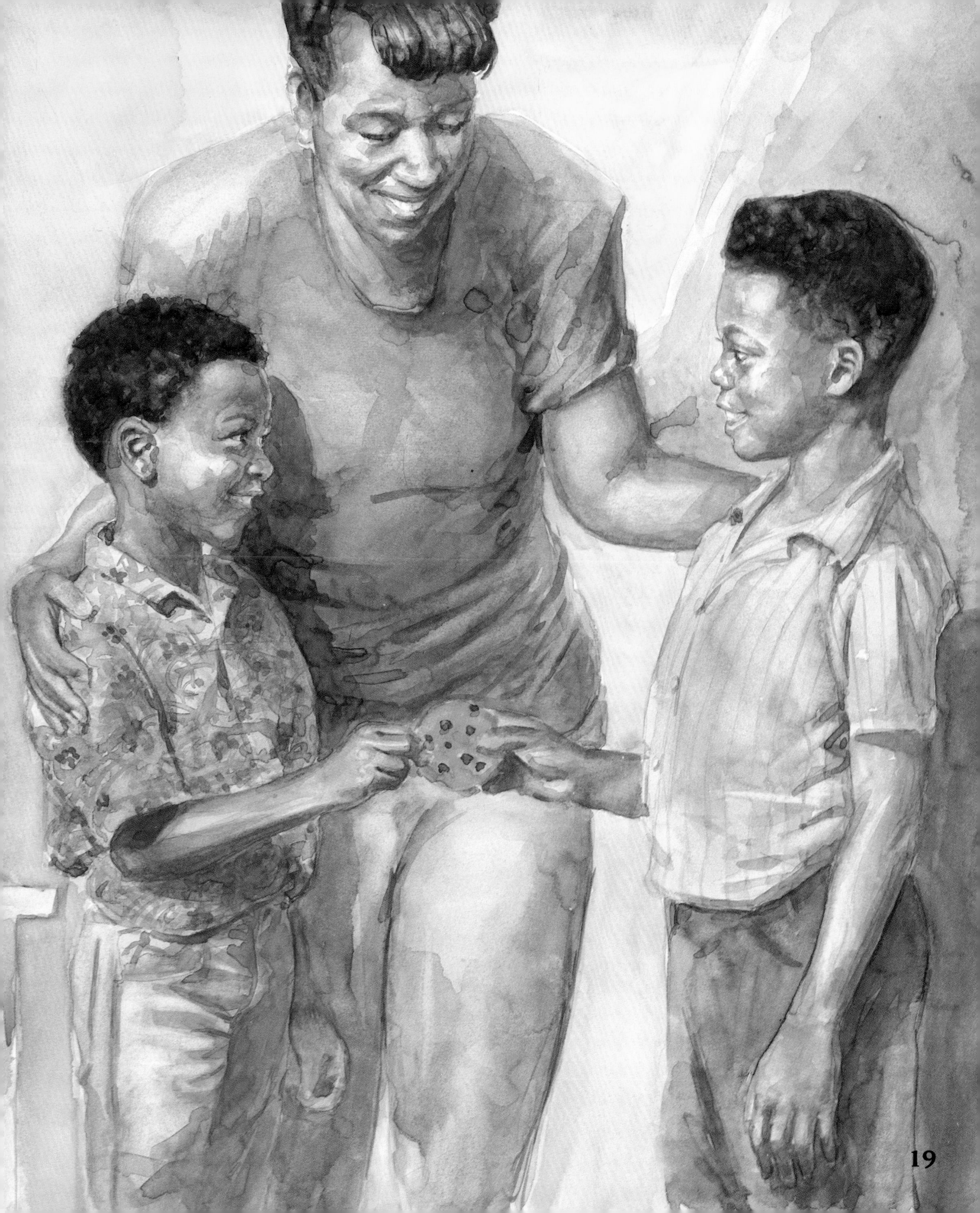

We said good-bye to the cousins all day long.

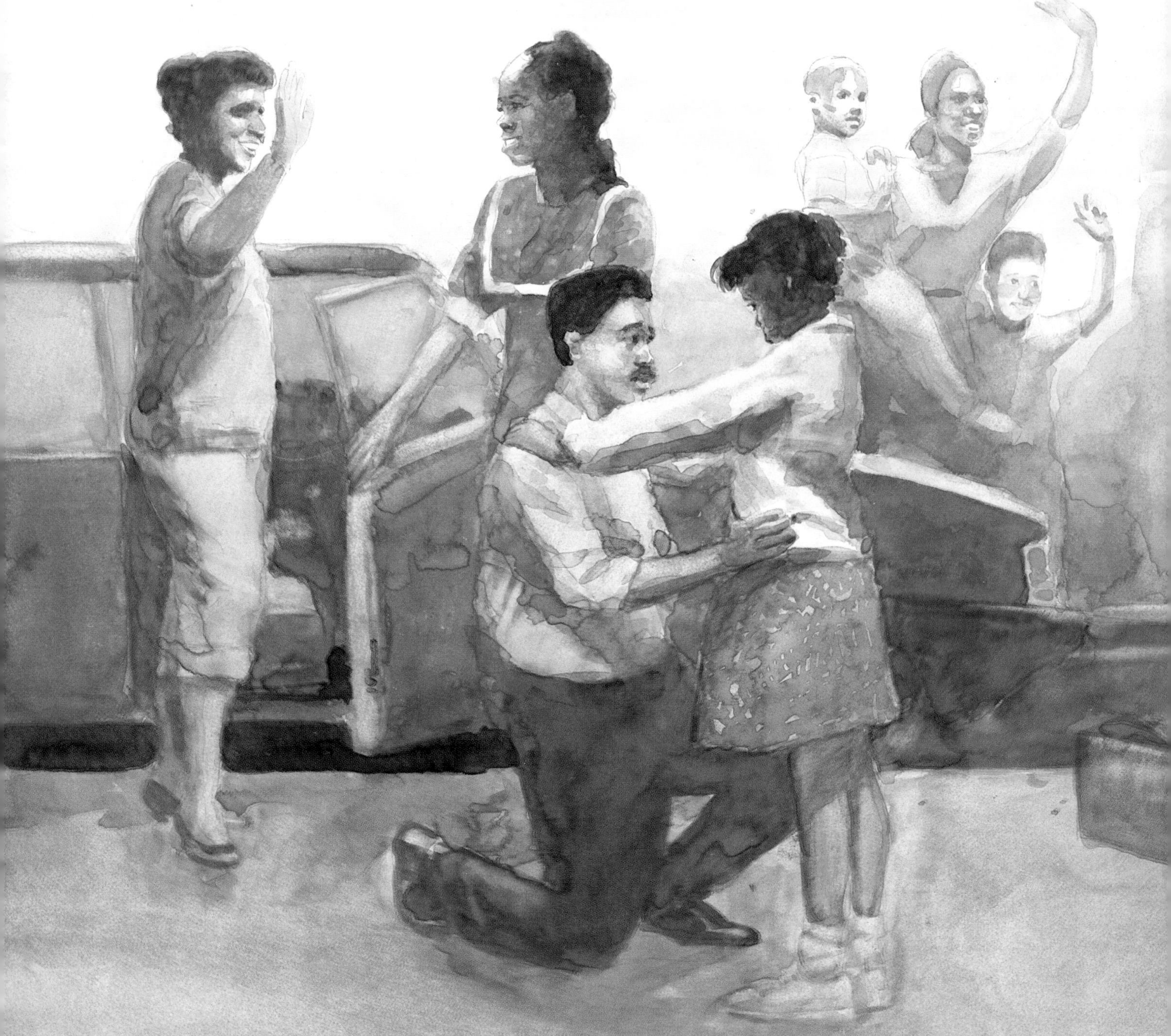

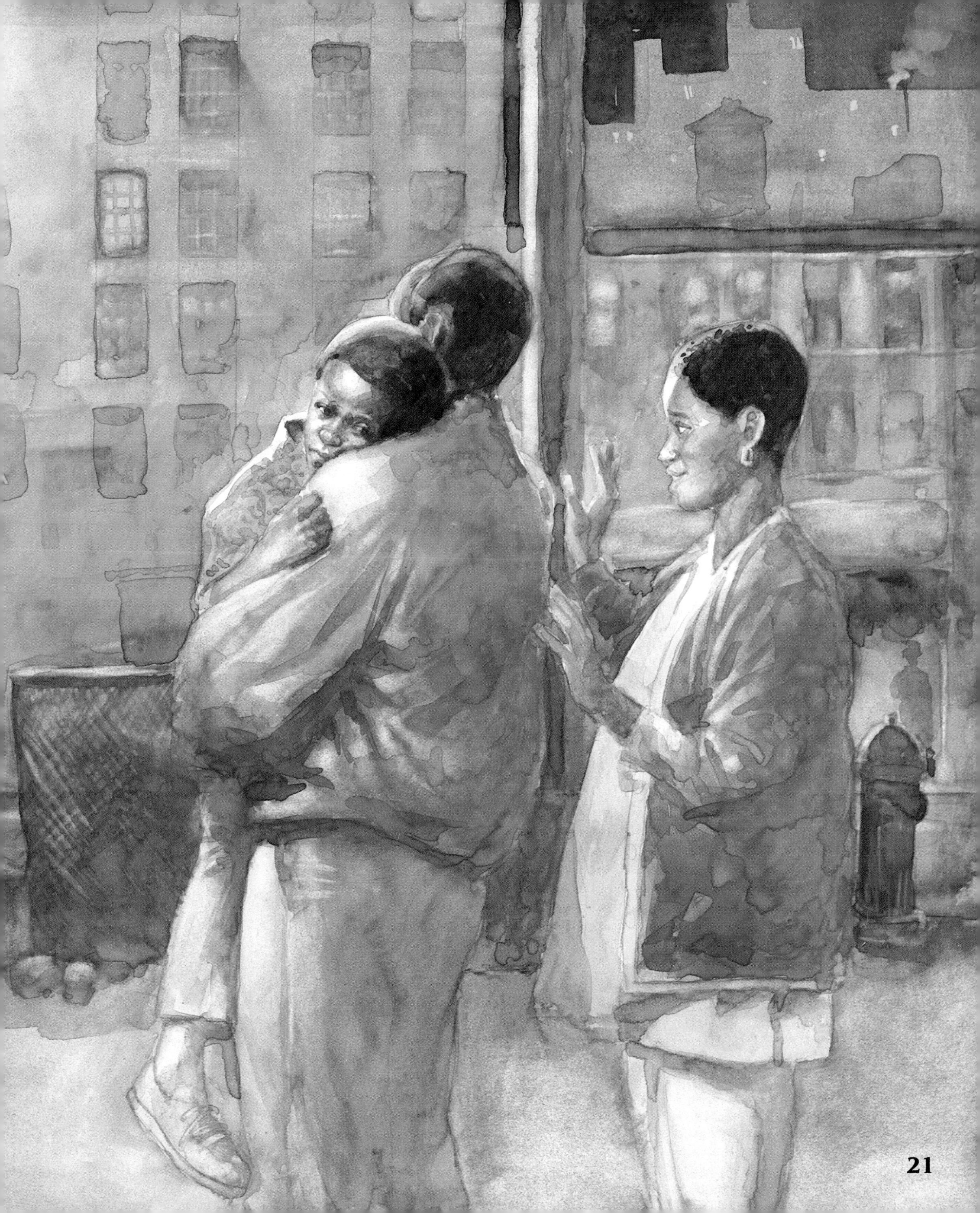

Mama said the people in a truck would move us
and take care of everything we loved,
on the leaving morning.

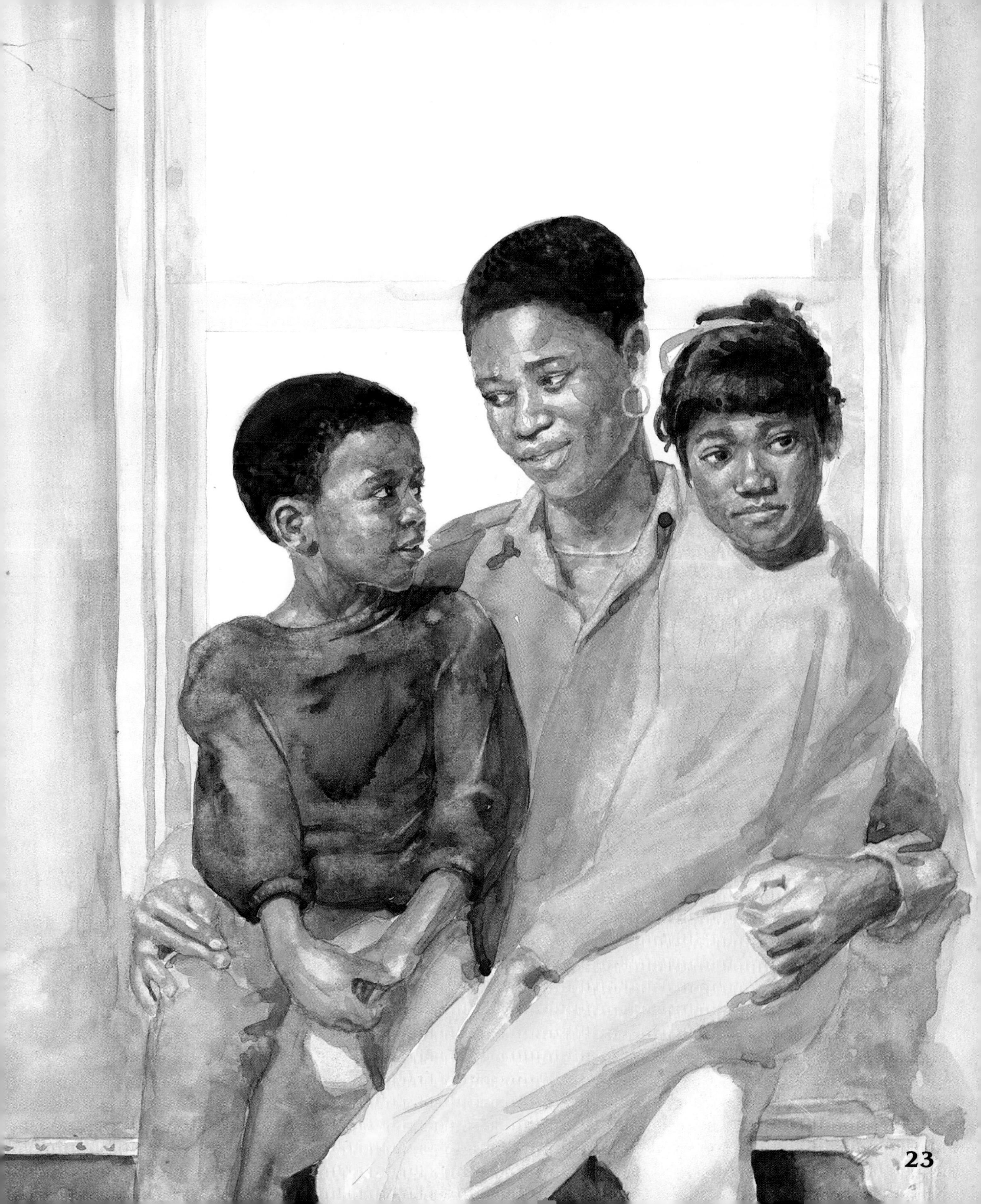

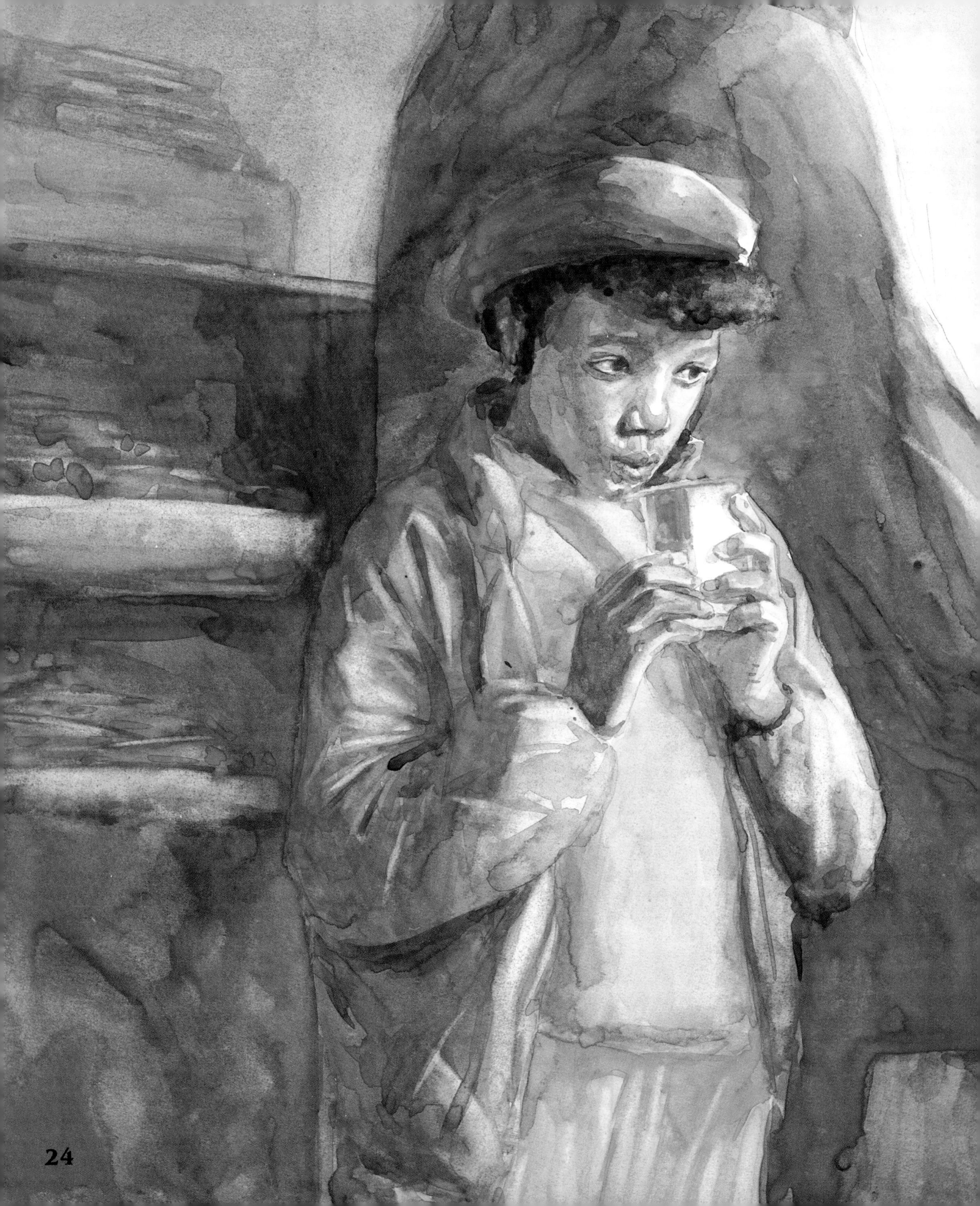

We woke up early and had hot cocoa from the deli
across the street.
I made more lips on the deli window
and watched for the movers on the leaving morning.

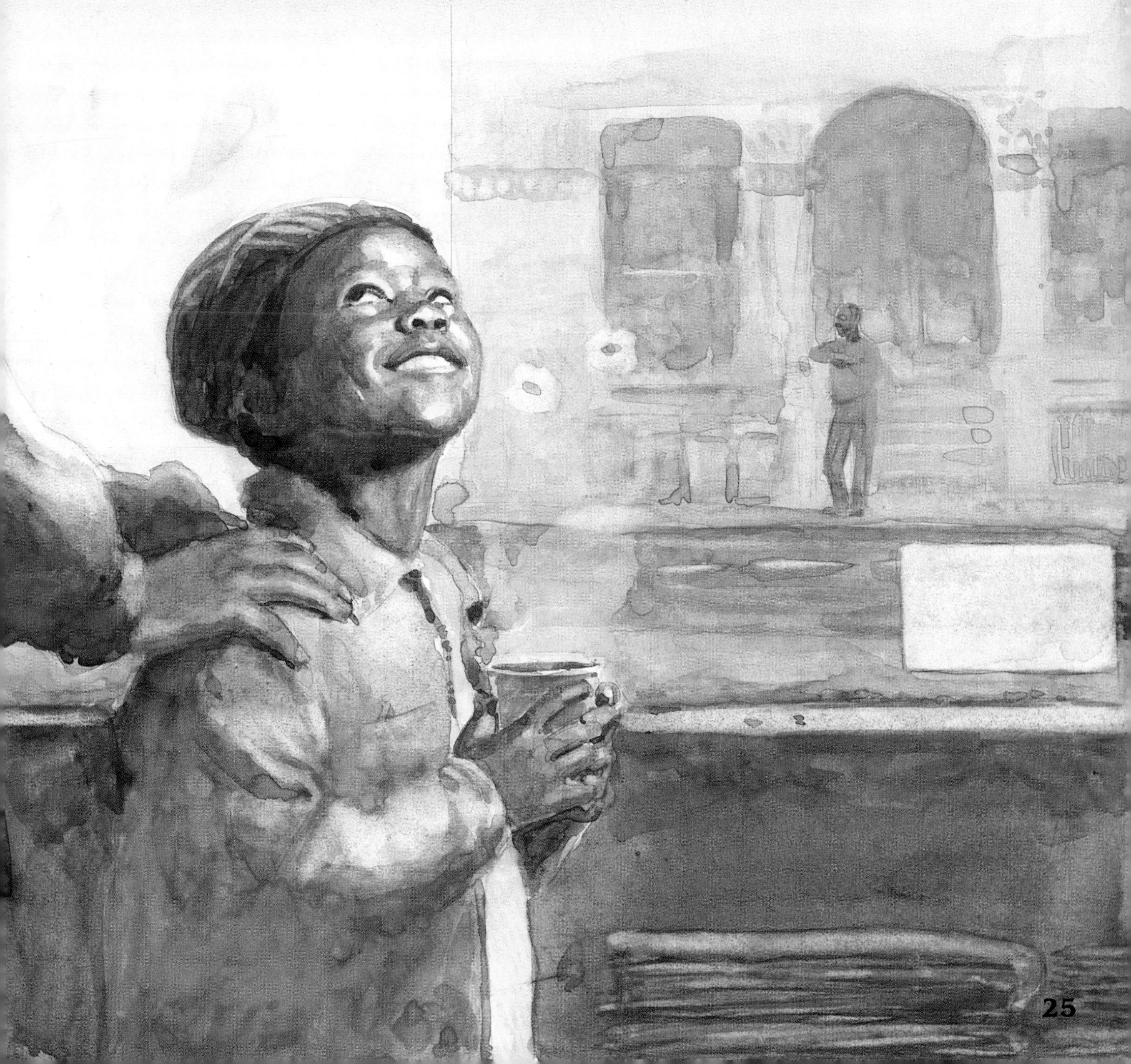

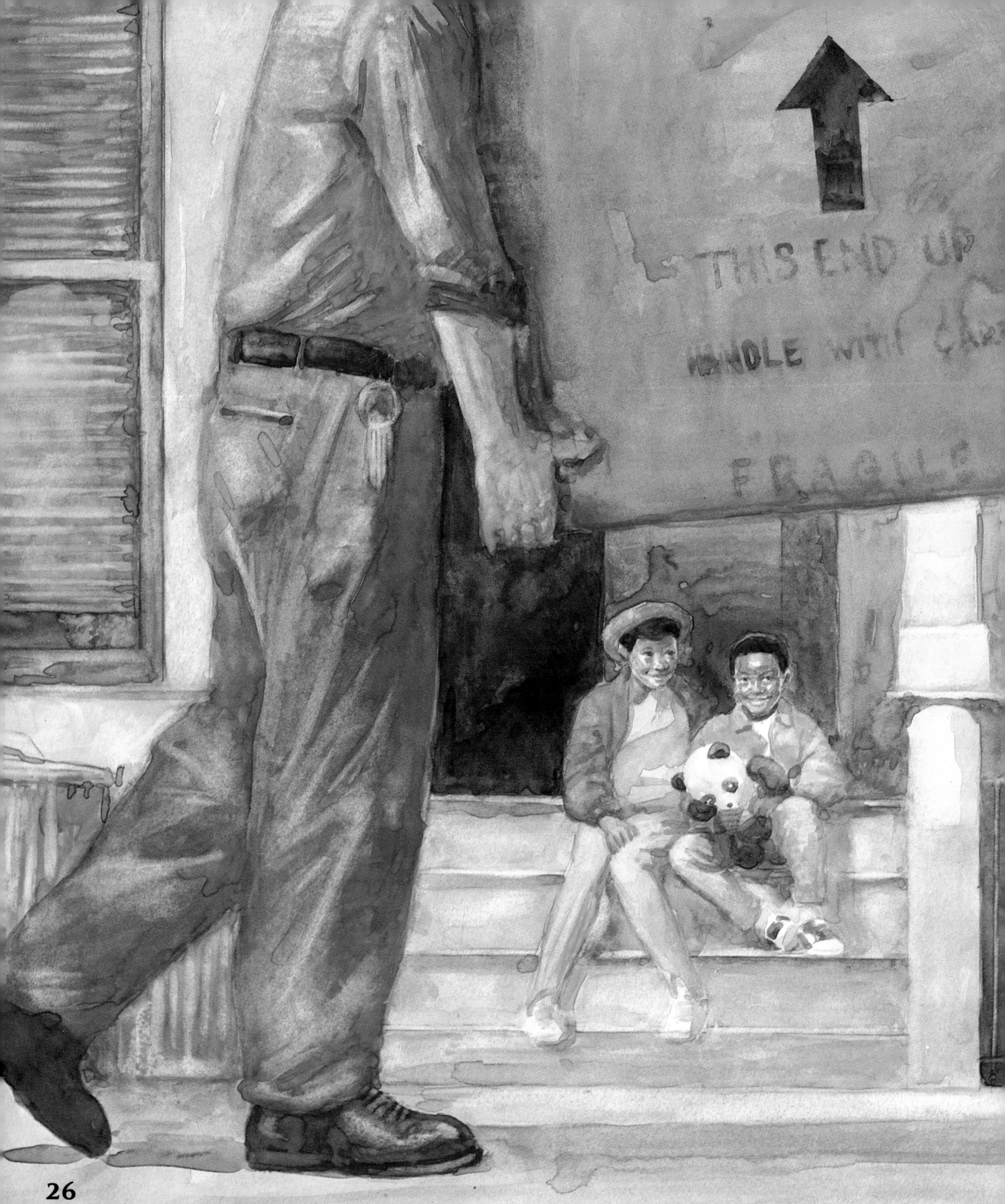
THIS END UP

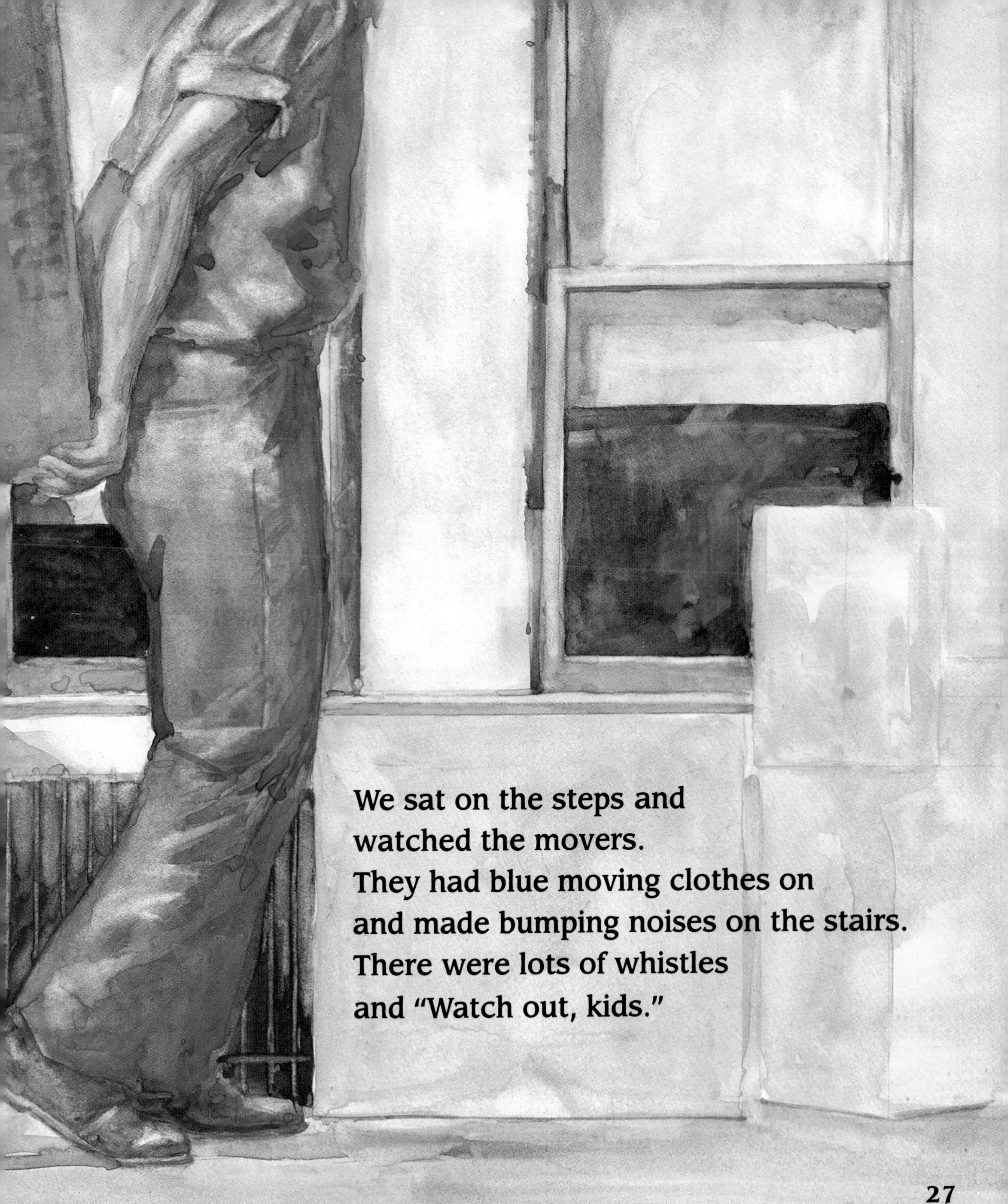

We sat on the steps and
watched the movers.
They had blue moving clothes on
and made bumping noises on the stairs.
There were lots of whistles
and "Watch out, kids."

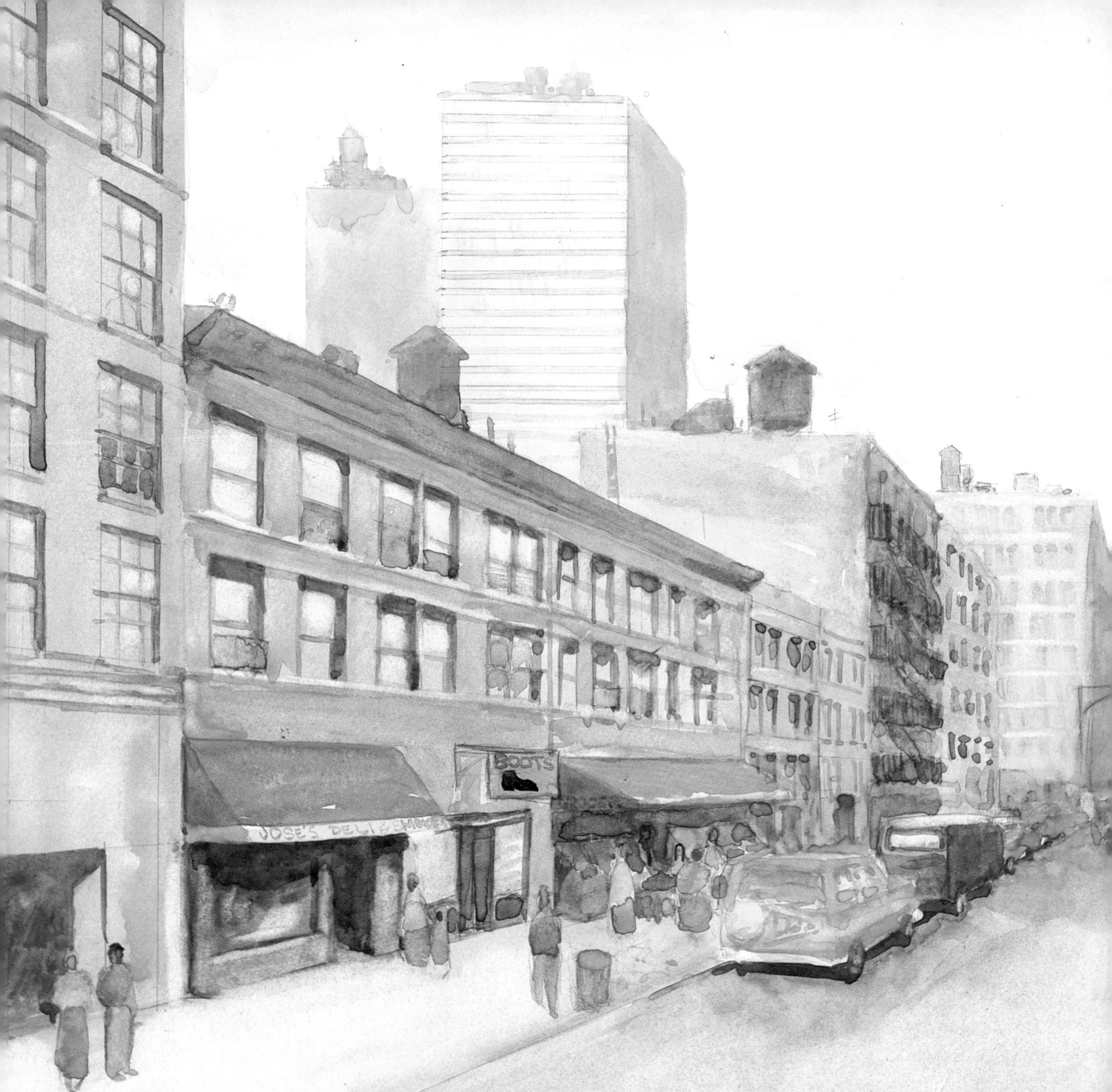
BOOTS
JOSE'S DELI

Got me a moving hat and a kiss on the head
from Miss Mattie, upstairs.
And on the leaving morning she told me
to watch myself in the new place when I crossed
the street, and think of her.

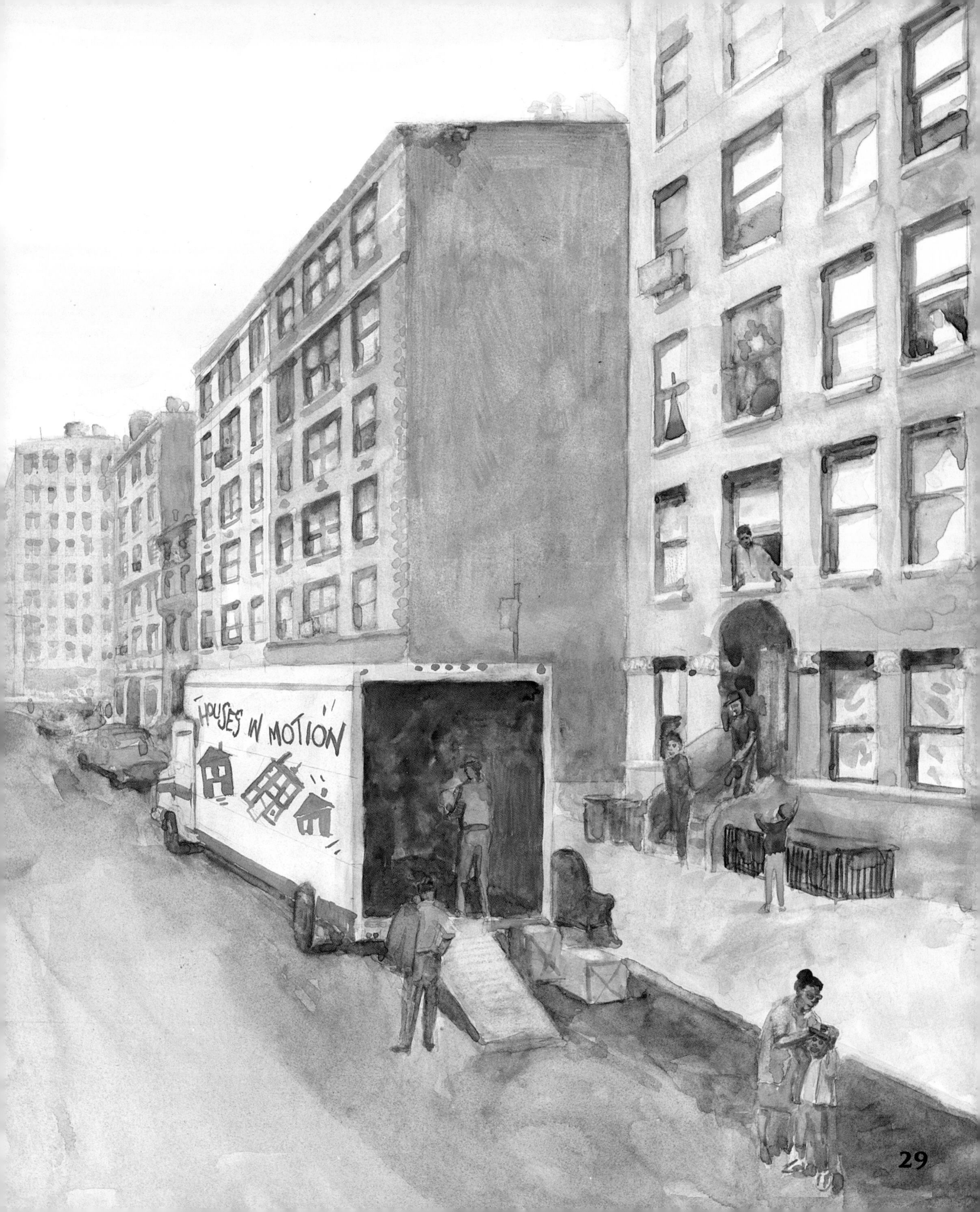
HOUSES IN MOTION

I sat between my mama and daddy,
holding their hands.
My daddy said in a little while we'd be someplace
we'd love.

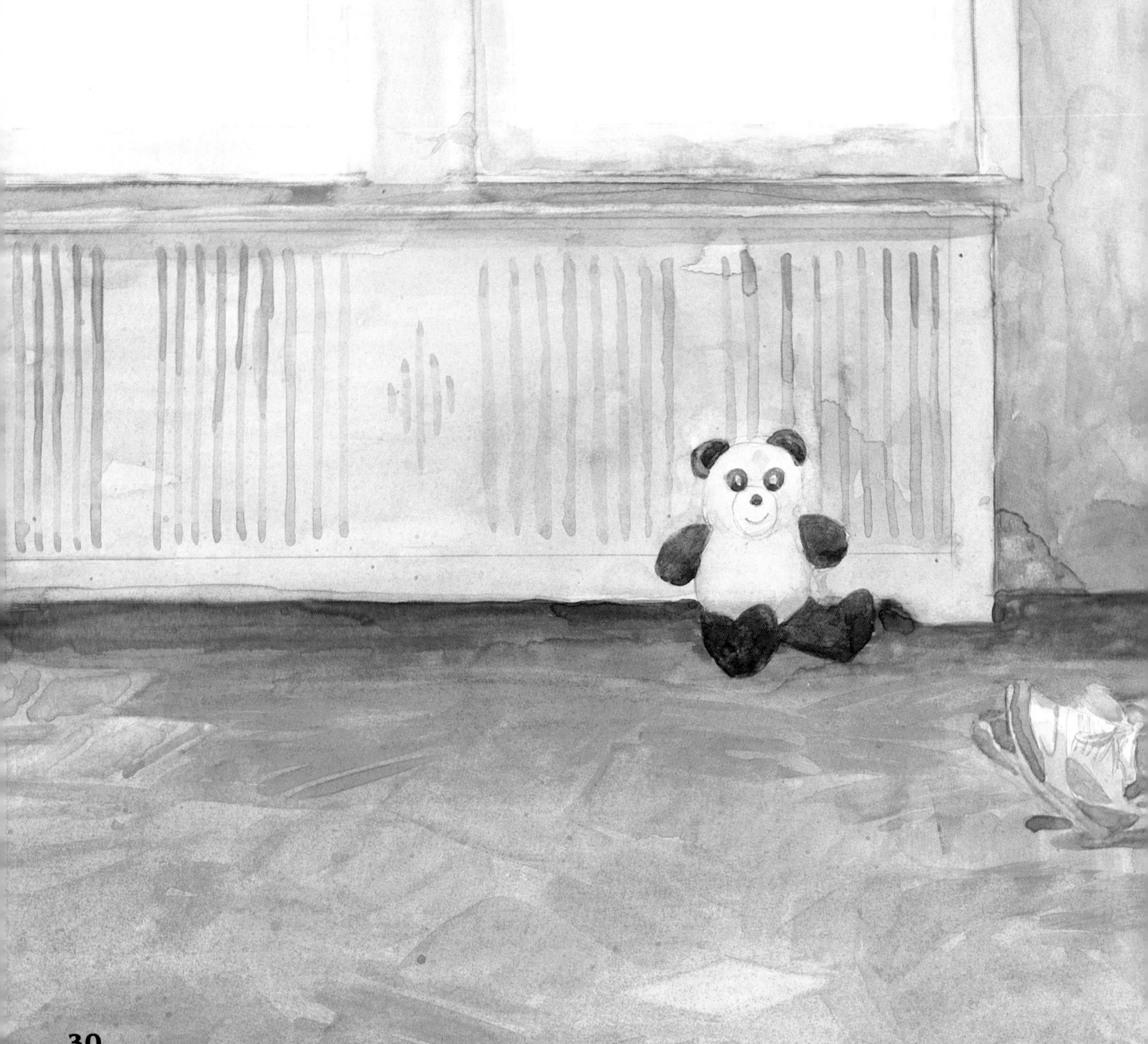

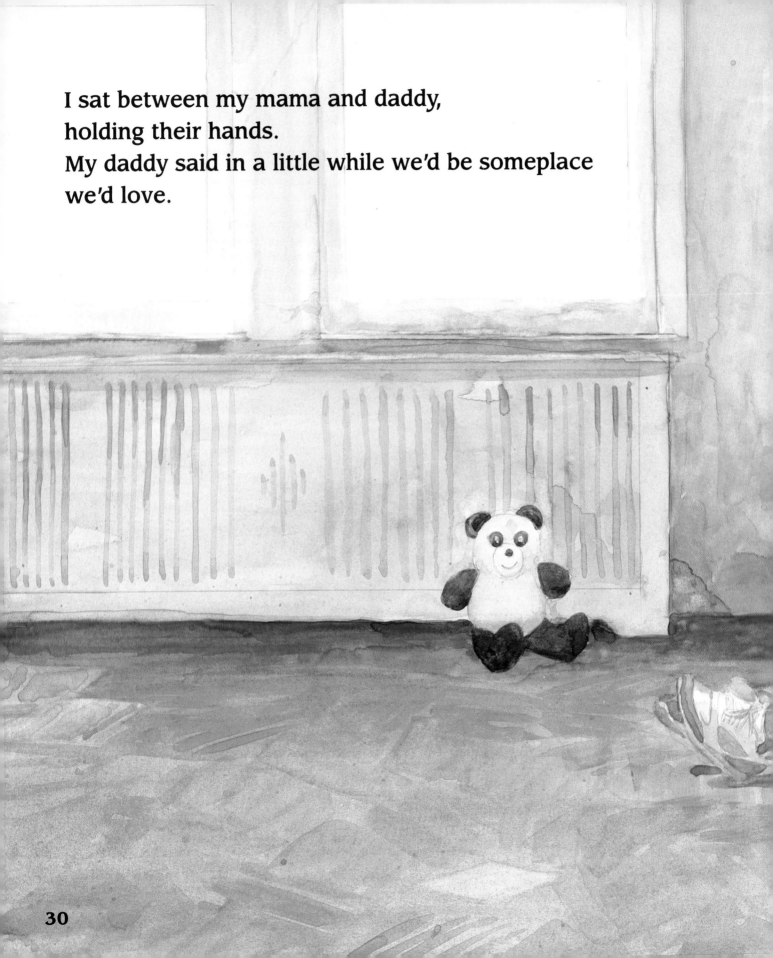

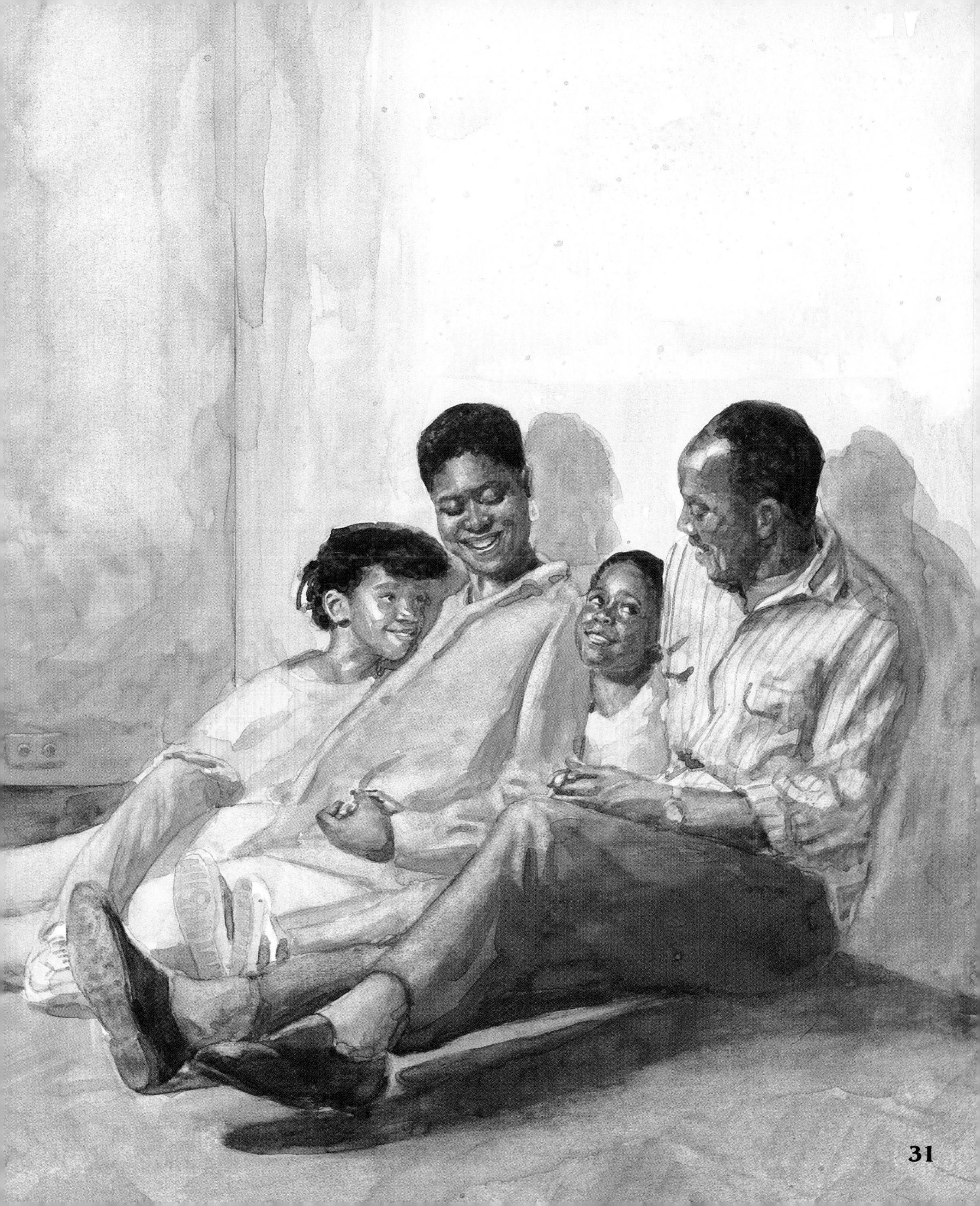

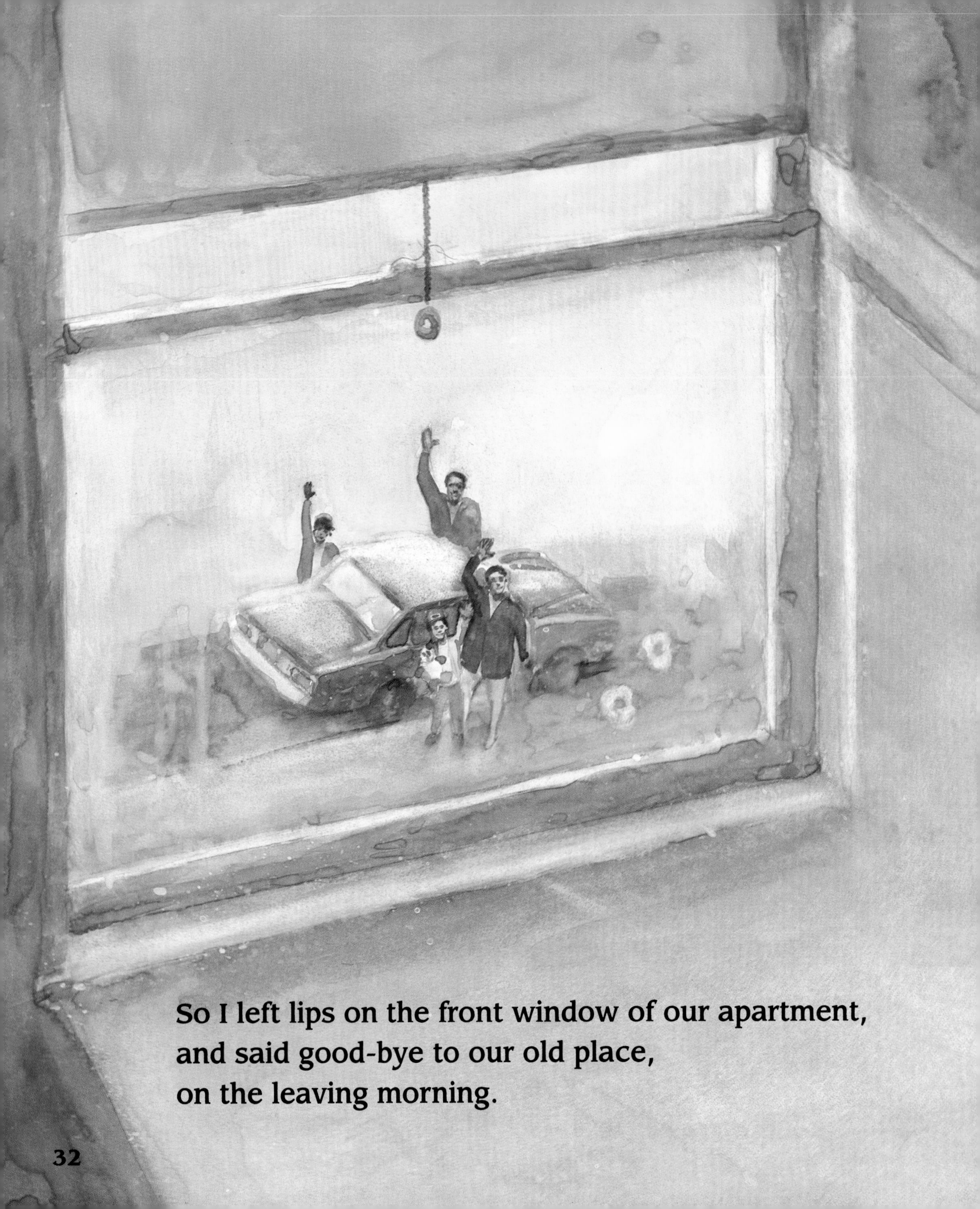

So I left lips on the front window of our apartment,
and said good-bye to our old place,
on the leaving morning.